NAPOLEON

Ronald Frederick Delderfield was born in Greenwich in 1912 and worked as a reporter and editor on the *Exmouth Chronicle* from 1929 until the Second World War. He served in the RAF until 1945, when he returned to the *Exmouth Chronicle*, resigning two years later to devote himself to writing.

For over forty years he was a prolific writer both of novels and plays, many of which were filmed. Among his later novels which have received world-wide recognition are the 'Swann' sagas, *God Is an Englishman, Theirs Was the Kingdom* and *Give Us this Day*, which he completed just before his death in June 1972.

He made a lifelong study of Napoleon, who fascinated him. Among his few non-fiction books Delderfield, in addition to *Napoleon in Love*, wrote an account of Napoleon's Marshals called *The March of the Twenty-Six*.

By the same author in Pan Books

COME HOME CHARLIE AND FACE THEM

NAPOLEON IN LOVE

R. F. DELDERFIELD

PAN BOOKS LTD
LONDON AND SYDNEY

First published 1959 by Hodder and Stoughton Ltd
This edition published 1974 by Pan Books Ltd,
Cavaye Place, London SW10 9PG

ISBN 0 330 23881 7

2nd Printing 1974

For my wife
('Valence to St Helena!')
this book is dedicated

*Printed in Great Britain by
Hazell Watson & Viney Ltd,
Aylesbury, Bucks*

Contents

List of Illustrations
(Between pages 128 and 129)

*Illustrations reproduced from photographs supplied by
the Mansell Collection*

CHAPTER I

Husband and Lover

'The ivy winds its tendrils round the first tree it encounters and that, in brief, is the story of love.'

This somewhat banal statement was written down by Napoleon when he was eighteen years of age. At that time his experiences with women were limited to a single encounter with a prostitute and a brief summer idyll with a pretty, sixteen-year-old girl.

In the years that followed his rise to a position of enormous personal power, he had at his disposal the favours of countless women, many of them possessed of beauty, grace, charm and wit. Discussing women with his intimates on St Helena he admitted to seven mistresses, but he does not seem to have considered his more casual encounters as worthy of inclusion in the reckoning.

From the wide choice available to him he chose, in fact, two wives and at least a dozen mistresses, exclusive of some twenty others whose names were linked to his by rumour during the fourteen years that he occupied the centre of the world stage. Thus, in a period of twenty-five years – that is, from the date of his first marriage until his death in exile – he made love to at least fourteen women; all were young, attractive and extremely eager to please.

At first glance his conquests in the field of love are impressive and there is no Waterloo to offset them. It might be claimed that his successes here equalled those in the fields of battle and statecraft, yet this is not so, for there is a curious sterility about his love-affairs and only two of them influenced his character development to any appreciable degree. In spite of this he took each of them seriously enough at the time and the mild cynicism expressed in his adolescent summary of love never showed itself in later years. To the end of his life his attitude to women was, in the main, as uncomplicated as that of a schoolboy and often nearly as tender. His much-publicized brusqueness when addressing certain women was part of a charade; at heart he lived and died a romantic. Women's tears and women's supplications moved him to a frenzy of tenderness and solicitude, and towards the majority of the flint-hearted opportunists who clamoured for his favours he displayed matchless generosity, unfailing kindness, thoughtfulness and a remarkable lack of recrimination.

Napoleon's associations with women cannot be judged from the moral standpoint of today. If one so judges them he is entitled to instant dismissal as a voluptuous and sensual despot, lacking all standards of civilized conduct towards wives and subjects. Neither does one seek to excuse his sensuality on grounds that he was some special kind of being, not in any way subject to the codes of lesser men. He himself occasionally claimed such immunity but only when he was in a childish temper and endeavouring to justify himself to his wife. Whenever he sought to explain away any of his shortcomings as a man, a husband, a soldier or a statesman he talked – as most of us talk – a great deal of nonsense. Because he was who he was his irresponsible utterances were jotted down as he said them by a cohort of eavesdroppers. The majority of us are luckier in this respect. Our self-pitying bleats are jeered at and at once forgotten.

In order to judge his character objectively one is obliged to view it in relation to his times and the singular position he occupied in his day and age. He grew up in a period of frantic social upheaval and in a country where sexual morality had been steadily undermined by that country's leaders. Neither the Bourbon aristocrats nor the seedy politicians who replaced them regarded the married state as a barrier to the enjoyment of mistresses. Napoleon's views in this respect did not differ from those of his immediate predecessors. In addition, his opportunities to indulge himself were unlimited. If one compares his use of those opportunities with that of certain of his contemporaries one is led to think him modest in his demands. Barras, Talleyrand, Metternich, Masséna and his own brothers, Joseph and Lucien, were coarse, disreputable and licentious men if judged by the standards of today. Some of them kept half a dozen mistresses at one time, whereas Napoleon usually moved from mistress to mistress, often under the impression that he was genuinely in love.

It is his astonishing power of self-deception in this respect that makes his love-affairs interesting. He was a man who lived the whole of his mature life under a spotlight yet the record of his associations with women is not a sordid record. Instead it has a kind of rhythm, obedient to a main theme and although casual notes do occur in the theme it is not by any means casual in essence. It is measured and strangely repetitive.

Probably no man in history has been more written about than Napoleon. His private life has been the subject of countless memoirs, reliable and unreliable, dull and amusing, admiring and bitterly censorious. Almost every literate person who came close to him during the quarter-century when he was the most-discussed man in the world has recorded, or caused to be recorded, his considered opinions, his love-affairs, his preferences, his moods and, above all, his hundreds of tongue-in-cheek observations made during idle moments around the court. A painstaking historian might devote a lifetime to a study of this avalanche of words yet emerge with little more than a moderately accurate character sketch of the man behind the legend. This is not because of the multiplicity of tongues that tell the story but because no human being has ever succeeded in living for ten years at the pace Napoleon maintained for twenty. His field is so vast. Geographically it stretches from the coast of Portugal to the eastern suburbs of Moscow, from the North Cape to the Nile and South Atlantic. Functionally it embraces almost every human activity, from that of wooing to that of conspiracy, law-making and Empire-building.

A painstaking and deliberate man might have spent his entire life doing what Napoleon often achieved in a few hours yet still have had reason to be proud of his labours. His conclusions were arrived at by intuition rather than by the process of sustained thought. In a matter of months he climbed from unemployment to a position of dictator over thirty million people; in a year or so more he extended his dominion over the greater part of the Western hemisphere. He has gone down in history as a soldier, yet soldiering was but a by-product of his fantastic nervous energy, generated by a powerful dynamo of self-confidence. In fields of human endeavour he had, and has since had, no real equal. The victor in sixty fields, he was a superb administrator with the supreme quality, entirely absent in most good organisers, of inspiring the unswerving devotion of millions of men.

Men! His genius fell away altogether when he came to deal with women and his record in this field is strangely pitiful. He paid court to women of every type. He was passionate lover to a few, a tolerant husband to two and a generous friend and protector to scores. They repaid him with at best the dutiful compliance of a Victorian wife, at worst black treachery and shameless ingratitude.

How did this come to be? Why was it that Napoleon could inspire men to die blessing him without being capable of inspiring more than a tepid, self-seeking affection in the hearts of women?

One writer on the subject suggests that the reason lies in the fact that women cannot love a man who is truly their master, that domination by a man of Napoleon's stature could inspire awe, fear, respect even, but never genuine devotion.

This theory can be ruled out for two reasons. In the first place millions of women have shown steadfast devotion to men who have treated them with barbarity. In the second place Napoleon did not behave towards a woman as a master; in most cases he elevated her to a position out of all proportion to her true merit, either as a charmer or as a human being. His letters to Joséphine are the letters a passionate young man might have written to a sweet, unsullied girl, yet he must have known that she had won her place in Paris society by harlotry. His breathless pursuit of the Polish countess, Marie Walewska, was an echo of his wooing of Joséphine. 'When I press my hand upon my heart you will know that it is dreaming of you,' he wrote. Yet Walewska, for all her fragile charm and her early resistance to temptation, was a shrewd woman whose surrender was part of a policy – patriotic policy it is true but a policy for all that.

It is the same with all the women who play an important part in his life. To the end of his days he remembered every detail of his youthful idyll with Caroline Colombier, in the early morning of his career, yet she only remembered him when she wanted a favour. For as long as he was master of France he remembered with gratitude the embraces of Pauline Fourès, his blonde camp-follower during the Egyptian campaign, yet she was for ever pestering him for material reminders of their transitory affair. In the extreme stress of the campaign of France, in 1814, when his Empire and dreams were falling about him, he found time to make special provisions for the love-child he had fathered on Eléonore, seven years before. Towards his second wife, Marie Louise, he displayed a gentleness and tolerance that would be astonishing in the fondest of rustic husbands, and when she became the mistress of a one-eyed seducer he never once referred to her in terms other than those of love and respect.

Reviewing his relationships with women – all kinds of women – one is driven to the conclusion that, as regards the opposite sex, he never really grew up, that the man who readily forgave a wife's sordid treachery when he was over fifty was at root the boy who ate cherries with the pretty little brunette in a provincial orchard thirty-five years previously. Naïve this may be but it is also rather comforting. It is pleasant to learn that the man who sped across Europe in the bitter winter of 1812, abandoning the wreck of one army in order to be first in the field with another, retained to the end of his eventful life a tenderness for a woman's smile and a concern for a woman's tears that might be sought in vain today among the male staff of a city office.

It is now more than a century and half since Napoleon Bonaparte was laid in his first grave in the Valley of Geraniums, on the tropical island where he spent the last six years of his life.

During that hundred and fifty years the Napoleonic legend has reflowered for each successive generation. This book is just one aspect of the astonishing source of that legend. It is neither a condemnation nor a justification of him as a man, merely a partial survey of his many-sided character – a character that is in some respects pitiable.

This is the story of an odyssey, a journey made by a lonely man in search of the ideal mate. It is a long and eventful journey that ends in disappointment but disappointment without bitterness.

CHAPTER II

'Be assured of my desire . . .'

On the morning of 20 August, 1804, a courier delivered the
morning's mail to the Headquarters of Napoleon at his
camp, outside Boulogne.

It must have been a bulging satchel and its contents, if
they could be reassembled today, would probably tell us a
great deal we have yet to learn of the First Consul's plans to
invade England.

The means to invade were readily available. Round him,
based at Boulogne, were a hundred and ninety thousand
trained men, poised for descent on the coasts of Kent, Sussex
and Hampshire.

British naval officers, cruising up Channel, could see the
vast array of tents and hear the roll of the *rappel* as the
troops assembled for morning manoeuvres. In the harbour
below were scores of invasion barges, not unlike those assembled by Hitler in the same harbour a hundred and thirty-
six years later.

A group of secretaries sorted the mail. There were letters
from contractors, letters from cranks, letters from Paris
politicians, flatterers, Royalists, Republicans and the agents
of foreign powers. There was one from the persistent Mr
Fulton, who had come all the way from America in order to
offer Napoleon a steam navy. There were letters from staff
officers and the wives of staff officers, letters from experts of
every kind, including balloonists who were trying, without
much success, to persuade the conqueror of Italy to essay
the conquest of the air.

Each letter was read, noted and set aside. Only one, a
brief note in feminine handwriting, delayed Napoleon for

more than a few moments and sealed his mind against the clamour of war that surrounded him.

It was a simple request from a lady living near Lyons, a young lady called Caroline Bressieux. She wrote asking if something might be done for her brother, a Monsieur du Colombier.

The name 'Bressieux' meant nothing to the First Consul but the name 'Colombier' meant a great deal. It set him musing, taking him back nearly twenty years to a summer morning in Valence and a cherry-gathering expedition in the company of a pretty girl his own age.

He read the letter twice. Then he called the nearest secretary and dictated a reply.

Madam,
     Your letter was a source of great pleasure to me. The memory of your mother, as well as of yourself, has never ceased to be of interest to me. I will avail myself of the first opportunity of assisting your brother. I see from your letter that you are living near Lyons, and I think it a little unkind of you not to have come over while I was there, for I shall always have great pleasure in seeing you. Be assured of my desire to be of service to you.
Napoleon

The letter, which might have been written by a country curate accepting a belated invitation to tea, was sealed and despatched. Within weeks the entire Bressieux family was on the broad highroad to fortune.

Caroline's husband became President of an Electoral College, owing his elevation far less to his abilities than to his good fortune in marrying the Emperor's partner in an early morning cherry-picking expedition. Caroline's brother was at once made a Lieutenant and she herself was attached as Lady-in-Waiting to the household of Napoleon's mother.

One thing more and this a mark of special favour. The

names of all the Colombiers' aristocratic relatives were at once removed from the list of *émigrés*.

It is strange that Caroline had not thought of writing to the First Consul before !

Caroline Colombier's name has survived in history as the very first of Napoleon's loves and there is no doubt at all that she did indeed fill this role.

He would have remembered her freshness and charm and the emotion she had once stirred in him, whether or not she had written after an interval of twenty years. In his terrible isolation at St Helena, when his triumphs and his disasters were behind him and he was awaiting slow death from cancer, he was still able to recall every detail of that innocent romance against a summer background in Valence, his first garrison post.

The world owes something to Caroline Colombier. The music she played in the heart of a sixteen-year-old starveling never quite died away. Notwithstanding his imperial prattle of harems, his propensity to reduce women of the court to tears by brutal comments on their fatness or the redness of their elbows, his basic attitude to womankind was softened by the sweetness of this obscure girl, who was gentle and flattering to a gaunt, lonely, awkward boy, hundreds of miles from home and friends, a boy who, despite six years in military school, still used an accent that made the more aristocratic among the cadets exchange sly, superior smirks.

Caroline came from a family that had nothing to gain from revolution.

In 1785 the Colombiers were middle-class gentry, the élite of the district in which they resided, but although Mamma exercised a careful watch over the men Caroline was likely to meet among the younger garrison officers, Madame Colombier was no snob. When her friend the Abbé of St Ruffe recommended this unkempt youth to her notice, she accepted him into her home as an equal and placed no ban on his association with her pretty daughter.

By so doing she did the young Corsican an immense service. He had been away from home and family for more than six years, had just passed out of the military school at Paris and had received his commission as a Sub-Lieutenant in the artillery. He was barely sixteen, thin and pale after years of concentrated study and possessing no scrap of influence of any kind. The only income he enjoyed stemmed from his meagre pay and it would have required a very discerning eye to perceive that his prospects were anything but drab and all but hopeless.

Promotion in the Royal Army was slow and owed little to merit. At twenty-five he might be a full Lieutenant; at thirty, with luck, scars and a good record, a Captain. He was not a very promising suitor to a mother on the lookout for a match. Despite all this the young cadet was made welcome and he never afterwards forgot the kindness shown him, any more than he forgot Caroline's chestnut hair, her graceful figure or her fresh, country complexion.

All that summer, the summer of 1786, the adolescent romance prospered.

'No one could have been more innocent than we were,' wrote Napoleon, at St Helena. 'We often used to arrange little assignations and I recollect one in particular, which took place at daybreak one morning in the middle of the summer. It may not be credited but our sole delight on that occasion consisted of eating cherries together.'

Notwithstanding the gallant reputation he earned for himself in the years ahead it was credited by someone who saw these two together almost exactly twenty years later.

There seems to have been some talk of marriage, but as the summer wore on the first thunderclouds of the revolution gathered over Lyons and Napoleon's regiment was despatched to the city to suppress a militant strike among the silk workers.

Three workmen were hanged and the rest driven back to work. It was his first experience of mob violence and in the excitement of the event even Caroline's shy smile was forgotten. When the trouble was over and his regiment moved to Douai, he took his first leave and returned to his native Corsica after an absence of nearly seven years. Almost twenty years were to pass before he was to see Caroline again.

Their reunion was a direct result of her letter to the camp at Boulogne. Sweet and innocent as she might have been at sixteen, at thirty-five she had learned to take hints. Napoleon's rebuke respecting her long silence and probably the flattering promptitude he had shown in replying to her begging letter, led her to write again 'enquiring after his health'. Again he replied promptly, and in April of 1806, soon after he had made himself an Emperor, she was among the first to greet him when he passed through Lyons on his way to be crowned at Milan.

Madame Junot, one of the most amusing and indefatigable diarists of the First Empire, saw her about this time and has recorded her impressions. It would appear that the Emperor's eager interest in his first love had become generally known and Madame Junot, who seldom missed a trick, watched Caroline Colombier with a keen, sophisticated eye. Afterwards she wrote :

'. . . I found her witty, agreeable, mild and amiable, not handsome but with a graceful pleasing figure. I can well understand that Napoleon should find pleasure in gathering cherries with her, without an improper thought !'

And then, after this somewhat cryptic comment, comes the tailpiece of a born columnist :

'She watched his every move, her eye following him with an attention which seemed to emanate from her very soul.'

Well it might, for here was the most important man in the world, the man of whom all Europe was talking, the conqueror of Italy, the master of kings, fresh from his coronation and his resounding triumph over the combined armies of Austria and Russia at Austerlitz. And this was the man she might have married ! Just a little more faith and foresight on her part or her mother's, a few tender letters after his hurried departure from Valence, a softer glance or a kiss or two as the sun came up that summer morning and she, not the widow Beauharnais, would have been running up dress and jewellery debts in Paris to the tune of twelve hundred thousand francs!

It would be interesting to know what Caroline said to her husband on her return to their country-house outside Lyons that night. It would be even more fascinating to learn whether Monsieur Bressieux entertained any feelings of jealousy or whether, like a sensible man, he was content to congratulate himself on the prospect of the endless by-products that attended his wife's first romance.

It is recorded that Napoleon was disagreeably surprised by the effects of time upon poor Madame Bressieux's face and figure. Like all men in similar circumstances he made no allowance at all for the passage of time upon his own appearance but saw himself as young, spry and eager, regarding with some misgivings the strange transformation in the appearance of the woman who kissed his hand. Other famous men have undergone this chastening experience and it is to his credit that his disappointment did not prevent him from continuing to interest himself in the Bressieux family. Four years after this meeting Caroline's husband was made a baron of the Empire, but Caroline and the Emperor made no attempt to follow up their reunion. Perhaps she was happily married, or perhaps he preferred to leave her in the orchard of his youth.

CHAPTER III

'And what shall we do there?'

Napoleon was 'emancipated', as he himself might have put it, in November 1787, and we are fortunate in possessing an interesting account of the incident (or the encounter that led up to it) from his own pen.

Like most imaginative young men, particularly those possessing more than the usual share of ambition, he was an ardent diarist up to the period when he found too many other things to do.

His own descriptions of the incidents of his youth are always alive and clearly set down. The extreme loneliness and poverty of his early years encouraged him to spend time expressing himself on paper. It was during this period that he tried his hand at writing romance.

It was a search for 'local colour' to use in a projected novel, that led to his brief association with the prostitute in the Palais Royal, then the Paris equivalent of London's Shaftesbury Avenue or Piccadilly Circus.

He had the normal youth's curiosity about this class of women and the same tendency to mark his approach to them with the veiled pomposity one has now learned to expect from a special enquirer on a television jag.

Fortunately prostitutes as a class are well-accustomed to this approach, particularly when it emanates from an inexperienced youth, and they often play up to it, recounting the hard-luck story with their tongue in their cheek. This one would appear to have been no different in this respect and consequently the young Lieutenant's solemn report of the discussion has plenty of unconscious humour.

Napoleon had arrived in Paris in October and was staying

at the Hotel de Cherbourg, in the Rue du Four-St Honoré. He had already spent a year in the Paris area, but during that period he had little time or opportunity for sight-seeing and was scarcely more than a child.

On this occasion he was much more of the man about town. He had just returned from a visit to Versailles and on the night of 22 November when a bitterly cold wind was sweeping through the streets of the city, he visited the Italian opera and was moved by the performance, so much so that he did not notice the inclemency of the weather until, as he himself puts it, 'my imagination cooled'.

Thinly clad and with little flesh on his bones, he sought the shelter of the colonnades in the Palais Royal and here he came face to face with a young street-walker. He was at once struck by her youth and 'encouraged by her timidity'.

Had she been a brazen type, who accosted him openly and cheerfully, he would have been glad to exchange the comparative shelter of the arcades for the windswept street and make his way home at top speed.

This woman, however, was ready to accommodate him in more ways than one. They discussed, of all things, the weather! The girl led off with a remark that, low temperature notwithstanding, she was obliged to complete her evening's business and that 'the cold refreshed her'.

Napoleon then began to preach, remarking on the delicacy of her appearance and the unhealthiness of her calling. Her willingness to discuss her profession delighted him and they fell into step along the colonnades.

She told him that she came from Nantes, in Brittany, and went on to describe her fall from virtue in terms of almost incredible banality. All the usual stage properties were solemnly wheeled out, the callous seducer (inevitably an army officer), his ultimate desertion, her mother's anger, the shameful flight that followed it, a second seducer and then a third, with whom she lived for a period of three years. One can almost see the officer-protector twirling his moustache and the girl waiting in a fireless garret for the wedding contract that never arrives. Having finished her story the girl returned briskly to business and asked Napoleon to take her home with him to his hotel.

Napoleon then made a remark which can hardly be forgiven an eighteen-year-old youth, engaged in his first attempt at emancipation. He said, blandly :

'And what shall we do there?'

The girl must have been fairly new to the game. Instead of telling him bluntly she suggested that 'they should warm themselves' and that is what they did, although how they went about it must be imagined, for at this point Napoleon's modesty leads him to resort to the line of asterisks so essential to the modern novelist.

He has the honesty to add, however, a final paragraph to the story, and here we find a slight concession to his sense of humour. He says : 'I had led her on in order that she might not be able to escape when pressed by the train of reasoning I had prepared, while counterfeiting a severity I determined to show her was not natural to me !'

They went back to the Hotel de Cherbourg and there can be no doubt that the affair ended as it was meant to end. One can be equally certain that this was his first experience of the sexual act. It did not, however, spark off a series of encounters among the women of the Palais Royal, for almost immediately Napoleon left Paris to spend an extended furlough in his native Corsica. On his return he was posted to Auxonne.

Shortly afterwards Paris exploded and the mobs poured from the slums to sack the Bastille and create a state of affairs inside the capital that led, step by step, to the bloody anarchy of '92, the flight and death of the Royal family, and finally the Terror of Danton and Robespierre.

There are no more musings about women in the scribblings of Napoleon at this time. He was far too occupied with the business of keeping up with the times and climbing the ladder of his profession. When he did come to think of women again he did so in terms of a steady and respectable young man on the lookout for a dutiful wife, who could provide him with a happy home and hearth. The idyll in the cherry-orchard, and the incident in the Palais Royal, were now succeeded by an extraordinary yearning for domesticity.

CHAPTER IV

'How happy that rascal is!'

This change of heart and the example of his recently married brother almost led Napoleon into matrimony at the age of twenty-four.

In June 1793, when the Revolution was at its height and the guillotine in Paris and elsewhere was claiming as many as eighty victims a day, the impoverished Bonaparte family landed in Marseilles owning nothing but the clothes they wore.

Even these clothes were much the worse for wear. Closely involved in the struggle for Corsica, the family had backed the losing side and had barely escaped with their lives. Bonaparte's father was dead and the refugees, seven in number, were in dire straits. All their Corsican property had gone, they were penniless and almost without friends in a country convulsed with the Terror and at war on every frontier.

It is a pity that no one was at hand to prophesy the rosy future for the harassed mother of the brood. Of the seven children who queued for municipal bread in Marseilles that summer six were to occupy thrones in the next fifteen years! All three girls – Elise, Pauline and Caroline – were to make brilliant matches.

Letizia Bonaparte, however, had far too much commonsense to indulge in crystal-gazing. She at once set about organizing the family life and was ably assisted by her second son, Captain Bonaparte, the only member of the group who was already self-supporting.

Napoleon took his younger brother Louis to live with him and maintained him in lodgings, besides making himself responsible for the child's education. On thirty pounds a year this says a good deal for Napoleon as a son and a brother.

For more than a year the Bonapartes were numbered among the submerged victims of the Revolution. Then, quite suddenly, things began to improve. Joseph, the eldest boy, obtained a job as a commissary, whilst Napoleon leaped into prominence as the artilleryman whose brains and dash had swept the Royalists and the English clear of Toulon. Rapid promotion followed and he at once set about helping his impoverished family.

Brother Joseph had already helped himself. He had wooed and won the elder daughter of a Marseilles soap-merchant named Clary and his wife, Julie Clary, brought him a dowry of six thousand pounds sterling !

To the refugees, with the Marseilles soup-kitchens less than a year behind them, this dowry must have seemed like a key of King Solomon's mines and it may have been the prospect of laying his hands on a similar sum that encouraged Napoleon to look towards the Clary family for a bride.

Joseph's wife was an amiable girl, somewhat addicted to pimples and by no means as pert and pretty as her younger sister, Désirée, who was then sixteen years of age.

Désirée has been variously reported as 'a frivolous coquette' and 'an utter nonentity'. Her portrait inclines one to accept the less charitable estimate, for although possessing a certain dark charm, her expression lacks vivacity. Madame Junot, who knew her very well, says that her character was colourless and 'although harmless she was without a spark of appeal'. As events turned out she did not prove harmless to Napoleon. She ultimately married the most unrelenting of his enemies and she never quite forgave Napoleon for failing to press his suit with more resolution.

At this period, notwithstanding his success at Toulon, Napoleon's prospects were still dubious. He had distinguished himself in battle and had risen to the rank of Chef de Brigade, but the tide of Terror was receding, Robespierre was dead and Napoleon's personal friendship with the tyrant's brother was an obstacle to further promotion under the seedy gang who had replaced him – expert schemers like Barras and vacillating scoundrels like Tallien.

He himself did not think a great deal of his chances and was inclined to play for safety. He cast longing eyes at Joseph's domestic bliss. 'How happy that rascal Joseph is,' he wrote, and in the uncertain period preceding his next upward leap we find him writing to Joseph and urging his brother to woo Désirée on his behalf.

In June 1795, he was still pestering his brother to bespeak Désirée, but either there was truth in the story that the soap-boiler's second daughter was a flirt, or Napoleon's continued absence prevented the romance from developing. In July, after telling Joseph that she had asked him for his portrait and that he is getting one done for her, he adds : 'You can give it to her if she wishes it; if not keep it for yourself.'

Shortly afterwards he complains bitterly that he has had no word from Désirée and later still he plagues his brother to give him an account of her silence. Poor Joseph was evidently in a quandary about the projected match. It is said that the Clary family were against it, and that Désirée's father, when sounded on the proposal, snorted : 'No, no! One Bonaparte in the family is enough !'

Joseph, who doubtless felt slighted by this remark, has denied that it was ever made, pointing out that his father-in-law had been dead a year when he was said to have made it, but it is obvious that the Clary family did not view Napoleon's suit with much enthusiasm. Why should they? Joseph had not been much of a catch and it was not long before he was indulging in the one form of indiscretion that appealed to his bucolic nature, a taste for pretty mistresses. He was a heavy, dull, ineffective sort of fellow, doomed to be chivvied along by his terrible brother for the next twenty years. It was not until Napoleon was safely tucked away on St Helena that Joseph had a soul to call his own, and Napoleon's stream of letters about Désirée must have distressed him almost as much as the thrones he was forced to occupy in the years ahead.

He did what people of his type usually do in this kind of situation – nothing at all – and in yet another letter to his wretched brother Napoleon expresses indignation at Joseph's failure to assist him in reaching a decision. 'I have received a letter from Désirée which seems as if it had been written ages ago,' he says, adding peevishly, 'you never said a word about it!'

Reading between the lines of these letters, and judging by Désirée's subsequent behaviour, it is clear that Napoleon cannot be accused of jilting this young lady. What almost certainly happened is that she blew hot and cold through the summer of 1795 and made only the feeblest efforts to overcome the opposition of her family to the marriage.

Then, when Napoleon suddenly leapt into prominence by saving the Directory from a Paris mob, she (and most probably her mother also) bitterly regretted her hesitancy, but it was then too late. Not only had Napoleon fallen deeply in love with a sophisticated woman, he had arrived at a point in his career where the choice of a wife was a matter of considerable importance to him.

Désirée was a provincial. She was coltish and inexperienced and spoke with a strong Marseilles accent. This was not the kind of partner who could be of much assistance to a man whose skill and promptitude had just saved a government, who was now certain to go far in the Republican armies. It is true that he was still penniless and the Clary dowry, had it been forthcoming, would have been very useful to him, but what he needed more than money at that particular time was someone with influence in high places, someone who could beguile his employers in Paris into giving him an important command.

Joséphine Beauharnais, the widow of a victim of the guillotine, was ideally placed for this maneouvre. She was the ex-mistress of Barras, then the most influential man in France.

* * *

What happened to this girl whose tardiness in love cheated her out of so great a destiny but not, as it turned out, of founding a hereditary line of Princes?

Napoleon never forgot her and treated her with that patience and generosity he reserved for every woman who had touched his heart.

In 1779, when the whole world was ringing with his incredible successes as an exponent of the new style of warfare, when he had become the darling of France and the White Hope of Republicanism everywhere, he remembered that she was still husbandless and sent her a handsome young soldier, General Duphot, together with a warm letter of recommendation.

'Duphot', he wrote, 'is a distinguished officer, a man of the highest character', and then, because one of his favourite occupations was match-making, 'a marriage with him would be most advantageous!'

This was never proved, for although Désirée took the hint and hastened to make the best of a bad job by becoming betrothed to the obliging Duphot, the poor man was cut to pieces before her eyes during a popular insurrection in Rome that same year.

The shock of thus losing two possible husbands in under two years caused little Désirée so much distress that she tearfully rejected a whole string of proposals. It was as well for her that she did, for in the end she chose General Bernadotte, at that time Napoleon's most fancied rival.

It was the best thing either of them ever did. Because Napoleon always maintained a warm affection for her and because he had a slight conscience about the rapidity with which his love for her had cooled after his meeting with Joséphine, he showered favours on Désirée and her husband right up to the moment when Bernadotte accepted the offer of the Swedes to become heir to the throne of their childless king.

She played her strong hand very cleverly. She hurried to meet him when Napoleon returned from Egypt. He became the godfather of her son, Oscar, a son in whom he himself would have delighted. He raised Bernadotte to the rank of Marshal and later Prince. He gave them everything they wanted and for his wife's sake forgave all Bernadotte's intrigues and failures on the field of battle.

In spite of all this neither Désirée nor her despicable husband ever forgave the Emperor, the one because he failed to marry her, the other because he was Napoleon's debtor for as long as Napoleon wore a crown.

The strain they put upon Napoleon's affection was very great and sometimes the small flame of nostalgic love that continued to burn in his heart was almost extinguished by the successive cold douches of Bernadotte's indiscretion, Bernadotte's arrogance, Bernadotte's incompetence and, at length, Bernadotte's disgusting ingratitude.

In 1813, when shadows were falling over the Empire, this man, who owed everything he had to the Grand Army and its chieftain, marched his Swedes into the camp of the allies, who already outnumbered the French by three to one. It is pleasant to record that his old comrades-in-arms never forgave him this treachery and that he lost the prize he longed for – Napoleon's empty throne. He and his wife reluctantly left a Paris occupied by Cossacks and Uhlans and drifted back to their capital in the north, where they both died comfortably in their beds.

One might search history in vain for a parallel to such baseness.

CHAPTER V

'The all-absorbing business of life ...'

In May 1795, eight years after his stay at the Hotel Cherbourg as a down-at-heel Lieutenant, Napoleon Bonaparte walked the streets of Paris once more, this time as a down-at-heel General.

He found the city much changed. In 1787 Paris had been full of starving idealists. In 1795 it was full of starving opportunists. Rhetoric and lofty sentiments were confined to clubs and cafés, and the men and women who had beaten the dust out of European dynasties continued to address one another as 'citizen' and 'citoyenne', and to think of society in terms of liberty, equality and fraternity. For all that their outlook had undergone many radical changes since the day the Bastille had fallen. The vast majority of them were now concerned less with the doctrines of human rights than with the humdrum economics of three square meals a day and a chance to consume them in comfort.

Everyone, from the chastened survivors of the Convention to the lowliest pike-wielder in the hovels of Saint Antoine, had had more than enough of revolution. Everyone was sick and tired of patriotic speeches, bread riots and legalized murder. All the politicians wanted was a breathing-space to entrench themselves in lucrative posts. All the people wanted was bread, a chance to go back to work, and a government that was stable enough to consolidate the two undoubted gains of the Revolution – the breaking of feudal chains and the opening up of opportunities to young men with talent and ambition. Paris would have voted for a return of the Bourbons if these exceptionally stupid exiles had possessed enough commonsense to guarantee such simple demands.

Napoleon had changed, too. The rapid promotion that had followed his share in the taking of Toulon had whetted his appetite for power, power to make something of his career and to exercise some intelligent authority over the fools, scoundrels and ditherers who occupied the executive posts of the capital. All around him was chaos, and Napoleon hated chaos. That was why he had flatly refused to command the Army of the West and embroil himself in a fratricidal war against peasants still loyal to the dead King.

The war in the west was the graveyard of military reputations. It was true that Generals who failed in that area no longer went straight to the guillotine. Since the final upheaval of Thermidor, in the previous July, Parisians had developed a profound distaste for the guillotine. All the same, nobody made a name for himself in a civil war, and Napoleon, who was now on the threshold of his twenty-sixth birthday, preferred to kick his heels in the capital until he could be certain which way the cat was going to jump.

The decision was neither as easy nor as indolent as it sounds. Cats were jumping in all directions and nobody knew which cat had lethal claws.

Two observant women have left us pen portraits of Napoleon as he appeared to passers-by at this particular phase in his life, and the portraits have an astonishing similarity.

'He was by far the thinnest and most singular-looking being I ever encountered,' says one, and goes on to describe how his lank hair hung down on his shoulders 'like a hound's ears'. This, far from conveying an impression of sombre genius, gave her the kind of misgivings a lady entertains when she meets a disreputable character on the edge of a wood at nightfall! His greatcoat was threadbare and his general appearance wretched and neglected. In spite of this both ladies were struck with the 'remarkable refinement of his expression', 'the soft lines of his mouth' and his 'singularly winning smile'. All his life people were to remark upon his smile and the time was coming when Europe was to wait for it as eagerly as cold, hungry children await spring sunshine.

There was something else these ladies noticed about him. He never wore gloves, at a time when the dandies were beginning to strut once more and the patriotic rags of revolution were going out of fashion. The truth of the matter was that he could not afford gloves or good boots either, so he affected to scorn fine dress as unbefitting a soldier and a man.

In spite of the feverish gaiety and the almost hysterical obsession of Parisians with pleasure and frivolity, Napoleon was greatly impressed with the new Paris, particularly so by the women he saw, young, beautiful, sophisticated women, like Madame Tallien, universally known as 'Our Lady of Thermidor' after the romantic part she had played in ending the Terror and emptying the prisons.

'Here alone,' he wrote, 'among all places on earth, women mightly justly aspire to dominion. A woman needs six months in Paris to learn what is due to her and what her empire might really be! Women are more beautiful here than anywhere in the world; they are the all-absorbing business of life in Paris!'

They were indeed. Our Lady of Thermidor was queening it among deputies, speculators and bankers at her pseudo-rustic house in the Cours la Reine. It was she who had initiated the post-Terror fashions of transparent muslin, worn *à la Greque* and more revealing than any fashion since the fig-leaf. It was she, aged twenty-one and so serenely beautiful that she had hardbitten men like Ouvrard the banker grovelling at her feet, who presided over the *Merveilleuses*, with their fantastic hats, monstrously high cravats and striped pantaloons; it was Thérèse Cabarrus, now Citoyenne Tallien, who was hostess at the salon of Barras, the principal inheritor of Robespierre, for her role as the Angel of Mercy had captured the imagination of all Paris and cheering crowds greeted her wherever she went.

Bonaparte was not admitted automatically to this feckless

but exclusive society. His scroll of destiny had unrolled a little at Toulon but not far enough. He was still on the fringe, shaking his 'hound's ears' and pocketing his gloveless hands, while other soldiers, heroes like Hoche and Joubert, hogged the limelight. He was awaiting his turn. By this time he was confident that that turn would come.

It came in the autumn, when the Paris mob, driven to new frenzies by starvation and a worthless currency, rose on behalf of the Royalists and threatened to overwhelm the Directory.

In wild panic the corrupt politicians shouted for a sword and they found Napoleon waiting patiently in the wings.

With his famous whiff of grape-shot he blew away the new revolution overnight, and the Directors, sighing with relief, admitted him into their circle on equal terms.

The scroll had unwound another few inches and Napoleon, in addition to finding the broad road to destiny, had also found himself a wife!

He had been thinking and talking of marriage for a long time now, so persistently and so embarrassingly that his friends began to wonder if this untidy little man had received a damaging wound in the head on the hills around Toulon.

Not long after his arrival in Paris he had pounced upon Madame Permon, a widow some twenty-five years his senior and the only true friend outside the barrack-room that he possessed.

The Permons, a pleasant, hospitable family, were friends of his mother, and Madame Permon, a jolly, well-preserved matron with a grown-up family came from his native Corsica.

In his lean Academy days this charming woman had gone out of her way to be kind to the lonely youth and he now sought to reward her in a dramatic way.

Soon after the death of Madame Permon's husband he proposed a visit to the theatre 'in order to cheer her up' and here, to poor Madame Permon's intense astonishment, he blandly proposed a triple union of Permons and Bonapartes!

Madame's son, he suggested, should marry his sister Pauline, Madame's daughter Laure (later the famous Madame Junot) should wed one of his younger brothers – either would do – and he, here he drew a deep breath, he would marry the widowed Madame Permon!

For almost a minute Madame Permon gazed at him in speechless astonishment. Then her sense of humour came to her rescue and she reeled against the partition of the opera box, helpless with laughter.

Napoleon was understandably annoyed and showed as much. The moment Madame Permon had succeeded in composing her features he pointed out that the age of his bride was a matter of complete indifference to him for 'although she had a son of twenty-five, she certainly did not look more than thirty'!

Madame Permon's maternal heart was touched by this compliment but she seems to have had little difficulty in talking him out of the project, for we next find him exploring the possibilities of marrying an even more mature lady, this time the roistering Mademoiselle Montansier, directrice of the Théâtre du Palais Royal.

There is not much evidence for this proposal but it certainly matches the little Corsican's mood of the moment. Barras, in his unreliable memoirs, makes something of it and even claims that he introduced the two with a view to matrimony. He also adds that at this time the gay old trouper was not less than seventy but was nonetheless 'unafflicted by the infirmities of old age'. He was in a position to know for he had recently made love to her himself.

Another adventuress crossed Napoleon's path about this time, none other than the famous Englishwoman, Grace Dalrymple, who had been mistress to both the Prince of Wales and Philippe Egalité, the Duke of Orleans.

Philippe had been struck down by the guillotine (it was he who advised Sanson, the executioner, to leave his boots because 'they would come off better dead'), and at the height of the Terror pretty English Grace found herself in prison, awaiting the final summons.

The prisons were crammed with beautiful women that summer and Grace was spared by the same reprieve as Madame Tallien and Joséphine Beauharnais, a pair she soon joined in the diverting game of bewitching Paris.

The editor of Grace Dalrymple's memoirs claims that Napoleon included her in his wild volley of unsuccessful proposals, but as this claim was ultimately made by most of the women Napoleon met not too much reliance can be placed on it.

There is no doubt however that once he had turned his back on hesitant little Désirée, he showed the same determination to marry as he was soon to show in driving the Austrians out of Italy. It was the whiff of grape-shot that widened his field and brought him into personal contact with the vice-queen of Madame Tallien's salon, the thirty-two-year-old widow, Joséphine Beauharnais.

At first sight of her his vague longing for domestic bliss, which had shown itself in gusts and sighs aimed in all directions, increased to a hurricane that swept the none-too-eager lady off her feet and at last provided him with an outlet for emotions that had been bottled up since boyhood. In the embrace of the handsome Creole his passion ceased to be a subject for farce, it swept into the orbit of classical romance.

CHAPTER VI

'How strangely you work upon my heart!'

Who was this shrewd, stately woman, who inspired some of the most tender love-letters in the history of marriage? Why is her name for ever linked with Napoleon's, even in the realm of the TV sketch and the bar-parlour joke?

She was already the mother of a fourteen-year-old boy and a twelve-year-old girl when she first attracted the admiring glance of the General in the threadbare greatcoat. She was handsome rather than beautiful, graceful rather than alluring. Her figure was good, she had a pleasant voice, regular features and bad teeth, so bad that she had learned to smile without revealing them. She knew all there was to know about how to make the very best of such charms as she possessed. She had exquisite taste and never wore an item of apparel that did not become her. She was worldly-wise without being intelligent. She could write a good letter but that was the limit of her educational equipment. She had an extraordinarily kind heart, very little nerve and an absolute disregard for the economies of housekeeping. To the last day of her life she was utterly incapable of retaining money, any money. It slipped through her fingers like handfuls of fine sand. She was loyal to her friends but curiously haphazard in her morals. For a woman with such a highly-developed sense of fitness about what to wear, how much rouge to apply, what to say to the right people and how to dispose of the wrong ones, it is astonishing that she was unfastidious when it came to choosing a lover. She seems to have acquired bedfellows much in the same way as she collected jewels and once acquired they ceased to interest her.

Parted from her first husband she went her own way. She

was the mistress of General Hoche whilst in prison and of Barras as soon as she was safe from the guillotine. In the early days of her marriage to Napoleon she undoubtedly took other lovers, yet she seems to have regarded the act of love as the most trifling incident in a woman's everyday life. This is all the more strange when one learns of her qualities as a mistress. After her first, impulsively generous response to Napoleon's passionate advances, her lover wrote : 'I awake all filled with you. Your image, and the intoxicating pleasures of last night, allow my senses no rest. Sweet and matchless Joséphine, how strangely you work upon my heart ... a thousand kisses but give me none back for they set my blood on fire !'

This is not the kind of reaction one would expect of a young and passionate Italian if he had spent the night with an unresponsive woman. Rather it is indisputable evidence of Joséphine's easy familiarity in the courts of love and an eagerness on her part to enslave a man by every means in her power.

Joséphine Tascher de la Pagerie had learned how to please men in the hardest of schools – that of marriage to a man who considered her his social inferior.

Her grandfather, originally a nobleman from the Blois district, was the ne'er-do-well who appears in every generation of most aristocratic families. He, and his eldest son, Joséphine's father, were a pair of lazy, useless men, expert only at sponging. Grandfather Tascher used his aristocratic connections as stock-in-trade. He had no other and never acquired any. Like most men of his kind he drifted overseas in search of better luck and settled on the French-owned island of Martinique, but even here, in a paradise of sun peopled only by men of his stamp and by slaves, he was a dismal failure, and his son Joseph grew up to be exactly like his father, a well-born idler content to support himself and family by expert cadging.

Joseph tried his hand at soldiering but not very seriously, leaving the island as a youngster and returning a few years later as a mere Lieutenant. There was then nothing left for him but marriage to someone with plenty of money and luckily for him there were islanders to whom noble blood meant far more than a promise of industry in a son-in-law.

He married another nobleman's daughter and went to live on his father-in-law's plantation, but in 1766, when his daughter Joséphine was a small child, a hurricane destroyed the establishment and the family, Irishlike, moved into a vacant storehouse.

The Lieutenant accepted the hurricane as a sign from Heaven. He smiled, yawned and shrugged his shoulders. He never repaired the plantation or built himself another house but became what we should now call a beachcomber, an ideal subject for one of the stories of Somerset Maugham. Doubtless he quite enjoyed the remainder of his life in the sun for he did absolutely nothing but eat, sleep, game, talk or solicit. He was always in debt and he must have been a really hard case, for the islanders do not seem to have viewed him with that half-contemptuous esteem so often extended to wasters of this type. His reputation in the island was bad.

Notwithstanding a grinding poverty, Joséphine's childhood was an extremely happy one.

Untrammelled by strictures that would have narrowed her horizon at home she grew up like a young gazelle frisking about a luxuriant reserve. Almost her only companions were the children of Negro slaves, who worshipped her as a little white goddess, a deity who could descend to their level without losing caste.

Delighting in the beauties of nature, passionately devoted to flowers and butterflies, untaught and gloriously unrestrained by her parents, she romped through an idyllic girlhood until she was old enough to be packed off to the convent school at Fort Royale.

Here, in the next four years, she learned a few ladylike accomplishments – singing, dancing, reading, writing and playing upon the guitar but she was never much good at these pursuits. Ballroom dancing was too formal for her taste and the only music she liked was the clack of the flattering tongues of plantation mammies or the uninhibited laughter of their piccaninnies.

Fate, however, had a bunch of rods in pickle for Joséphine and the first of them was homegrown. In the same island another noble family was rearing children and one of them was to play a vital role in Joséphine's future.

Alexandre de Beauharnais, eldest son of the Governor, was three years Joséphine's senior. They had met as children, but when Joséphine was seven Alexandre's father, who had very different ideas on how to rear children, sent the boy to France in order that he could be properly educated.

By the time Joséphine had left her convent Alexandre had grown into an attractive youth of seventeen. He had spent a good deal of his boyhood in the household of the Duke of Rouchefoucauld and it was here that he imbibed the liberal ideas that were to raise him to eminence and cost him his life on the scaffold.

Soon after his seventeenth birthday he joined the army and his family began to think it was time he married.

Their choice of a bride was guided by a watchful relative of the penniless de la Pageries, a member of the Tascher family who had managed to infiltrate into the Beauharnais family when the boy's father was Governor of Martinique, some years before Joséphine was born. She must have been what modern Americans would call a smart operator for this was certainly a catch for a family still snug in their storehouse, waiting for somebody to come along and rebuild their plantation.

The first choice of a bride fell on Joséphine's younger sister but the child died of fever before the proposal could reach the West Indies. As the youngest daughter flatly refused to leave her mother, Joséphine, scenting luxury from afar, promptly volunteered to fill the gap and began to pack her scanty wardrobe.

Father and daughter (the former no doubt much relishing a little jaunt with all expenses paid) sailed in October and landed at Brest the following month. Here they were met by the matchmaking aunt and the young groom, who was disappointed by his bride's appearance but agreeably surprised by her mild temper!

The couple were married in Paris in December and made their home with the Marquis de Beauharnais. To Joséphine, fresh from the plantation, it must have seemed like transportation to Aladdin's Cave.

Disenchantment, however, was not long in coming her way. Utterly untrained for life in aristocratic society and having no weapons in her armoury but youth, freshness and a natural dress sense, the little Creole was cold-shouldered by her husband, who was soon seeking the society of more sophisticated girls.

Joséphine's tearful scenes (scenes that were to be staged by the dozen in the Tuileries in the future) did not upset him as much as they were to upset Napoleon, but her constant flow of tears maddened the young man and he was happy to exchange her society for regimental duty within six months of marriage. He wrote her long, scholarly letters, advising her, optimist that he was, to study and improve her mind!

Joséphine's first child, named Eugène, was born in 1781 and her second, Hortense, two years later but the children did nothing to mend the marriage and it was not long before Alexandre found himself an ambitious mistress and began to explore the possibilities of divorce.

His family openly sided with Joséphine but in spite of this check he achieved a separation and settled down with his mistress on his return from abroad.

Joséphine was given a pension and the temporary custody of both children.

Wretched and depressed by all that occurred she spent a year in a refuge that was maintained for women of nobility who had fallen among thorns.

It was the wisest thing she could have done. At the refuge, the Abbey of Panthemont, she learned in a few months all that her husband had expected her to know when she came to him as a sixteen-year-old bride. The manners and customs of aristocratic life were thus acquired almost incidentally and in search of a finishing school Joséphine moved on to Fontainebleau, where her loyal father-in-law maintained a large establishment.

She was not the kind of woman to sit and brood over the past. Once the initial shock of the broken marriage was behind her she thoroughly enjoyed her freedom and the substantial pension that the courts had awarded her. She is rumoured to have enjoyed other consolations in Fontainebleau, and in view of the ease with which she slipped into an unconventional mode of life during the Revolution this seems extremely likely. She was, however, devoted to her children and so agreeable to everyone around her that she soon won many good friends.

The year before the Revolution broke out she went back to her beloved Martinique, taking with her her daughter Hortense. Her father died about this time and she remained overseas for two years. When she returned, in 1790, the Revolution was in full swing and her errant husband, Alexandre, had espoused its principles and already made a name for himself among the small group of French nobles who supported a constitution on the English pattern.

The chaotic state of the country helped husband and wife to get their personal differences into perspective and they became almost reconciled to one another. They continued to live apart but they met very frequently and the Viscount, now a member of the National Assembly and playing his part in forging the new society, was quick to notice the changes that had taken place in his wife's character during their years of separation.

She was now an elegant woman of twenty-eight, renowned in the society in which they moved for her grace, charm and sweetness of disposition. When the royal family made its celebrated attempt to fly the country Alexandre was for a time the virtual head of the Assembly, but when the courts of Europe declared war on the Republic he exchanged the politician's gavel for a sabre and hurried off to the front.

Joséphine kept in close touch with him but a moderate like Alexandre soon lost his hold on the public. The pace of the Revolution increased with every hour, so that Joséphine was constantly occupied exerting her influence to save friends from imprisonment for the dreaded crime of *incivisme*.

To mask her growing horror of events like the terrible September Massacre of 1792, she dressed her Republican shop-window with a bold display of pedantry, respectively apprenticing her nobly-born children to a carpenter and a dressmaker.

It was of no avail. Nothing could arrest the vicious spiral of extremism and when the Girondins fell and 'the Revolution began to devour its own children', General Beauharnais was seized and thrown into the prison of Les Carmes.

Joséphine's reaction was typical. Instead of laying low lest she should invite a similar fate, she moved heaven and earth to get him out. The inevitable result was that within a month she, too, was in prison and awaiting the summons for a trial that would be nothing but a prelude to death.

Every prison in Paris was crowded and Les Carmes was no exception. In here, living cheek by jowl, were ex-aristocrats like Alexandre, humble little tradespeople who had incurred the spite of someone with influence, the former servants of royalty and minor gentry, unsuccessful soldiers of the Republic, cooks, hairdressers, journalists, poets and a few genuine criminals.

An extraordinary atmosphere prevailed. Once behind the walls the prisoners were allowed to intermingle (there was no space to keep them apart), to entertain friends from outside, even to conduct little love-affairs in the limited privacy of the airless cells.

Joséphine managed to forget her terror of death for a while in an affair with General Hoche. Her husband indulged a romantic passion for another woman prisoner but husband and wife remained on cordial terms. In the shadow of the guillotine, which claimed a fresh batch of their companions every evening, their domestic squabbles must have seemed very trivial.

The knife continued to fall. Towards the end of June Alexandre's name was called and he was taken before the tribunal, condemned, and executed the following day. Joséphine's grief was tempered by her own terrible situation. She wept continuously, showing none of the stoicism displayed by the majority of the prisoners.

All over Paris men and women, distinguished and obscure, were waiting to die, to 'sneeze into the sack' as a Jacobin Terrorist described it, and every evening a convoy of the doomed rumbled towards the guillotine set up in the vast open space now known as Place de la Concorde.

Almost all the Girondins went down and so did Danton and his friends, killed for the unforgivable crime of moderation. The Revolution had developed into a terrible game of musical chairs with no one, not even the executioners themselves, daring to prophesy who would survive the slaughter.

The end came unexpectedly, on 9 July 1794.

Fearful of their own impending doom a gang of ruffians arrested Robespierre and his intimates and had them guillotined in less than twenty-four hours. They had no intention whatever of stopping the Terror but had merely acted to save their skins. The Parisians, however, had now had more than enough blood-letting. It would have been checked long before had the victims shown less courage on the scaffold and screamed and wept, as Joséphine was doing in Les Carmes, and the Thermidorians discovered to their bewilderment that they were regarded by the vast majority of their fellow citizens as saviours and deliverers.

They did what one would expect of them in the circumstances. They accepted the credit, preened themselves, set

44

up their Directory and arrested the least savoury of their former companions, beasts like Carrier, the Butcher of Nantes, and sadists like Le Bon, the Butcher of Arras.

The prisons emptied rapidly and one of the first to step into the summer sunshine was Joséphine. She had survived a terrible experience and it taught her a great deal. She at once set about looking round for a protector.

Latterly she must have learned far more than the nuns had taught her at the far-off convent, or the troubled gentle-women had imparted to her during her sojourn at the Abbey of Panthemont. Aiming high she secured the interest of Barras, the leading man in France, and it was not long before she, who had been without a change of clothes, was installed in a pleasant house in the Rue Chantereine with her own carriage and pair from the royal stables of the dead King!

There was a kind of rough justice in the appropriation of this equipage. On going to the front two years before, Alexandre, her husband, had presented the Army of the Rhine with his own carriage and pair.

Joséphine made the most of her good fortune. The shadow of death had been miraculously lifted from her and all she wanted to do now was to relax, to wear pretty clothes again, to attend parties, to gossip and to forget the dreadful past.

General Hoche, her prison lover, was a very useful con-tact. He had been set free at the same time and obligingly took his mistress's fourteen-year-old son, Eugène, on his staff. Hortense was packed off to Madame Campan's famous school for girls at St Cloud and life went merrily on until a certain little Corsican General, with far too much intensity and a hound's ears coiffure, arrived on the scene, having been called in by Protector Barras to stop yet another revo-lution from breaking out.

The manner in which these two dissimilar people met is as odd and romantic as everything else in Joséphine's life.

After the insurgents had been mown down by Napoleon's

strategically-placed cannon he made the wise decision to disarm the Sections. If somebody had done this before, the Revolution might have steered itself into still waters while the King yet lived and a sound constitution was still a possibility. Among the arms surrendered was Alexandre Beauharnais' sword, dutifully handed in by Joséphine, who, as a mistress of Barras, was anxious to set an example.

Her boy, however, had a soldier's blood in his veins and was quick to make a personal appeal to Bonaparte for the return of the weapon. The triumphant little General was greatly struck by the boy's manner and at once returned it. Joséphine, never slow to miss opportunities of this sort, at once called on Napoleon in order to thank him for the gesture.

One look, one brief, grateful word of thanks on the woman's part and Napoleon was head over heels in love. Within days he had returned Joséphine's call. Within a month she had become his mistress and was at her wits end how to prevent herself from becoming his wife!

Why did this indolent, pleasant, experienced courtesan agree to marry Napoleon?

Did his frenzied wooing arouse some genuine response in her, or was she so insecure that she welcomed the chance of marrying any man eager to offer herself and her two children a home in a city gone mad?

It would appear from correspondence attributed to her at this time that neither reason is valid. She was, in fact, extremely reluctant to yield to his importunities and that despite the cynical Barras' advice. Barras was growing tired of her and wanted her off his hands for good.

The Corsican's passion bored her and she was very easily bored. She confessed to a friend that she neither loved nor disliked the man whose ardour of affection 'amounts almost to madness', that she admired his courage and intelligence, his ability to understand thoughts before they were expressed but was nevertheless 'somewhat fearful of that control which he seems anxious to exercise over all about him'. Her 'spring of life', she goes on, was past and when his love cooled, 'as it certainly will after marriage, he will reproach me for having prevented him from ultimately forming a better match!'

Her ultimate decision was probably influenced by Barras, who assured her that if she married Napoleon he would appoint him General of the Army of Italy. There was, after all, a limited security in this assurance. Joséphine always found it very difficult to think more than a month or two ahead and she might have reasoned that, even if Napoleon did nothing spectacular in the south, his appointment would at least keep him out of the capital and leave her free to enjoy herself in his absence.

Her capitulation threw Napoleon into transports of joy and they were married almost at once, the purely civil ceremony being performed at the Registry Office of the Section, on 9 March 1796.

What a strange wedding it was!

It was scheduled for eight o'clock in the evening but for some reason that has never been explained the groom was two hours late!

The witnesses were Barras, Tallien, a lawyer friend of Joséphine called Camelet (who was brought along to watch her interests) and Napoleon's aide-de-camp, a young soldier called Lamarois.

The bride's party, which included Barras and Tallien, both Directors who owed their survival to Napoleon's whiff of grape-shot, arrived on time. For two hours they and the bride sat kicking their heels in the *Mairie*. The mayor himself went to sleep and was only awakened by the rattle of scabbards on the stone steps as groom and aide-de-camp came bustling in. Napoleon made no apology for the delay. He merely shook the mayor by the shoulder and demanded that the ceremony be performed at once.

There was not much to do, the contract having been

drawn up the previous day. It still survives and is surely one of the most interesting Napoleonic documents in existence.

The groom added eighteen months to his age and the bride, not to be outdone, knocked four years off hers! Thus the six-year gap between them was appreciably reduced, Napoleon writing himself down as twenty-eight, and Joséphine pretending to be twenty-nine.

There were other inaccuracies. Napoleon, besides giving a wrong birth date, stated that he was born in Paris and produced a birth certificate to prove it! Perhaps this fact accounts for his delay in getting to the *Mairie* for he might well have been occupied in forging a birth certificate. The aide-de-camp had no right to stand as a witness for he was still a minor, but, as the painstaking author Lenôtre points out, 'who of those present would ever imagine that future historians would criticize these minutiae? Was not the document destined to lay forgotten in the registrar's dusty office?'

There was a kind of studied carelessness about the entire proceedings, as though nobody present, least of all bride and groom, expected the marriage to last more than a few weeks or were anxious to hurry off somewhere else and resented loss of time and the lateness of the hour.

When it was over they all shook hands and went their several ways. Barras returned to the Luxembourg. Tallien went off to find the adored Thérèse at their sham rustic house near the Champs Elysées (he was not to have her much longer, poor fool, for she was soon to abandon him for the wealthy banker, Ouvrard) and the aide-de-camp and the lawyer strolled off for a drink. The newly-married pair climbed into Joséphine's carriage and drove off to Joséphine's little villa in the Rue Chantereine.

Even then the story of this unconventional wedding was not complete, for Napoleon found that he was expected to share his wedding night with Fortuné, Joséphine's spoiled and snarling poodle.

He tried, and who will blame him, to dispose of the dog

but both bride and pet put up a brisk and successful resistance to this act of tyranny. Commenting ruefully on this experience he wrote : 'I was informed that I must make up my mind to sleep elsewhere or consent to the division. That rather put me out : but it was either one thing or the other, and the favourite was less accommodating than I was !'

Astonishing amiability on the part of a man who was to hold Europe in thrall for nearly two decades !

The poodle possessed a good deal more rashness than some of Napoleon's subsequent opponents. It is reported that he 'bit the happy husband's leg, yet without incurring his malice'. Writing from Italy some weeks later the victor says : 'A million kisses, and some even for Fortuné, notwithstanding his viciousness.'

If all the details of the story of Fortuné are true, and there seems no reason at all to doubt them, then it cannot be claimed that Napoleon lacked a sense of humour.

The following day, 10 March, was all that the couple were able to spare for the honeymoon and they spent most of it at Saint-Germain, visiting Joséphine's children in school.

Both Eugène and Hortense had already met their stepfather, Eugène having made his acquaintance when he called on the General for his father's sword.

The boy took to him as readily as Napoleon took to his stepson. They had something in common, a longing for military glory, and their friendship endured throughout Napoleon's career and was strong enough to survive the putting aside of his mother for the daughter of the Austrian Emperor. The early promise Eugène had shown was amply fulfilled in the years to come. He emerges from the cesspool of betrayal in 1814 and 1815 without a stain on his character. Napoleon's high opinion of the young man was maintained to the end.

The girl was not so easily converted. From the first she was greatly intimidated by Napoleon's manner, having met him shortly before the marriage at a dinner-party given by Barras. On that occasion she had sat next to him and Napoleon, who could be very charming indeed with young people, appears to have frightened Hortense very badly, so much so that for years their relationship was in jeopardy.

Afterwards Hortense was always shy with him and it is reported by one of her school-fellows that soon after the dinner-party the child burst into tears in front of her companions, exclaiming that '... General Bonaparte frightened her and she feared he would be very severe with her and Eugène!'

The visit to the school, however, went off without incident. Notwithstanding his encounter with the poodle Fortuné, Napoleon was in high spirits. After putting several questions to the nervous pupils he playfully pinched his stepdaughter's ear, a mark of affection he subsequently bestowed upon scores of Imperial guardsmen who had earned decorations under fire.

The proprietor of the school – the celebrated Madame Campan – was an undoubted gainer by this honeymoon visit, for Napoleon promised her that he would send his youngest sister Caroline to be a pupil. He kept his promise and Madame Campan's school became as fashionable as the modern Cheam and Gordonstoun, counting among its pupils many of the young women who flowered into the wits and beauties of the Empire. Almost anybody who was anybody among women of the Imperial court spent a period at Madame Campan's school.

On the following morning, 11 March, a coach drew up outside the newly-weds' home in the Rue Chantereine. The groom emerged from the house loaded with maps, writing materials and military accoutrements of one sort and another. There were last-minute embraces, a whip cracked and the coach rattled off down the road to the south on the first stage of a journey that was to set millions of men on journeys that were to end on the field of Waterloo.

At every stage the twenty-six-year-old General sat down

in a tavern to write to his beloved and some of the most passionate letters in the ageless history of love were penned at these wayside inns. Each had a single theme that whirled across the pages like a tongue of flame. 'You will come,' he begged, 'and quick! If you hesitate you will find me ill ... take wings ... come ... come!'

But Joséphine did not take wings. She folded the letters and yawned.

CHAPTER VII

Notre Dame des Victoires

Napoleon joined the famished Army of Italy at Nice on 26 March 1796. It had been stationary for three years and disease and desertion had reduced it to thirty thousand mutinous men. Its opponents numbered at least twice that number.

By 8 June the French had occupied Milan, bundled the Austrians out of Lombardy, knocked their Sardinian allies out of the war, won eight battles, any one of which would have earned the victorious General a reputation, and established Napoleon as virtual dictator of Northern Italy.

Paris went mad with joy. Here at last, after nearly a decade of upheaval and a succession of governments composed of monsters, sadists, windbags and nonentities, was a real, live hero! The man himself was hundreds of miles distant, winning still more victories and sending home coachloads of trophies and loot but his wife was at hand; the jubilant Parisians determined to make the most of her.

All through the month of May, when a stream of couriers bringing news of fresh triumphs were galloping up from the south, Joséphine warmed herself in the sunshine of her odd little husband's reputation.

She was not a vain woman but she was an extremely sociable one and she enjoyed every moment of her triumph, the more so perhaps because it was totally unexpected.

Everywhere she went cheering crowds assembled and bystanders exclaimed: 'There she is! That's his wife! Isn't she beautiful?' Almost everyone who came close to Joséphine was prepared to accept grace and charm as beauty.

It was soon common knowledge that he was madly, hopelessly in love with her, that in the midst of planning complicated movements of his tattered legions he turned aside to write not one but a whole spate of love-letters, that in every courier's bag containing demands for reinforcements and terms of an enemy's surrender, were three or four such letters for her. Just as the twentieth-century newspaper-reading public devours the latest developments in a film-star's romance, so the Parisian's, who had been fed on blood and rhetoric for six long years, were eager to discuss their hero's passion for this smiling, elegant woman, who rode out from her modest home to the Luxembourg in order to inspect the batches of captured colours her husband sent home as proofs of his triumphs.

Junot, the General's gay young aide-de-camp, came galloping in with a stand of twenty-one one morning and immediately sought her out in order to inform her that the only thing needed to crown her husband's success in Italy was her presence soon. *Soon! Now! At once!*

Joséphine pouted and went home to think up an excuse. She loved Paris and was enjoying herself. She sighed at the prospect of crossing France in a dusty coach and burying herself in a camp, where pretty clothes would become rumpled and unfashionable in a matter of days. She thought of saying that she was too ill to travel but put aside this idea as ridiculous. How could she plead ill-health when she went to a fête or a reception every day and a dinner-party each night?

Then she hit upon something more plausible and wrote saying that she was expecting a child. Napoleon was delighted.

'How shall I ever atone for all my hard thoughts of you?' he scribbled. 'You were ill and I accused you of lingering in Paris ... a child, sweet as its mother, is soon to lie in your arms!'

There came a time, however, when even this excuse was insufficient cause for further delays. Reluctantly she set out for Milan and with her went a cohort of companions and a small baggage-train of trunks and boxes.

The villagers on the road down into Italy must have scratched their heads when her cavalcade clattered by. Accustomed by this time to the constant passage of marching troops, squadrons of hussars, artillery trains, and a ceaseless stream of couriers, they had not seen anything like this procession since the pre-Revolution progresses of grand seigneurs, travelling between Versailles and their provincial châteaux.

With Joséphine was her confidential maid, Louise Compoint, the irritable poodle Fortuné (licking its lips, no doubt in anticipation of another bite at its rival), Napoleon's brother Joseph, handsome young Junot, General Leclerc, soon to marry Napoleon's sister Pauline, and Leclerc's Adjutant, this last an extremely personable Lieutenant who went by the name of Hippolyte Charles.

Hippolyte was what we should now describe as 'quite a card.' He was exceptionally handsome and his figure was displayed to advantage in a gorgeous cavalry uniform. He was full of brash self-confidence and had acquired a great reputation as a wit and a clever punster. He was equally at home in the saddle or when organizing original party games in a drawing-room. He had something else to recommend him, something which is always appreciated by women in wartime, a whole crop of 'contacts' with slick army contractors who were handling goods in short supply.

Had Hippolyte Charles been born a century-and-a-half later he would have known exactly where to go for nylon stockings and unrationed petrol; instead of a horse he would have used a noisy sports-car and referred to his decorations as 'gongs'. Every army in history has produced its crop of Hippolytes and ladies have never ceased to prefer them to austere husbands who are inclined to take war a shade too seriously.

During the journey down into Italy, Adjutant Charles was the life and soul of the party, although young Junot played his part, making great headway with Joséphine's maid, Louise. This conquest, by the day, did little to endear him to the General's wife, who was fond of her Louise but did not welcome competition.

Meanwhile Napoleon was skirmishing in the valley of competition.

Established in Milan as a conqueror and the Commander-in-Chief of an army pledged to establish liberty, fraternity, equality and uncomplicated divorce laws, he was surrounded by every attractive woman who entertained hopes of improving her position in life.

Here was a man, not yet twenty-seven years old, passionate by nature and brilliantly successful in everything he undertook! He was married to be sure, but his wife was a long way off and, it was rumoured, in no great hurry to join him. Surely a woman owed it to herself to make the most of her opportunities before the young conqueror was caught up in some fresh campaign or went galloping off home to rejoin his ageing wife!

Thoughts such as these found a permanent perch in the pretty head of Madame Grassini, the most eminent contralto of her time, who was then drawing enthusiastic audiences to the Scala Opera House.

Grassini, besides being the possessor of a wonderful voice, was a also a beautiful woman. If she was unable to capture the attention of the hero then who could?

The answer to this question was no one. Grassini did her very best and as an Italian Napoleon was not slow to appreciate her remarkable merits as a singer but in all other respects she courted him in vain. Her beauty and her endearing little artifices (she had a trick of saying shocking things in a childlike way and then hurriedly excusing herself on the grounds of unfamiliarity with the language!) meant less than nothing to him. He complimented her gravely on her performances and then turned aside to write yet another letter to his matchless Joséphine. It was not simply that he was heart-whole. His reticence was also due to an acute appraisal of his position. He had lived through a Revolution and had seen too many hard-won reputations come crashing down on the orange peel of scandal. 'My success or failure depended on my behaviour,' he wrote years later, in St Helena. 'I might have let my caution slumber for one brief hour and how many of my victories depended on no longer time than that?'

So Grassini dashed herself upon the Corsican rock in vain and at last retired, bruised and breathless, but not wholly convinced of his impregnability. Had she but known it there was nothing wrong with her attack but its timing. Her opportunity came three years later, when his passion for Joséphine had spent itself and he was high enough above the ordinary man to snap his fingers at scandal.

One other beautiful woman set her cap at Napoleon during this spring of success. She was Madame Visconti, formerly the widow of an Italian Count, who had made a second marriage to a noted diplomat.

Visconti was no singer but she was one of the most beautiful women of her time and remained so, up to the day of her death. There is hardly one diarist of the time who fails to remark upon Visconti's lovely skin, the classic mould of her features, or the seductive grace of her figure. She was the Italian Récamier but far more accessible to admirers. Alas for her charms! Her advances met with even less success than Grassini's. He would not give her a second glance.

Visconti was more practical than the opera star. Having failed to capture the Commander-in-Chief she switched to his Chief of Staff, forty-two-year-old Berthier, an ex-Royalist officer whose brilliant staff work had played an important part in the French victories.

Poor Berthier, who was small, shock-headed and at a grave physical disadvantage to the handsome young men of his staff, was speechless with delight. Hardly able to credit his good fortune he mooned about Italy in an ecstatic trance and it would not be surprising to learn that, while in this up-lifted mood, he had despatched the entire reserve cavalry in the wrong direction. Everybody chaffed him but he did not mind. His Chief had found world acclaim and the junior officers had found glory in abundance, but he . . . middle-aged, scrubby-haired and not by any stretch of imagination, handsome, had won Madame Visconti, the most beautiful woman in the world!

The association endured for the rest of his life. When Napoleon insisted that his Chief of Staff married a Bavarian Princess, Berthier managed to persuade his wife to share a house with his mistress and all three lived happily together whenever the Maréchal was able to snatch a moment from maps and compasses. In the great days that followed this was regarded as a rich joke among the roysterers of the Grand Army.

Joséphine's cavalcade arrived in Milan in July but hus-band and wife did not have time for an extension of the one-day honeymoon.

Almost at once Napoleon was off again to meet a new Austrian threat and the history of Joséphine's stay in the theatre of war is one of tiresome darts and dashes about a countryside disorganized by the constant passage of armies.

Several times during this period Napoleon's fate hung in the balance and at least once he came close to being killed in action. Whenever he could spare half-a-day he rushed back to Joséphine, who was being fêted as a kind of queen by the Italian aristocracy and the rich business interests in the conquered territory.

Sometimes, in response to his continued requests, she joined him in the field and once, when the enemy was press-ing too close, she came under Austrian fire at Brescia.

This alarming experience was more than enough for Joséphine, who had lived under a suspended knife during the Revolution and sought no repetition of the experience. She left the firing-line at once and scuttled back to safety in tears. Contempt for physical danger was never one of Joséphine's characteristics.

Napoleon accepted the situation and ceased to plague her into making actual appearances at his side but he continued to complain bitterly of her shortcomings as a letter-writer. 'I do not love you . . . you are a wretched, stupid, awkward little thing,' he scolded. 'You do not write to me at all . . . what are you doing all day long?'

He exploded when he found out, for two activities on the part of the beloved had at last filtered through to the Commander-in-Chief. One was Joséphine's devotion to Adjutant Charles, the handsome punster, the other concerned her large-scale acceptances of gifts from interested parties, gifts that were really nothing but bribes.

It is doubtful if at this period anything but a gay friendship existed between Joséphine and Charles. His conversation amused her and she liked amusing conversation. He managed to remain at her side despite his military duties but as soon as their association was brought to Napoleon's notice the husband acted with his customary despatch. Charles was arrested, dismissed from the army and sent packing : his irregular dealings with crooked contractors made this part of the business very simple. The rumour of bribes, however, was a more serious matter, for Napoleon had a strict code in these matters and could not afford to have it whispered abroad that his wife was guilty of nepotism. He found time, Heaven knows how, to investigate these 'gifts' and a stormy scene resulted. Joséphine talked him round and was allowed to keep the jewels, pictures and other gifts already received but she was told that on no account whatever was she to accept any more. She got over the difficulty by accepting everything that was offered and then bluffing him into believing that each new gift was something out of the original consignment ! She was always extremely clever at this wifely manoeuvre and later on, when her crazy extravagance caused other and more terrible scenes, she not only used the same trick but persuaded Bourrienne, Napoleon's solemn secretary, to play her hand in the game.

Admirer Charles turned his expulsion from the army to very good advantage. He had learned a thing or two about contracting and he at once went into business on his own account and soon made a fortune. He must have smiled to himself when the Empire fell and he stood watching the scarred veterans sitting at the café tables, too poor and discredited to order anything more than a litre of *vin ordinaire*.

Fresh campaigns were crowned with fresh victories and at last the whole of Italy lay at the conqueror's feet. It was time to return to Paris and plan fresh ventures, so, in the autumn of 1797, Napoleon set off for France, where he was received as few returning soldiers have ever been welcomed by a civilian population.

Joséphine did not accompany him. Capriciously she chose this very moment to tour other parts of Italy and her husband was either too busy or too irritated to reason with her. She completed her little tour and came back a month after his arrival. He was still madly in love with her and she was beginning to appreciate the undoubted advantages of this fact, for she wrote of him as 'the dearest husband in the world who can refuse me nothing'.

It was true. They settled at their house in the Rue Chantereine, which he had bought and she had furnished out of the proceeds of the Italian campaigns.

Napoleon always claimed that he came out of Italy with nothing but his General's pay but this is very unlikely. The acquisition and furnishing of their home must have cost far more than he could have saved from this source.

She accompanied him to all the fêtes and receptions given in his honour. He would not attend one without her and would not leave her side when they arrived. Part of his initial passion had spent itself but in its place there grew an appreciation of her value to him as confidante, friend and hostess. The Directors hated him, for his triumphs had reduced them to the size of pigmies. There were storms ahead and he knew that he would need all Joséphine's skill at winning friends and allies. When they chaffed him for his devotion he replied, quite simply, 'I love my wife', and he was speaking with all sincerity. Signs were not lacking that the marriage was now settling down and if Joséphine could have had a child she might never have heard of names like Austerlitz, Jena and Waterloo. Unluckily for everybody Joséphine was past the age of child-bearing and no one regretted this more bitterly than her husband, who was already thinking in terms of a dynasty.

He mastered his disappointment. If there was to be no child then there must be fresh triumphs. He withdrew from the social round and sat down with Berthier to study the maps, maps of the Orient.

CHAPTER VIII

'Vive Clioupâtre!'

In the early spring of 1798 there was brisk bustle in and about the offices of the Paris theatrical agents.

The theatre had boomed during the Revolution. Ever since war had broken out, more than five years before, a steady flow of soldiers, always enthusiastic supporters of drama and comedy, had passed through the capital, but here was something that promised high adventure to enterprising actors and actresses – an extended tour, not into the sleepy provinces, not even to Italy, but to the land of the Pharaohs!

Napoleon was expected to be away some time and with an eye on army welfare he set about recruiting his own theatrical company. Invitations were issued to all actors of note but few qualifications were needed for aspiring actresses. Any attractive girl possessing limited stage experience was offered a free passage out and full employment for as long as the campaign lasted.

In the event only one actress, an Italian who had married an officer, volunteered. There was great enthusiasm in the profession when the invitation was issued but second thoughts induced a marked cooling off among the ladies of the theatre. The more they thought about Egypt the less the prospect of a tented theatre in the desert appealed and when the expedition sailed from Toulon, in May of that year, only one of the four hundred vessels in the armada carried a woman who was neither a regimental cantinière nor the wife of a high-ranking officer. Even these ladies were not listed as orthodox passengers. Having failed to recruit a stage troop, Napoleon settled for a contingent of servants and

Egyptologists and issued strict orders against the embarkation of the kind of camp-followers who accompanied all field armies of the eighteenth century.

Three months in Paris, following his triumphs in Italy, had persuaded Napoleon that no General, no matter how successful, could build a permanent reputation on two campaigns.

The leading politicians hated him, and their fulsome addresses of congratulation did nothing to mask their obvious desire to be rid of him as quickly and quietly as possible. For his part he, too, was restless. His eye searched every horizon for a new field of glory. He even considered an immediate invasion of England but ultimately rejected the venture, pointing out to enthusiastic Directors that it would be at least six years before the French fleet was strong enough to dispute the Channel crossing with Nelson's Band of Brothers.

It was essential, however, that some sort of blow should be struck at the Revolution's most tenacious enemy and when he revived the old scheme of a sally against England's trade routes in the East the Directory gave him every encouragement. They probably reasoned that this would be the last they would ever see of him, that he would disappear into the Orient and either be killed fighting the Turks, struck down by some Oriental disease or carried away to languish as a prisoner-of-war in a Portsmouth hulk. Even if he triumphed in the field his ambition would certainly lead him still further east into India, so that whatever transpired he would cease to strut about Paris, robbing the dingy survivors of the Terror of every gleam of limelight.

The General organized the vast expedition with his usual efficiency and at first it was arranged that Joséphine should accompany him. Like the actresses, however, Joséphine hastily backed down, pleading ill-health. It had been difficult enough to get her down to Milan. To persuade her to face flies, scorpions and the steamy discomfort of the Nile Valley was beyond even Napoleon's powers.

He accepted her refusal philosophically. By this time he

was fully aware of his 'star' and although he was still in love with her she no longer enslaved him in the way she had done when he rode down into Italy less than two years ago.

She roused herself sufficiently to travel to Toulon and wave him goodbye. Standing with thousands of other women she watched the huge armada cast anchor and sail into the south-east, after which she tripped away to take the waters at a health resort. It was eighteen months before she was to see him again and then she was to come within an ace of losing him altogether.

Floods of tears must have been shed on the Toulon quays that May morning but Joséphine's were not among them. Why should she weep? She was already uncrowned Queen of France and being an incurable optimist she could read nothing but success in the future. She could weep, and none more easily, when things were going badly, as in the Carmes prison or under the raking fire of Austrian batteries in Italy, but a lover's parting left her dry-eyed.

Another soldier's wife shed no tears that morning. Her name was Margaret Pauline Fourès. She was petite, violet-eyed, flaxen-haired and newly-wed. Her husband was a newly-commissioned Lieutenant in the 22nd Infantry of the line.

Pauline's cheerfulness was not attributable to lack of affection for her husband. She was happy because she was one of the few who did not remain on the quay to wave a handkerchief. Attired as a soldier she was now standing beside her husband, Lieutenant Fourès, watching the coast of France recede in the heat haze. Like the Commander-in-Chief she, too, had a rendezvous with destiny.

Marguerite Pauline, surnamed Bellisle, was the illegitimate daughter of a gentleman and a cook. She was born in the pretty, walled town of Carcassonne, in the valley of the Aude, and her presence on board the troopship in a soldier's uniform was the second of a series of adventures that were to enliven her long and bizarre journey through life. Many of her fellow passengers had less than a year to live but Pauline's future stretched far into the unpredictable future. She was to survive almost until a regenerated Prussia overthrew Napoleon's nephew and his legend-buttressed Empire, in 1870!

Between then and the day on which she waved farewell to less enterprising wives at Toulon she was to have many lovers and three husbands. In between her love-affairs she was to write several novels, paint many pictures and make several fortunes. She was, in fact, to lead an extraordinarily full and colourful life and to die with a sigh of fulfilment at the ripe old age of ninety!

Marguerite's early life reads like that of a heroine in a mid-Victorian novel. Exceptionally pretty, possessing a small but dainty figure and a strong sense of humour, she soon overcame the handicap of an obscure birth. She had an elfin charm that appealed to every man she met and not only to young men, who were at once attracted by her soft mouth and abundant fair hair – 'Enough', says a contemporary, 'to cover her entire body'. She also attracted elderly men, who sometimes took a fatherly interest in her, men like Monseigneur de Sales, the lawyer of Carcassonne, who employed her about his house as a dressmaker and needlewoman.

M. de Sales was an amateur song-writer and soon discovered that his wife's pretty little dressmaker had a small but charming voice. He persuaded her to make her début at one of his dinner-parties and sing some of his verses set to music. So prettily did she perform on this occasion that she at once acquired a reputation as an entertainer, attracting, among others, the attention of a certain Monsieur Fourès, son of a prosperous local merchant.

Fourès, who had served as a soldier but had recently got his discharge, fell head over heels in love with 'La Bellilotte', as she was nicknamed, and at once proposed marriage.

Pauline hesitated, influenced by her employer's paternal advice to accompany him to Paris (possibly in the role of needlewoman) in order to explore the chances of a better match. The glimpses of prosperity afforded her at M. de Sales little dinner-parties, however, had made Pauline very impatient for a home of her own. She, too, wanted to entertain and play hostess to a group of admiring friends and young Fourès was not without means, so in the end she accepted the proposal and would probably have settled down in Carcassonne to a life of domestic bliss had not her unfortunate husband been tempted to re-enlist in the army when Napoleon asked for officer volunteers to accompany him to Egypt.

Acccepted and restored to his original rank, Fourès was accompanied by his wife to the rendezvous at Toulon. Here, unable to part from her after so brief a spell of married life, the Lieutenant disguised the girl in a soldier's uniform and smuggled her up the gangway to the troopship.

Under the crowded conditions on board, her identity could not have remained a secret for very long, but the military authorities seem to have winked at the young couple's stratagem and no disciplinary action was taken against the husband.

On arrival in Egypt the pair disembarked and set up house in Cairo, the Lieutenant concerning himself with his military duties and his wife, now in feminine attire, enjoying the limited delights of garrison life in occupied territory.

We might never had heard of them had not a certain letter from France slipped through British blockade and reached the aide-de-camp of the Commander-in-Chief.

Ashore in Egypt Napoleon soon swept everything before him, just as he had done in his previous campaigns. The famous Mameluke cavalry was annihilated at the Battle of the Pyramids and the whole country fell under French dominion in a matter of weeks.

Nelson, however, after missing interception of his enemy en route for the Orient, took his revenge in the Delta and almost exterminated the French fleet, isolating the invaders from their home base. After the Battle of the Nile Napoleon might as well have been in Java or Botany Bay for all the contact he was able to maintain with Paris but he remained undismayed, confident of returning home by a prodigious land march, in the style of Alexander.

His confidence in his 'star' and talents remained but his personal pride and his faith in his marriage received something like a deathblow when his aide-de-camp, Junot, sought a private audience with him one morning and handed him a letter that had evaded Nelson's cruisers.

The letter was a circumstantial account of Joséphine's shameless liaison with Hippolyte Charles.

Junot must have searched his heart very thoroughly before he made up his mind to break the news. The two men were much more than Commander-in-Chief and military aide. They were close personal friends and had been so for the past five years, ever since Junot, as a Sergeant of hussars, had flatly refused to enter Toulon and accomplish a spying mission in civilian clothes. 'Are you disobeying my orders?' Napoleon had asked him. 'No,' said Sergean Junot, lightly, 'but if I go at all I'll damned well go in my uniform!'

His courage and assurance had impressed his Chief and they fought the Italian campaigns side by side. Junot, it will be recalled, was the same gay young hussar who had escorted a reluctant Joséphine down into Italy in 1796 and incurred her grave displeasure by directing his battery of charms at the maid instead of the mistress. Hippolyte Charles, the personable punster, had been there on that occasion and Junot had watched him captivate Joséphine. Now, in his mail, was reliable information that the ex-Adjutant had moved in again the moment Napoleon was out of the way and Junot's loyalty (throughout his entire life he never ceased to adore Napoleon) proved too strong to allow him to burn the letter and keep silent.

Judging by the letter it looked as though Our Lady of Victories had been persuaded to share the Paris politician's view that the Whirlwind had now whisked himself out of their lives for good. She had bought an extensive estate outside Paris and Charles was actually sharing it with her. Whilst the husband was making war under the Pyramids the wife was making love under the chestnuts at Malmaison, a mansion that she had acquired, redecorated and equipped on Napoleon's credit!

Her brazen infidelity outraged Napoleon's family but it was not her disloyalty that made them choke with rage. What brought their fury to the boil was her fantastic extravagance, an extravagance that was already becoming a byword in Paris.

Before leaving for Egypt, Napoleon had appointed his brother Joseph to watch over his interests and to keep a discreet eye on Joséphine. Poor Joseph was finding this assignment an even more disagreeable task than the previous one set him by his terrifying brother – that of wooing little Désirée by proxy.

The Bonaparte family had never liked Joséphine. They resented having to share a gold-mine with a total stranger. Napoleon, they felt, was an exclusive family asset and they alone were entitled to share his glory and the material benefits that attended it.

All their lives Napoleon's mother, brothers and sisters were to be outraged by Joséphine's carelessness with family money. It was, they argued, one thing to climb into bed with a handsome young man the moment her husband's back was turned but quite another to spend money – *their* money – with a prodigality that was causing Paris tradesmen to fall over one another in their eagerness to open accounts with Citoyenne Bonaparte.

The family yearned for Napoleon's return so that he might put an end to this ridiculous marriage once and for all. They watched Joséphine like a row of angry buzzards and at last dispatched Joseph to reason with her and attempt to steer her back, if not to the path of virtue, then at least to that of careful housekeeping.

Joseph failed in this as he was doomed to fail in everything he undertook. He did not succeed in persuading her to break off her affair with Charles. He made even less progress in the field of finance.

Joséphine heard him out and then laughed at him. For the first time in her life she could indulge in endless shopping sprees and not all the Bonapartes in Corsica were going to stop her from buying one hat or one piece of jewellery that caught her fancy.

Joseph puffed and fumed and his mother, the solemn Letizia, presided over endless conferences of glum-faced Bonapartes. The family turned over one plan or another, all aimed at stopping up this terrifying leak in the family coffers but their discussions were barren. Nothing could be done until Napoleon came home and if that did not happen soon all the gold in France would be needed to extricate his wife from the clutches of creditors.

Napoleon took the news badly and sat down to write Joseph a long, despairing letter. 'Look after my interests I beseech you,' he begged. 'I have a great deal of trouble at home; the veil has been torn off once and for all – I have no one left in the world but you . . . greatness bores me . . . at twenty-nine I find that fame is vanity . . . I've got to the end of everything . . . !'

Thus he wallowed in a sea of self-pity, reminding us vividly of the outpourings of the lonely, half-starved youth of the previous decade.

There is no doubt that he had made up his mind to divorce Joséphine as soon as he returned. In the meantime he saw no point in maintaining the role of adoring husband and in a sullen mood he ordered a parade of oriental beauties, in order that he might look them over like a pasha seeking a wife in the slave-market. Thus far had he travelled since the night a little over two years before, when Grassini, the opera star and Visconti, the most beautiful woman in Italy, had exerted all their appeal to win him.

The dusky beauty parade was a great disappointment, at all events as far as he was concerned. He found the beauties of the Nile far too obese for his taste but Junot and some of the other staff officers were not so fastidious. The handsome aide-de-camp selected an Abyssinian slave called Xraxarne, whom he nicknamed 'Jaunette', and his wife tells us that this woman bore him a son, christened Othello. Junot was not married at this point and in ten years to come his wife treated Xraxarne as a family joke, an illustration of the broadmindedness of Frenchwomen at this period.

Napoleon, however, was not long in finding compensation for the loss of his wife's affections and the obesity of the local girls.

Returning from a festival outside Cairo one day the Commander-in-Chief's entourage overtook a caravan of donkeys conveying a party of European women into the city.

The women were the wives of officers who, in one way or another, had contrived to join their husbands in the field and Napoleon's quick ear caught the sound of a particularly attractive peal of laughter. He made enquiries and was informed that the silvery laughter was that of Madame Fourès, the wife of an obscure Lieutenant of infantry. When next at the Tivoli Gardens, the rendezvous of all the Europeans in Cairo, he managed to take a discreet peep at the little needlewoman. He instantly made up his mind to seduce her.

In these matters, as in all else, Napoleon acted as methodically as he acted on the battlefield.

General Dupuy, commander of the Cairo garrison, was ordered to give a little dinner-party and to invite Madame Fourès to attend. The garrison-commander knew his business. He invited 'La Bellilotte' but conveniently forgot to invite her husband, a circumstance that caused the latter bewilderment.

Madame Fourès, who also knew her business, accepted the invitation and no one was much surprised when the Commander-in-Chief dropped in on the party and took a long, careful look at the demure guest. So long and steady was his scrutiny that he did what nobody had been able to do before. He caused the little lady to blush furiously.

He was in no great hurry, however – nobody had been in a hurry since Nelson had destroyed the fleet – and he went away again. At a second dinner-party the help of the obliging Junot was enlisted. The aide-de-camp managed to upset a cup of coffee on Madame Fourès' gown and the gallant Commander-in-Chief at once leapt up in order to convey the lady to another room and repair the damage to her dress.

The repairs occupied the couple exactly two hours, during which period the other guests tried to make polite conversation. Nobody appears to have remarked upon the fact that Junot, a dead shot with a pistol, seemed to be losing his steadiness of hand but the remainder of the evening must have been a trifle embarrassing to those among the guests who were not in the secret.

The rest is pure French farce. A day or two after the dinner-party Lieutenant Fourès received the shock of his brief military career. He was summoned to the Headquarters of Berthier, Chief of Staff, and informed that his zeal had attracted favourable notice, so favourable indeed that the Commander-in-Chief proposed to reward it by sending him back to Paris with important despatches! The wretched Fourès was tremendously flattered and asked for leave in order to say farewell to his wife.

Berthier looked sad and shook his grizzled head. 'No time for that, I'm afraid,' he said, but added : 'You are more fortunate than any of us for you are to set out within the hour. Adieu, my dear fellow, I wish I were in your place!'

Berthier was only half a hypocrite. In one sense he did indeed wish that he was in Fourès' place, for he hated every moment of this prolonged separation from the captivating Madame Visconti. He kept her memory green by worshipping at an altar erected to her honour in his tent. Bourrienne, Napoleon's secretary, surprised him there one night, kneeling devoutly before her portrait and reciting a litany of love. So engrossed was he in this curious act of homage that he did not even notice Bourrienne's entry and was in no way embarrassed when the secretary coughed in order to make his presence known.

Fourès went off in high glee, convinced, poor fellow, that he was now on the high road to rapid promotion. He did not get very far along it. The day after he left Alexandria (where another old friend of Napoleon, General Mormont, had been waiting to speed him on his way) his cutter, the *Chasseur*, was overhauled by the British cruiser *Lion*. The cutter's entire company was hauled aboard and all were searched to their shirts.

The Lieutenant's bulky despatches were soon located and studied. Fourès was in despair. Twenty-four hours before his prospects had looked so promising, yet here he was, his despatches in the hands of the enemy and he himself doomed to spend the remainder of the war in captivity.

Again, however, he was jumping to conclusions. The British Commodore turned out to be a most agreeable fellow. He pointed out that he was about to commence a grand tour of the Pacific and had no accommodation on board his ship for prisoners-of-war. This being so he was ready to land the Lieutenant at any convenient point on the coast and if the prisoner had any preference he had only to state it and be set ashore at once.

Fourès must have rubbed his eyes. How was he to know that crowds of spies and shiploads of captured mail had acquainted the blockading British with every detail of life in the French camp, or that this bluff, good-natured naval officer was far better informed on the reasons for Fourès' voyage than was that officer himself?

In view of what followed it was soon clear, even to Fourès, that the Englishman was not bluff and obliging at all but a deep, far-sighted man with a sense of humour not at all common on Nelson's quarterdecks. His gesture was simply one more manoeuvre aimed at the discomfiture of the enemy but one, moreover, that would not have been found written into the Articles of War.

So Fourès popped up again in Alexandria almost as soon

as he had left it and his presence threw Napoleon's old friend Marmont into a panic. In vain the General tried to persuade the Lieutenant to remain in the port. Fourès, still elated at his good luck, insisted on returning to Cairo and reporting what had taken place to a Chief of Staff who appeared to think so well of him as a junior officer.

Reluctantly Marmont let him go. He could not order him to remain without a great deal of embarrassing explanation and he soon persuaded himself that he was not the person from whom explanations were due.

Fourès rushed off to Cairo and hurried straight to his lodgings, eager to embrace his violet-eyed wife. To his astonishment and alarm she was not there and all enquiries respecting her were met with evasive answers and sly, pitying grins.

At long last the truth began to penetrate Fourès thick skull and the moment it did he rushed off to the hotel alongside the palace of the Bey, where Napoleon had his headquarters.

Several well-meaning folk tried to head him off but he would take no hint and succeeded in forcing his way into his wife's presence. The apartment was soon echoing with howls of rage on the part of the husband and shrill, unrepentant avowals on the part of Marguerite Pauline.

The result of this lively interview was an immediate divorce, pronounced by the army Commissary-general in his capacity of a civilian lawyer. Fourès, boiling but by no means speechless with indignation, was packed off again and his wife became the acknowledged mistress of the Commander-in-Chief.

Once her husband was out of the way she settled down to enjoy her good fortune. Napoleon, harassed by thoughts of the army's future, nagged by countless problems of administration and living under the constant threat of assassination by Moslem fanatics, found solace in her amusing company and she became extremely popular with the troops, who, being good Frenchmen, relished the affair as an exceptionally good joke.

When Napoleon was occupied with work, Marguerite went for drives in a carriage and pair, escorted by a couple of brilliantly turned-out aides-de-camp in the capacity of outriders. Wherever she went the troops shouted : *'Vive Clioupâtre! Vive La Petite Générale!'* She wore Napoleon's miniature round her neck, suspended on a long, gold chain and the fact that one of the young outriders escorting her carriage was Eugène Beauharnais, the son of her lover's wife, does not seem to have caused her a moment's embarrassment.

It was otherwise with seventeen-year-old Eugène, who up to this moment had been having a wonderful time with his distinguished stepfather. He stuck manfully to his outriding duties for a week or so but at length somebody persuaded Napoleon to give the job to someone with a less conspicuous name.

Napoleon undoubtedly derived immense pleasure from the company of this saucy, feather-brained, large-hearted little baggage and he might even have married her had she been successful in providing him with a child. As the weeks went by, however, and 'La Bellilotte' showed no promise of this, he began to get somewhat petulant on the subject and remarked to somebody 'The little stupid doesn't know how to have one !' This ungallant remark was at once reported to her by the camp gossips and she was almost as indignant as her husband had been. 'It certainly isn't *my* fault !' she complained with an air of having done her very best to oblige.

Heavier matters than the fruitfulness of Marguerite Pauline were now besetting Napoleon. After the spectacular failure of his march across Suez and the abrupt check to the army at Acre, where the Englishman Sir Sidney Smith beat back every attack launched by the French storm-troops, he at length made up his mind to abandon the East and return to France, no matter how great the risk of capture *en route*.

With a few chosen officers he embarked secretly in a frigate and hugged the coast all the way along the North African coastline to the waist of the Mediterranean. Here he made a quick dash for Corsica and thence to Fréjus, landing safely after a series of hair-raising escapes from Nelson's cruisers.

The little blonde did not accompany him on this risky voyage. When he had decided to go he confided in her, pointing out that he could not let her run the risk of being taken prisoner by the English. 'My honour is dear to you,' he is reported to have told her, 'and what would they say to finding a woman at my elbow?'

In view of the fact that he had been parading the streets in her company for weeks, and that not only did the entire French army but every Jack-tar in the blockading fleet know of the affair, this remark strikes one as being among the most fatuous ever uttered by Napoleon. Perhaps it was a jest, like his supplementary caution about the sensation she might cause among a crew of British seamen, most of whom had enjoyed no shore-leave for years on end!

He left instructions that she was to be sent home on the first available vessel but Kléber, who succeeded him to the command, was not inclined to lend himself to this arrangement. Kléber was a huge, truculent soldier, with a soldier's tastes and a soldier's manners.

He argued that since he had inherited all the dangers and troubles of the Commander-in-Chief he should not be denied any of the perquisites that went along with the appointment. His view was that he should take over Marguerite with the job and he made all manner of difficulties regarding her voyage back to France. 'La Bellilotte' would doubtless have been in Egypt when Kléber was assassinated had not the kindly physician-in-chief, Desgenettes, befriended the girl and persuaded the new Commander-in-Chief to carry out Napoleon's instructions regarding her.

She sailed at last, on a neutral vessel, the *American*, and her fellow travellers included Junot (who seems to have been singularly fortunate in the matter of travelling companions) and some of the Egyptologists who had recently discovered the Rosetta Stone.

This party were not so fortunate as their predecessors. In spite of the neutrality of the American flag they were soon scooped up by the British Navy. The seamen, notwithstanding Napoleon's misgivings on the matter, treated 'La Bellilotte' with great consideration and after a short delay returned her to France under a safe-conduct.

Once in France she immediately set out for Paris, determined to pick up the broken threads of her happy association with Napoleon. A bitter disappointment awaited her. Great historical events had taken place in Paris during their brief separation and not only was her lover reconciled to Joséphine but was now First Consul and virtual dictator of France. The public who were ready to wink at the off-duty behaviour of a soldier serving in the field, were not likely to look so tolerantly upon the private life of the first citizen of the land and no one knew this better than the man who had seized supreme power. From now on he knew that he would be obliged to use backstairs, and although his associations with women would always be public knowledge they could no longer be openly displayed, as in the streets of Cairo.

For some weeks the disconsolate Cleopatra sat sulking in the capital, a city now showing signs of settling down after a decade of riot and revolution. She could not even obtain an audience and men who had flattered her in Egypt now pretended not to recognize her in the streets and theatre. Then she ran into Duroc, the Grand Marshal, and Duroc's warm heart was a byword in Paris, both then and subsequently. He mentioned her plight to Napoleon, who seems almost to have forgotten her, and the First Consul's response was immediate. Although he refused to see her he granted every request she made, sending large sums of money and marrying her off (nobody was better at finding husbands for ex-mistresses than Napoleon) to a recently returned nobleman, now serving with the artillery.

Her marriage to Henri de Ranchoup took place within a year of her return to France and like all the husbands of

Napoleon's women friends Henri received a handsome wedding-gift from the seat of power. On this occasion it took the form of a vice-consulship of Santander, in Spain, and when things in Spain became difficult on account of the war the couple moved to a similar post, in Sweden.

'La Bellilotte', however, could never be happy for long outside of France. Like Joséphine she loved her Paris and spent a great deal of time there throughout the years of the Empire. She moved in polite society and managed, somehow or other, to hold her place in it when Napoleon was overthrown and the Bourbons returned to hunt down and persecute the Emperor's old friends.

About this time she tried her hand at the writing of novels and published a two-volume story entitled *Lord Wentworth*. The novel does not seem to have made much stir but Marguerite Pauline was a resilient creature and after a spell of painting she tried again, publishing a mediaeval romance entitled *A Chatelaine of the Twelfth Century*. The book was completed in middle age, when she had settled in Paris again.

Her skill as a painter, particularly as a portrait painter, was above average. Her self-portrait, which reveals her vivacity and charm, is an excellent piece of work and gives us some indication of the soothing effect her elfin prettiness must have had upon a frustrated genius commanding a marooned army in conquered territory.

Despite artistic occupations her love-life continued its erratic course. The year after Waterloo, when she was about thirty-six and still as pretty as a Boucher shepherdess, she separated from her husband, de Ranchoup, and sailed off to South America as the mistress of an ex-officer of the Imperial Guard called Bellard.

There was a strong rumour in Paris at this time that her object was to rescue the eagle from his prison-rock at St Helena and that in order to accomplish this she had realized on her entire fortune. Madame Junot believed this and was smartly rapped over the knuckles for reporting it in her memoirs. Nothing, in fact, was further from the lady's mind and her voyage was a mere business venture. It proved a very successful one, for she came home with a shipload of rosewood and mahogany, then in great demand among the highly-skilled *ébénistes* in Paris. It is interesting to learn that some of the exquisite French furniture of this period, now sold by auction at Christie's and Sotheby's, was made from fine woods imported by Marguerite and bought with the interest on Napoleon's money.

The guardsman Bellard soon disappeared from her life but she continued to live on in Paris, right through the convulsions of 1830 and 1848 and throughout the entire period of the Second Empire, when her former lover's nephew occupied the Imperial Throne.

She was a very happy old lady, with her novels, painting, Bohemian friends and a horde of pet canaries and monkeys. In the final year of her life she must have smiled to herself when she saw the Painted Emperor ride by, with his escort of steel-clad cuirassiers, an accurate yet somehow unconvincing reincarnation of the man whom she had held in her arms in Egypt exactly seventy years ago.

When she died, in 1869, she left her large collection of valuable pictures to the museum at Blois and it was discovered that one of her final acts had been to burn all her letters from Napoleon, letters written to her when she had ridden about the streets of Cairo to the accompaniment of laughing cries of *'Vive Clioupâtre! Vive La Petite Générale!'* It is a pity that she did burn her letters for they might have thrown a stronger light on the association but the act does her more credit than reflects upon other Imperial mistresses : women who hoarded their letters and published them for profit the moment Napoleon was safe in exile.

Marguerite Pauline's story is not a creditable one but it does provide a curious contradiction to the claims of moralists. She had betrayed one husband, voluntarily chosen to become a famous man's mistress, abandoned a second husband, and was quite without a sense of shame on account of her actions, yet she died a wealthy and respected woman at the age of ninety! She was, moreover, remembered with affection by everyone who knew her.

There seems no record of any children so perhaps Napoleon was right after all, perhaps 'the little stupid' never did learn to have any!

CHAPTER IX

The Threshold and the Voice

When news of Napoleon's unexpected return from Egypt reached Paris one of the French deputies uttered a shout of joy and dropped dead with a heart attack.

This is a fair illustration of how the General was received by a population so sick and tired of muddle and inefficiency that one thing they desired, to the exclusion of every revolutionary slogan and philosophical principle, was the establishment of a strong man in power, someone who could bring order to an exhausted and distracted realm.

His journey north was a triumphal progress. At every town and village he was welcomed with cries of delight. It did not matter that his Egyptian campaign had been a gilded failure, or that he had abandoned a decimated, plaguestricken army to make its own terms with the enemy. He was here, in France, ready to do instant battle with the discredited government and Frenchmen welcomed him into their hearts.

Joséphine heard the news whilst she was dining with Gohier, one of the Directors. It must have come as a profound shock to them both for neither had really expected him to return and, if at all, then certainly not in triumph.

Joséphine abandoned the quaking Director and made her own dispositions with the speed and skill of a pupil of a Napoleon.

She rushed home, packed her prettiest clothes, ordered her fastest coach team and galloped off to intercept him before her in-laws could head him off and pour a stream of poison into his ear.

She forgot the handsome Charles and her mountain of

debts and concentrated solely on getting to his side as rapidly as possible, there to exercise once more the charm that had seeded those wonderful love-letters from Italy.

She was to come within a hairsbreadth of losing him and the fact that she did not is an illustration of the hidden strength of their relationship.

In her race along the autumn roads she missed his caval-cade and he arrived at their home in the Rue Chantereine to find not his wife but his mother awaiting him.

Letizia was soon joined by the entire flock of Bonapartes. The family jostled round, recounting every detail of José-phine's infidelity and criminal extravagance. He went down under this torrent of truth, half-truth and falsehood, inform-ing them brusquely that he would at once set about getting a divorce. His sisters squealed with triumph and the clan dispersed to spread the good news over Paris.

The moment they had gone he had Joséphine's luggage packed and placed in the entrance hall, where it could be collected without its owner having to face an outraged hus-band. Then he went to bed, locking his door, not only against Joséphine but against the dismayed Jacobins and Royalists, who were already sharpening daggers for a man who was neither extremist, legitimist or politician-on-the-make.

The moment she discovered that he had passed her on the road Joséphine turned her carriage and came spanking back to Paris. Her thoughts must have been depressing during this return journey, for on the way south she had at least been buoyed up by the hope of flinging her arms round him and kissing away the memories of her follies. She had done it before and she was confident that, given the chance, she could do it again. Now she must have realized that her task had been rendered ten times more difficult by the clack of eight Corsican tongues. Could any woman make herself heard above such a fearful racket?

She jumped from the carriage and hurried into the hall, passing her packed trunks on her way upstairs. She hammered on his door and when he did not answer she threw pride to the winds and sank to her knees, holding on to the door-handle and crying out to him in her beautiful alto voice, pleading and pleading for a chance to be heard.

For a long time there was no response. Inside, wracked by her cries and wretched with indecision, sat a tired, harassed man, the man to whom the whole of France was looking for help. Outside, with tears streaming down her face, knelt his wife, a woman to whom he had once written 'My life has become unbearable since I have known that you are not happy!'

It is like a scene from a great tragedy.

The silence inside the room remained unbroken and at length terror gripped Joséphine, a terror hardly less numbing than that she had experienced when the grilles opened at Les Carmes and the names of the condemned were read aloud by the gaoler.

She had almost given up hope when her maid arrived with the last Beauharnais reinforcements – sunburned Eugène and his pretty, fifteen-year-old sister, Hortense, the children whom this great soldier had come to regard as his own.

They stood with their mother on the landing and added their powerful pleas to hers; this threefold assault was not to be withstood. The door opened and he stood there, tears streaming down his cheeks. He spread wide his arms and Josphine rushed into them. Then the door closed again and the children stole away.

Perhaps it had never been properly shut. Perhaps it was never to shut until the week before Waterloo, when a plump man walked softly round Malmaison and into the room that had been hers, to emerge with tears in his eyes.

The Bonapartes were staggered by the terrible news that he had relented but what could they do but swallow their disappointment, call a truce and hunt around for some aspiring beauty who might be taught how to take the place of this tenacious Creole?

In any case other events were afoot, great events in which Joséphine had a part to play, the part of coaxing a promise of loyalty or neutrality towards her husband from all the leading personalities of Paris.

For the next fortnight the little house in the Rue de la Victoire was a stock-exchange of gossip, intrigue, plot and counter-plot.

Veterans came and went, swaggerers like the cavalry-leader Murat, scarred infantrymen like Lannes still limping from Egyptian wounds, his oldest friend, Marmont the artillery expert, and after them the cautious politicians, schemers like the Abbé Sieyès and Roger Ducos.

Talleyrand was there, limping and smiling, as he moved from group to group, sounding loyalties and weighing chances. Brothers Joseph and Lucien were there, anxious to maintain the truce with Joséphine so long as she employed all her charm to flatter anyone and everyone who might help to hoist the Bonaparte family on to the steps of a throne. Bernadotte, the shifty, scheming husband of the jilted Désirée was there and nothing, not all the blandishments of Joséphine, the gruff pleas of brother-in-law Joseph, or the gross flattery of the hated little Corsican could prevail upon this arch-trimmer to commit himself one way or the other.

At last everything was ready or as ready as it ever would be and Napoleon struck.

Two days later he was First Consul and an hereditary throne was only two strides away.

No one can say exactly how much he owed to Joséphine for his successful seizure of power. Certain it is that she carried a great deal of weight with the people who helped him and equally certain that her immense popularity among the Parisians did much to persuade them that his abrupt overthrow of a government he had sworn to defend was a simple act of patriotism.

On his part forgiveness had been utter and complete.

There were no conditions made and no bargains struck. Not only did he forgive her infidelity but he never, then or later, took a single step to revenge himself on Hippolyte Charles or any other suspected lover. He paid her debts and they were big enough to make a lesser man cut his throat in despair. He paid for Malmaison to the tune of nearly a quarter-million francs. He paid another million and a quarter to upholsterers and decorators. He paid forty thousand francs for jewellery. Her personal bills totalled something over two million francs.

He did not, however, pay out this vast sum without first subjecting the accounts to the kind of scrutiny he made of enemy entrenchments, and the result of this survey was disconcerting to some of the tradesmen and professional men who had danced such a profitable polka around Joséphine during her husband's absence.

He found, for instance, that many of the items entered on the invoices had never been delivered and he struck them out with a grim smile. He found also that there were cases of gross overcharging and in these instances he summoned the suppliers and blandly sliced the accounts in two. The Paris tradesmen soon found a trick worth two of this one. Whenever they served Joséphine in future they charged twice the normal amount and still made a handsome profit. The return of the Bourbons in 1814 must have been mourned in many a Paris counting-house.

From this moment on there were no more lovers in Joséphine's life. She had at last learned her lesson and not all the scheming of the Bonapartes, or all her husband's subsequent entanglements with actresses, readers, countesses or casual adventuresses, weakened the bond of affection that was reforged on the threshold of the bedroom door in the last days of the dying century. From then on he was to indulge himself with any woman he fancied to entertain. There were to be tearful tantrums and wails of protest from Joséphine but no repetition of the scene that had followed his return from Egypt.

Napoleon is said to have declared that he never let his rage mount higher than his chin. If this is true then Joséphine had learned something else from him, for all the scenes that followed her discovery of his subsequent love-affairs have the air of having been carefully rehearsed and played as a sop to her pride but nothing more than that. Their relationship from 1800 onwards became that of a middle-aged bourgeois husband and his middle-aged wife. When he was over-tired and unable to sleep she sat by his bed and read aloud to him. When he was away campaigning she never thought of him or wrote to him without affection and she seems to have delighted in his embraces when he was disposed to spare her one. She even paraded his affection, telling her maid on several occasions, 'The Emperor spent the night with me,' knowing, no doubt, that such information would move out like a ripple on a pond, informing all Paris of the fact that he still found her desirable.

These were the happiest days either of them were to spend. He, on his part, was consolidating his power and moving rapidly towards the throne, while she had now entered upon that stage in life when the alarms and enthusiasms of youth had become a subject for reminiscent laughter. At the same time she was at last coming to realize that the man who treated her with unfailing kindness and asked her on occasion to read him to sleep, was not only the greatest soldier since Alexander, and the greatest administrator of all time, but a tolerant, good-natured husband, with the moods and the sensitivity of an affectionate child.

The estate at Malmaison absorbed her attention and she indulged in her love of flowers by populating it with hundreds of varieties of rare plants, the descendants of which still grow in many a French garden.

She continued to spend money as freely as ever but he never railed at her on this account, indeed, he seemed to expect her to spend liberally and offset his mother's extreme parsimony.

Letizia could never forget that she and her family had

once queued for municipal soup. In spite of Napoleon's protests she continued to hoard the vast sums her son showered into her lap, as though such largesse must be counted out in sous. 'One day this will come to an end,' his mother warned him, when he laughed at her caution. 'One day, my boy, you will come to me and ask for this money!'

She was a good prophetess. When he returned for his last throw he drew upon her vast savings in order to equip an army.

Sometimes the lawn at Malmaison was the scene of gay, pastoral picnics. Races were run, in which Napoleon joined and tripped over, to the amusement of himself and spectators. He enjoyed these occasions and would invent games and competitions, before he remembered the mountain of work awaiting him. Then he would say, briefly: 'Come then, I must put my head in the collar again! It is there awaiting me!'

Four years slipped away, years of war, peace and renewed war, years of abortive attempts on the part of Royalists to blow him up and shoot him down, years in which he indulged himself in a series of trivial little affairs with a procession of pretty women, girls from the Comédie Française, Women-in-Waiting, *lectrices*, but these incidents remained trivial, giving some point to his laconic remark that adultery was a sofa affair. This, in fact, was something he never really believed, for it was impossible for him to behave half-heartedly about anything, even a passing fancy for a woman's embrace.

It is easy at this period in his life to find in these casual love affairs proof of cynicism on his part and to claim, as many nineteenth-century writers have claimed, that he had the carnal desires of a beast in the field and the moral outlook of a Turk.

The record of this stage of Napoleon's life is a very full one but it runs contrary to this supposition. It is clear that he demanded something more of these women than the mere satisfying of a physical appetite. He wanted to escape for a few hours from the pitiless pressure of statesmanship practised on a global scale. He needed a means to seal off the abysses on each side of the knife-edge on which he walked, hour by hour. He needed, for a brief span of time, to shed the immense, dragging weight of decisions necessary to maintain his balance at the apex of world affairs and he wanted, above all, to thrust into the background the brooding thoughts of the infernal machine and the assassin's knife that lay in wait for him at every public appearance. In short, he sought by means of perfumed magic to transport himself back to a cherry-orchard at Valence and when the women he summoned were not equipped with this particular magic they were dismissed and seldom given a second chance.

One woman both obtained and made use of her second chance. She was Grassini, the lovely opera star, who had courted him in vain after his successes in Italy.

The Napoleon who rode into Milan in 1800, during the Marengo campaign, was only four years older than the young General who had entered the city after the first victories in Italy but in those few years he had aged ten in appearance and a century in experience.

Grassini sang for him and he received her graciously, overlooking the fact that she, too, had aged somewhat and although but twenty-seven was now putting on weight and losing some of the refinement of her features.

Her voice, however, was at its very best and Bourrienne tells us that his master could have listened to it for hours. Unable himself to sing in tune he had a deep appreciation of music and was always moved by it. When one examines his relationships with this famous star one cannot escape the suspicion that it was as a singer and not as a woman that she won him.

He formed a semi-serious attachment with her and when Bourrienne obeyed his instructions to awake his master for bad news (good news, said Napoleon, could always wait until morning) and brought him intelligence of Masséna's surrender of Genoa, he found the First Consul and opera singer together in bed.

Soon after the victory at Marengo, Grassini was ordered to Paris. She set off with alacrity, convinced that she was on the threshold of a political career, and confident that she had banished every other woman from Napoleon's thoughts. She even succeeded in alarming Joséphine by her sensational conquest of Paris during her first series of concerts.

Despite all this she never succeeded in acquiring a single jot of political influence and Napoleon's attitude towards her remained respectful but unemotional. Her disappointment was keen. Suddenly she became bored with Paris, so bored that she took a lover in the person of Rode, the Italian violinist. When love beckoned Grassini was always ready to let her career take second place. Together they fled into the night.

Rode, poor fellow, flattered as he was by Grassini's violent passion for him, was nonetheless terrified of possible repercussions. It seemed to him just as reckless to challenge Napoleon in the field of love as to throw down a gauntlet on the field of battle and he was not even a soldier, simply a poor and hopelessly infatuated fiddler!

His fears were groundless, for his great rival, although an Italian, bore him no malice, but treated him as leniently as he had treated the lover of Joséphine.

The affair caused a sensation in Paris and at once put a period to the association of Napoleon and Grassini, but far from visiting star or lover with wrath the First Consul invited them to return to the capital and even loaned them the Théâtre de la République for two special concerts, one of which proved a huge financial success.

Grassini, who was an exceptionally sensual woman, had as many love-affairs as Catherine the Great. Both before and after her fleeting conquest of Napoleon she was always madly and spectacularly in love with someone. In affairs of the heart she displayed all the traditional temperament of an operatic star and for as long as her interest in a particular man was sustained it was the grand passion of her life.

She never quite lost touch with her most distinguished lover and Joséphine entertained vague suspicions of her long after the affair had burned itself out. Grassini continued to revisit Paris from time to time, in between successful appearances at Berlin, Milan, London and other centres. Napoleon invited her there in 1807, when he was at the zenith of his career, and paid her huge sums to perform. He also allowed her to organize profitable benefit performances and gave her the official title of 'First Singer to His Majesty the Emperor and King'.

Grassini had one thing in common with most of Napoleon's mistresses. She attracted bizarre adventures wherever she went. She was once set upon by a band of deserters, near the town of Rouvrai, and not only robbed but barbarously assaulted into the bargain. The highwaymen showed very little foresight in their choice of victim. There was such a hue and cry after them when the bedraggled star had reached a place of safety that they were caught within forty-eight hours of the robbery.

Napoleon took a keen personal interest in the affray and awarded the cross of honour to the doughty National Guardsmen who killed two of the bandits and arrested the others.

Found among the loot on this occasion was a portrait of Napoelon, set in brilliants, and it is said that Grassini had urged the robbers to keep the jewels but return the portrait. This theatrical gesture is typical of her but it should not be taken too seriously. Grassini is one of Napoleon's mistresses who used the imperial interest as a means of amassing money and attracting notoriety. No one could call her cold-blooded but it cannot be established that she entertained anything but a professional interest in the man whose affections she sought so earnestly. Her passion for Napoleon, like that of so many other women, was extinguished by the tide of allied invasion, in 1814. Among her distinguished admirers after the French débâcle at Waterloo was the Iron Duke himself.

He is said, on excellent authority, to have taken her as his mistress during the British heyday in Paris. She could thus be said to have achieved the unique distinction of having the very best of both worlds.

Grassini continued to enjoy a considerable reputation for the remainder of her life but like most artists of distinction she was always in financial straits. In her case insolvency was due to a crazy passion for gambling. Perhaps it was the gambler in Napoleon that appealed to her.

Napoleon never forgot her enchanting voice but he seems to have forgotten everything else about her. In the great summing-up at St Helena he post-dates the occasion of their first meeting by nine years, stating that she first attracted his attention at the time of his coronation!

A man does not make this kind of error about a love-affair that has occupied an important place in his affections. He did not post-date the early morning idyll with sixteen-year-old Caroline Colombier in Valence.

CHAPTER X

Supper for Two

There is no stronger proof of the reality of the reconciliation between Napoleon and Joséphine than the former's lusty championship of his wife's rights during the weeks preceding their coronation, on 2 December 1804.

The moment Napoleon was firmly established as head of the government the Bonaparte clan opened a concerted attack upon his wife. During the four years that elapsed between Napoleon's election as First Consul and his decision to make himself hereditary emperor of the French nation, the battle between wife and in-laws had continued unremittingly. For a long time there was constant sniping and enfilading on their part, a dignified but dogged defence on hers but open war was not declared until the summer of 1804, when it became known that the vital word '*Adoptive*' was to be inserted in the proclamation relating to Napoleon's successor.

The question of succession had cost Napoleon a great deal of thought. It cost Joséphine, who now realized that she could never bear her husband a child, a great deal of sleep and many silent tears.

In the face of his wife's failure to produce an heir several alternatives faced the future Emperor. He could adopt Napoleon-Charles, the son of his brother Louis and Joséphine's daughter Hortense. He could appoint Eugène, his stepson, his successor. He could adopt Achille, the son of his youngest and most vitriolic sister Caroline and her soldier husband, Murat. Or he could continue to hope for a natural son of his own by another woman.

He had yet to prove his ability to become a father and

seems to have had serious misgivings in this respect. There was his petulant complaint against Marguerite Pauline, 'La Bellilotte', for her inability to conceive and although in the years since his return from Egypt he had had relations with various other women there was still no proof that it was not he rather than Joséphine who was responsible for their disappointment.

He finally settled on his nephew, Napoleon-Charles, only to encounter bitter and unexpected opposition from the child's father.

Brother Louis now found himself caught up in the tangle of divided loyalties. Up to the moment of his marriage to Joséphine's daughter, a marriage that neither bride nor groom had entered upon with enthusiasm, he had sided with his mother, his brothers and his sisters against the Beauharnais family. Since his marriage, and particularly since the birth of the boy, the Bonapartes had lost no opportunity of accusing Louis of breaking the family ranks.

Louis was an obstinate, sour-tempered man, as dilatory but far less pliable than the sombre Joseph. The result of the combined family pressure on him was to cause him to turn savagely upon his young wife and bludgeon her into joining the alliance against her mother.

From the first day of her marriage Hortense had led a wretched life. In her late teens she had fallen madly in love with the sweet-tempered Duroc, universally popular Marshal of the Palace, but Duroc did not respond to her love and her mother, with the object of dividing the Bonapartes dominant in her mind, continually urged her daughter to please her stepfather by marrying Louis.

Louis himself was loath to do anything to consolidate Joséphine's position but after noting the girl's pretty bearing at a party he allowed himself to be talked into the project by Napoleon, who, in turn, had been won over to the idea by Joséphine.

As a first reserve to the succession there was always Eugène, who was proving himself a suitable choice in every possible way, so that in the matter of naming the heirs Joséphine scored a double triumph.

The Bonapartes were sick with rage, not the least of them Louis, who was so outraged at being passed over in favour of his own son that he threatened to whisk the boy into exile.

As for Caroline and her dandified husband, Murat (he was born an innkeeper's son but had already made up his mind to become a king) their joint fury was terrible, their own little Achille having been passed over with the remark – 'Achille? Oh, he'll make a good soldier I've no doubt!'

This was how matters stood in the week preceding the coronation, and by expressing his preference for his wife's family Napoleon revealed to all France that a divorce from Joséphine was no longer in his mind. He showed further proof of this when he announced that she, too, was to be crowned in Notre Dame and was therefore expected to rule by his side for the remainder of her life.

This last decision threw Joséphine into transports of delight and encouraged her to tie a final knot in the link that bound her to her famous husband.

Abjectly she approached Caprara, the Papal Legate, and timidly confessed that her conscience was troubling her.

'We are not even married,' she said, 'not in the eyes of the Church.'

Questions and answers followed. Slowly, and with a great show of reluctance, Joséphine told the story of that gusty March evening at the *Mairie* more than eight years ago. To the Legate the marriage which, until this moment in history, the whole of Europe had accepted, must have seemed as binding as a verbal contract for the supply of army boots.

Pope and Legate were deeply shocked. For reasons of state Napoleon had insisted that His Holiness made the winter journey to Paris, in order to participate in the ceremony. In view of what happened at the high altar the journey was hardly worth His Holiness' time. It was Joséphine, however, who took advantage of the Pope's visit. On learning the true state of affairs he protested that he could take no part in the ceremony unless the situation was rectified at once. There could be no compromise. The couple must be properly married without a moment's delay.

Napoleon was piqued but cooperative. He had been hoping to keep this matter dark but now that the facts were in the open he was not averse to a second marriage, providing, of course, that it was carried out under conditions of the strictest secrecy. He wanted no sly grins on the boulevards when he drove to his coronation on the morrow.

Joséphine was delighted and it is easy to see why. Religious scruples that do not seem to have troubled her during eight years of marriage were now satisfied but in addition she had at last insured herself against an uncertain future. If she was going to be an Empress, then she wanted to be one who had been properly married. Now the blessing of the Church would raise one more barrier, and a formidable one at that, against the ceaseless efforts of the Bonapartes to bring about her ruin.

The somewhat overdue blessing of the union took place at the Tuileries on the afternoon preceding the coronation. Napoleon's uncle, Cardinal Fesch, officiated and only two witnesses were present. The ceremony, although a very quiet and simple occasion, was nevertheless a great contrast to the casual affair of March 1796, and it worked upon Napoleon's memories in a curious way, bringing to the surface of his mind an eight-year-old slight to his pride.

On the following morning, when the whole of Paris was running here, there and everywhere in preparation for an event of unrivalled pomp and display, the Emperor-to-be sprang his little surprise and once again he demonstrated to his wife that he was a very difficult man to hoodwink.

Half in jest and half in triumph he suddenly produced an old acquaintance of Joséphine's, someone who had once predicted nothing but disaster of their marriage, and his summons at such a moment had the air of a conjuror producing a shamed rabbit from a hat. It was made for no other purpose than to compel the old acquaintance to eat a large slice humble pie.

The rabbit Napoleon produced on this occasion was an obscure lawyer called Raguideau, a man in whom Joséphine had once reposed considerable trust.

Shortly before their first marriage in the early spring of 1796, Joséphine had asked her intended husband to accompany her to Raguideau's office, saying that she felt she ought to acquaint her old friend with news of the forthcoming event.

Napoleon agreed but on arrival at Raguideau's he was left in the outer office. It is clear that neither bride nor lawyer was aware of the man with whom they were dealing for they were careless enough to leave the door ajar and in this way Napoleon heard all the lawyer's earnest endeavours to dissuade Joséphine from going through with the marriage.

'Can you be so mad as to marry a young man who has nothing but his cloak and sword?' he demanded.

Napoleon, biting his nails in the outer office, said nothing, neither then nor subsequently, so that Joséphine had to wait eight years to learn that he had overheard the discussion.

She made the discovery on coronation morning. Whilst in the act of being robed Napoleon received the lawyer, who must have wondered why he of all people should be summoned to the Tuileries at such a time and at such short notice.

He was not long in doubt. 'Well,' said Napoleon, very pleasantly, 'have I nothing but my cloak and sword now, Raguideau?'

It is not recorded what reply, if any, was made by the wretched notary.

Napoleon, child of the Revolution, far outdid his royal predecessors in the pomp and display of this splendid occasion. In colour and spectacle the coronation made light of the Bourbon ceremonies.

The actual coronation lasted five hours and the procession

that followed it another three and a half hours. The weather was excessively cold and by the time the day had ended poor Joséphine was exhausted, as were all concerned, with the exception of her tireless husband. Tired or not the new Empress went to bed a happy woman for the events of the day had set her mind at rest, at least for several years to come.

Notre Dame had been newly-painted for the occasion and magnificently adorned galleries and pews had been erected for the notables, which included Napoleon's three sisters and his brothers Joseph and Louis. Brothers Lucien and Jerome were both in disgrace and did not put in an appearance.

The imperial throne was placed on a high platform at the end of the nave, facing the main entrance. The pontifical throne was in the choir, beside the high altar.

Eye-witnesses declare that the entry of the principals into the Cathedral was a never-to-be-forgotten sight. All the newly-created Marshals of the Empire were present, their chests blazing with stars and orders, and among them were some of the old Republicans, men like Augereau and Lannes, who disapproved very strongly of all this pomp. Augereau muttered that all that was needed to complete the occasion was the million Frenchmen who had died to get rid of such buffoonery.

Paris did not share his views. One and all the people, who not so long ago had lined the Rue St Honoré to watch the tumbrils pass, now revelled in this brilliant spectacle.

Joséphine looked enchanting, 'no more than twenty-five' says a female eyewitness, and among those who exclaimed with delight when she emerged from her rooms to begin the journey to Notre Dame was her husband.

Joséphine, whom none could rival in the exploitation of the arts of the toilette, surpassed herself on this occasion. The entire morning had been spent in dressing and thought had been given to each item of adornment.

Her gown was of white satin, elaborately embroidered with silver and gold, caught at the waist with a girdle of gems. Her white velvet train was similarly embroidered and at the neck, which was cut square and low, was a gold ruff, set into the top of the long sleeves and rising high behind her small, shapely head.

Rows of diamonds decorated her narrow corsage and sleeves but her principal item of jewellery was a necklace of sculptured stones, set in diamonds. On her head was a diadem of pearls and her white velvet shoes and gloves were also embroidered in gold.

The party made first for the Archbishop's palace, where Napoleon donned his coronation robe and Joséphine exchanged her pearl diadem for a head-dress of amethysts, also donning a red velvet mantle embroidered with her husband's insignia, the bee and a garlanded 'N'. Before they left Napoleon, who was in high spirits, tried Joséphine's crown 'to make sure it would fit'.

On arrival at Notre Dame the sceptre, sword, globe, crown and ring of the Emperor were placed on the high altar. Beside them were laid the crown, ring and mantle of the Empress. The anointment then took place and Mass followed, after which the Emperor mounted the altar steps, picked up the crown that had just been blessed by the Pope and to everyone's breathless astonishment placed it firmly on his own head !

The Holy Father (who had been forewarned of this novelty in coronation procedure) looked down at his feet and his eyes remained lowered when Napoleon set a crown upon the head of the kneeling Joséphine.

Thus, for the mere acts of anointing and witnessing, the old man had travelled all the way from Italy. Presently, however, he raised his eyes and pronounced the orison : 'May God crown you with the crown of glory and justice . . .' after which the Imperial couple moved down to the platform in the nave to receive his formal kiss.

A storm of cheers greeted them as they passed from Cathedral to carriage on the first stage of the long procession.

'Never have I seen on any face such an expression of joy, content and happiness as that which then animated the countenance of the Empress,' writes a girl who saw her come out into the open. 'Her face was radiant!'

When it was over Emperor and Empress retired to dine alone. What did they talk about on this, the second night of their second honeymoon? Whatever it was it must have been agreeable conversation for a single detail of that tête-à-tête has come down to us. Napoleon was so pleased with the grace and dignity she had displayed in wearing her crown during the procession that he insisted she continued to wear it throughout the evening meal!

The girl who had once ran barefooted among the picca-ninnies of Martinique had come a long way in forty-one years, almost as far and nearly as fast as the glum little gunner-cadet who sat smiling at her across the table.

CHAPTER XI

'It needs but a minute to love'

Napoleon was a lukewarm patron of the arts. He had an Italian's appreciation of a good voice and first-class music could always hold his interest. For the rest the arts exerted little influence on him. He much preferred to devote himself to the study of human beings. Fine paintings and statues roused no enthusiasm in him and once he had attained manhood he seldom or never read fiction. He was a frequent theatregoer but a play seldom stimulated him. He called drama 'a mongrel art' and comedies and farces not only bored but irritated him. He could, however, appreciate high tragedy and he once told Goethe that kings should make a habit of seeing tragedies performed – they could always learn something from them. This is why, whenever he sought the company of a woman of the theatre, she was almost certain to be a tragedienne.

During the four-year period of the Consulate, that is, between the time of his assuming political control of France and that of making himself an Emperor, Napoleon's extramarital associations with women were almost exclusively based on the theatre. The years 1800–1804 might be called his 'actress period' for the Consulate was the heyday of the Comédie Française. Actors like the famous Talma were drawing all Paris and the plays of Pierre Corneille, particularly *Mélite* and *Cinna*, were immensely popular, as were the actresses who played leading roles in them.

Three of these stars, Mesdemoiselles Duchesnois, Bourgoin and Georges, became mistresses of the First Consul but of these only the last-named achieved any sort of permanence in her relationship.

Mlle Georges deserves a special place in an account of Napoleon's love-affairs, if only because she proved to be one of the very few women in his life who retained a strong affection for him after his eclipse and thought of him with gratitude when he had passed from exile into legend.

Were it not for Mlle Georges, Napoleon's 'actress period' would be little more than a recital of casual, cynical affairs far more characteristic of Barras, Masséna or Talleyrand than of Bonaparte. As it is the sketchy and uncompleted memoirs that were set down in the form of jottings by this woman when she was old, penniless and monstrously fat, provide an insight into Napoleon's character that is naïve, charming and revealing.

Mlle Georges' real name was Marguerite-Joséphine Weimar and she did not use her German father's name, 'George', until she became a successful actress in the capital.

Both her father and mother were professional players and for many years they travelled about the provinces attached, as leading players, to a barn-storming fit-up company.

They played comedy, tragedy, and even vaudeville and their daughter was born in the theatre at Bayeux, if not in the proverbial basket of tights, then at least during a performance of *Tartuffe*.

The whole of Marguerite's infancy and girlhood was spent with the company of strolling players and she knew no other life but that of the theatre. Almost from birth she was familiar with long, uncomfortable journeys in bad weather, apathetic audiences in small, seedy towns, dismal one-night lodgings and the eternal shortage of ready money.

When she was still a child her father became manager of the theatre at Amiens and it was here, where his daughter was appearing in a play, that the traditional fairy-godmother of all young actresses materialized in the person of a talent-spotter, a Mademoiselle Raucourt.

Mlle Raucourt was a famous actress who happened to be travelling through Amiens and paid a fleeting visit to her father's theatre. She was at once struck by the girl's beautiful speaking voice and her certain promise of classic beauty. Then and there she agreed to accept her as a pupil and at the age of sixteen Marguerite was playing leads in maternal roles at the Comédie Française!

It says much for Mlle Georges' abilities that she made her debut, in the exacting role of Clytemnestra, at such a precociously early age but she had matured very quickly, both as an artiste and as a woman. Before her seventeenth birthday she was being described as one of the most beautiful women in Paris.

Her portrait, a very striking one, has come down to us from the brush of Gérard and it is easy to see why she achieved such popularity among people possessing a traditional appreciation of feminine beauty. She had a sturdy but voluptuous figure, a wealth of dark hair and, above all, features set in a superbly classical mould, so classical indeed that their owner might have served as a model for a Greek goddess. Long after her figure had become a subject for boulevard jokes her lovely profile retained the qualities revealed in Gérard's portrait.

She had, in addition, attractive hands, but unfortunately her beauty did not extend to her feet, which were large and very coarsely formed. She was entirely without the volcanic temperament so often found in the higher ranks of the theatre and almost everyone who knew her speaks of her placidity, her childish good-nature and her complete lack of malice.

She was hard-working but not particularly ambitious and never once went out of her way to gain money or professional advancement from any of her many admirers. It was this unusual characteristic, added to her childlike simplicity and light-heartedness, that caused Napoleon to rate her above all actresses in Paris and to retain for her, notwithstanding the follies she ultimately committed, a warmth of feeling that accounted for generous impulses on his part long after their association had come to an end.

The story of her first meeting with Napoleon is an amusing

sidelight on the First Consul's rapidly developing technique as a lover. It also throws light on the conditions prevailing among the tragediennes of that era.

In the first flush of her success on the stage, when she was still a few weeks short of her seventeenth birthday, she attracted two important men, both of whom were eager to extend to her that form of patronage politely known as 'protection'.

The first of these was a Polish prince, a Prince Sapieha. The other was Lucien Bonaparte, the most talented and tempestuous of Napoleon's brothers and the only one who could be said to have entertained any feelings of rivalry for him.

Lucien (he had married a widow who gave birth to his child the day before the ceremony) met the young actress at his sister Elise's salon and was quick to appreciate her possibilities. Besides sending her an expensive gift (a hundred gold louis placed at the bottom of a silver-gilt teapot) he kept an eye on her career and began to enter into a mutually beneficial arrangement with her teacher, Mademoiselle Raucourt.

Unfortunately for Lucien he was obliged to leave Paris just when he appeared to be making steady progress and the Polish Prince, Sapieha, moved to the head of a small but distinguished queue. He began by paying calls on Marguerite and giving her, among other things, a beautiful lace veil.

The Prince, however, was very leisurely in his wooing and matters had not progressed very far when something happened that caused the Prince and would-be successors to melt into the shadows.

Returning from the theatre one night the much-sought-after Mlle Georges came face to face with Napoleon's chief valet, Constant, who was awaiting her with the consular summons.

From now on Constant begins to occupy an interesting place in Napoleon's love-affairs. Jovial, urbane and thoroughly discreet (until Napoleon was out of range) he was the complete man of the world, the kind of knowing gentleman's gentleman without whom no stage-romance would be complete. There is something oddly two-dimensional about Constant, as though he never existed outside the pages of a book, and although he moves silently up and down the corridors of Imperial memoirs year after year one can never really believe that he was anything but a kind of stage-property.

Constant had, in a manner of speaking, taken over General Junot's duties as chief confidant of the Man of Destiny. Perhaps 'confidant' is too strong a word, but his duties were nonetheless of a highly confidential nature.

He was employed on missions of a private nature for many years and during this time he hoarded up a sufficiency of sensational material to make himself an accepted authority on Napoleon's love-life at a time when such details were in great demand by publishers all over the world.

Unfortunately Constant is not always a reliable source and one cannot help feeling that he had no scruples about sacrificing truth for sensational reading. He was a very good valet but had he lived a century later he would have made an even better feature-editor of one of the less-reputable Sunday newspapers.

Quietly and benignly he conveyed to Mlle Georges his master's message. The First Consul had seen her performance that evening and had been so impressed with it that he begged her to call upon him at Saint Cloud, at eight o'clock the following evening, in order that she might receive a famous man's congratulations. That was all and it was a message that Constant had already learned by heart.

Young Marguerite cannot have been under the slightest misapprehension as to what this summons implied. She had been reared in the unconventional atmosphere of a travelling stage company and Napoleon's name was a household word when she was ten years old. His reputation for casual gallantry was now a byword in Paris theatrical circles and it was a matter of speculation among the audiences at the

Comédie Française as to who was likely to be the next actress to receive the Consular summons.

Despite this the appearance of Constant at her lodgings threw the seventeen-year-old actress into a terrible state of indecision.

Writing of the incident some forty-five years later, when she had accommodated dozens of lovers, among them Alexandre Dumas, she declares that she was a virgin when Constant called on her that evening and there seems no reason to doubt her claim. Her memoirs, patchy and disjointed as they are, have about them a ring of truth and she makes no effort in them to apologize for her way of life. She was, in fact, rather proud of the effect her astonishing beauty had upon people, for Dumas declares that sometimes she took a bath in front of an audience of onlookers! At this point in her career, however, there were factors other than that of modesty to be considered and Marguerite's distress throughout the next day was so obvious that at least two actors, one of them Talma himself, remarked upon it and concluded that she was having serious trouble with the management.

It must have seemed to Mlle Georges that whatever course she followed was attended by formidable risks. If she disobeyed the summons she might not only lose an opportunity that would not present itself a second time but, what was more, alienate the ultimate source of her bread and butter. She was not to know at this stage that the man who had fallen under her spell possessed even less malice than herself. What she did know was that he alone was the source from which all favours flowed and that he was the most distinguished patron of the theatre in which she performed. On the other hand if she accepted the invitation and became Napoleon's mistress, then she would undoubtedly incur the vicious rivalry of all her fellow tragediennes. Was this worth incurring for a liaison that might endure less than a week?

In addition to all this there was the tardy Prince Sapieha to be considered. The Prince had already showered patronage and material benefits upon her and all he had so far demanded in return was to kiss the tips of her fingers. Doubtless he hoped for more and was content to bide his time. He could not however compete with the First Consul and neither could anyone else in Europe and this was a point to be taken into consideration. If she went to Saint Cloud she would turn her back on the Prince and any other likely protector who had moved into the open since Brother Lucien's departure from Paris.

It was a serious dilemma for a girl of her age but Marguerite's maid, Clementine, a girl to whom she at once turned for advice, expressed herself astonished that her mistress needed any! Clementine lost no time in pointing out that any actress at the Comédie Française would have been wildly delighted to have received Constant's message and that Mlle Georges would be mad to ignore it or send a message (as she proposed sending one) saying that she was ill and unable to obey.

After a restless night Marguerite came to agree with her maid but she nevertheless went to the theatre that evening in an extremely disordered frame of mind. She was not due to play that night and one of the other actresses, Mlle Volnais, looked into her box for a chat. Seeing Mlle Georges dressed for an occasion she asked if her colleague would be seeing the play through to the end. Marguerite said not as she had an appointment.

Mlle Volnais then said that she had one, too, and was leaving the theatre at nine. After this skirmish they admired one another's dresses and eyed one another like a pair of gladiators, each waiting for the other to make a false move. What made this exchange of pleasantries so memorable to Mlle Georges was that she happened to know where Volnais was going on that occasion but Volnais did not possess the same advantage over her. Volnais was, in fact, to spend the night with the redoubtable General Junot, now Governor of Paris, and Mlle Georges, uncharitably for her, remarks that the liaison between those two lasted quite some time and that in due course Junot had several children fathered upon him that did not, in fact, belong to him at all!

At eight o'clock the maid Clementine looked into the box, telling her mistress that Constant was now awaiting her at the stage door.

Marguerite went down and entered the coach driven by Napoleon's coachman, Caesar, a man renowned all over Paris for his ability to maintain his seat on the box no matter how much liquor he had consumed during the long intervals of awaiting passengers.

The journey to Saint Cloud was a lively one. Caesar, as drunk as a fiddler, drove at a furious pace and the violent motion of the conveyance did nothing to soothe Mlle Georges' nerves. At last she appealed to the silent Constant, begging him to turn the carriage, take her home and report to Napoleon that she was indisposed. If he would agree, she said, she would promise to come another time.

Constant merely chuckled and remarked 'Not likely!' When his charge protested that she was so petrified with fear that she would be unable to utter a single word and the First Consul would therefore dismiss her as an idiot, his chuckles increased to laughter, after which he pointed out that, once brought face to face with Napoleon, she would soon realize how her fears were groundless.

'Not only is he awaiting you with a lively impatience,' comforted the valet, 'but he is really a very kind fellow!'

With this information Mlle Georges was obliged to be content and when they arrived at the palace Constant conducted her across the orangery to a bedroom window overlooking the terrace. Here they found Roustan, the Consul's Mameluke, awaiting them.

Roustan was a legacy of the Egyptian campaign. Along with other Mamelukes who admired Napoleon's dash and glitter he had entered the service of his conqueror and remained attached to him throughout the years of the Empire, not only fighting gallantly in a dozen campaigns but doing duty in the intervals between them as Napoleon's personal bodyguard. He usually partnered Constant in the business of conveying young ladies to and from his master's quarters. His Eastern background must have made him particularly suitable for this kind of work.

Roustan lifted the curtain and closed the window, while Constant went off to inform Napoleon of the star's arrival.

Left alone in the large, ornate room the seventeen-year-old actress was submerged by fresh waves of panic. On exchanging Malmaison for Saint Cloud Napoleon had remarked that 'the rooms lacked seriousness and were suitable for a kept woman'. Marguerite had leisure to test this assertion. She noted the green silk curtains, the big sofa in front of the fire, the blaze of lights issuing from a huge candelabra and the equally large chandelier above the room's principal item of furniture, an enormous bed.

While she was contemplating the fact that even a spot of rouge could be detected under such a constellation of lights Napoleon entered, wearing a green uniform, white satin knee-breeches and silk stockings. He approached her with a charming smile and at once lifted her veil, the gift of the dispossessed Prince Sapieha. Without more ado he tossed it on the ground. Far from reassured by this cavalier treatment Marguerite began to tremble. He at once noticed her confusion.

'Are you afraid of me? Do I seem terrible to you?' he asked, with an air of surprise and then going straight to the point, 'I found *you* exceedingly beautiful yesterday and I wished to compliment you!'

Under the gentle directness of the man who could charm or terrify more mature people than coltish tragediennes Mlle Georges found some of her confidence returning. It was usually this way with men or women who met Napoleon for the first time. In a matter of seconds they found themselves feeling precisely as he meant them to feel, cowed, impressed or completely at ease. Soldier and actress then exchanged some light conversation and she told him that her real name was Marguerite-Joséphine. He confessed to liking the name 'Joséphine' but, without stressing why, said he would use neither name but invent another. From now on he would call her 'Georgina' and Georgina she became from that moment.

He then asked why she said nothing in reply and she at last plucked up sufficient courage to tell him that the excessive amount of light bothered her. He at once rang for Roustan and ordered the candles on the big chandelier to be extinguished. Georgina, much relieved, decided to press her advantage and asked for half the remaining candles to be snuffed. Roustan complied and in the comparative gloom they sat and talked, this thirty-four-year-old Caesar and the seventeen-year-old daughter of two strolling players.

The girl was to recall every moment of this rendezvous during a further forty years of public life.

He first enquired into her past life and she told him everything, not forgetting the leisurely courtship of the Polish Prince. When she had finished he complimented her on telling the whole truth. He knew that she had distorted nothing and had held nothing back for he had made it his business to discover everything about her in advance.

Mlle Georges gives us a sympathetic picture of this unpredictable man who, having invited a girl into his bedroom for the purpose of seducing her, was yet content to sit and talk trivialities until five o'clock in the morning!

'He was tender and delicate,' she says, 'he did not wound my modesty by too much fervour and was glad to find a timid resistance. Heavens! I do not say he was in love but quite certainly I pleased him. I could not doubt it. Would he have put up with all my childish whims?'

She had indeed pleased him. He had come to her after a twelve-hour day at the desk, in the exclusive company of men with shrewd, tortuous minds. Is it surprising that he found a welcome tranquillity in the company of a beautiful young girl, whose loveliness and simplicity had cast a spell over him?

In spite of this promising beginning the association did not progress very far that evening. At five o'clock she said that she was tired and he made no effort to detain her. She promised to come again the following night and when they stood up he placed on her head the discarded veil and shawl. This done he kissed her lightly on the forehead.

It was then that Georgina's inexperience in these matters led her to commit a terrible error. She laughed aloud and when he asked the reason she was stupid enough to tell him the truth.

'You have just kissed Prince Sapieha's veil!'

A terrible change came over him. Everyone who came to know him well has remarked upon these sudden and almost horrifying changes of mood that distorted his smooth, regular features. 'It was like,' says one observer, 'a sudden and awful blotting out of the sun by a tempest.'

His face was twisted with rage as he seized the veil and ripped it into a dozen pieces, hurling them to the floor and stamping on them. He then seized her shawl and threw that to the ground and as if these violent actions did nothing to vent his anger he pulled from her finger a crystal ring, a trumpery little thing set in cornelians. The ring, too, was flung down and ground under his feet. The girl looked on, speechless with terror.

As suddenly as it had begun, and before the wretched girl had a chance to exclaim, the childish rage ebbed and his features relaxed once again into a warm, winning smile. He said:

'Dear Georgina, you must never have anything now except what comes from me!'

'Then it was impossible to be angry with him,' comments Mlle Georges. 'There was so much sweetness and tenderness in his voice that one was forced to say "After all, he acted quite rightly!"'

How many Kings, Princes and Ambassadors, how many Generals of Divisions and Ecclesiastics, all equally convinced against their will, were to say just this in the years ahead?

Georgina's drive home, accompanied by the sleepy Constant, proved as distressing to her as the outward journey, for she was obsessed by the thought that surrender to such a man would amount to gilded slavery.

When Constant told her that he would call for her again at eight in the evening she compromised, saying that he had better call at three o'clock in order to learn whether she had made up her mind to come.

He said nothing to this, he was probably too sleepy to care and Georgina found a chance during the day to discuss the rapidly developing situation with Talma, the actor. Talma gave her the same advice as she had received from her maid, namely that it would be sheer lunacy on her part not to make the utmost of her enviable opportunities.

Eight o'clock found her once more on her way to Saint Cloud. Napoleon received her just as warmly but opened their conversation by informing her that, from now on, she must see nothing more of Prince Sapieha. He had, in fact, already issued instructions that the visits of the Polish Prince must cease.

Mlle Georges admits that on this occasion the First Consul was as tender as he had been the previous evening but was also 'more pressing'.

She, on her part, found to her dismay that she was falling in love with him, not merely as a 'protector' but as a man! He wooed her with great delicacy and when in spite of this she still hung back, he said : 'See, Georgina, let me love you altogether; I want you to have complete confidence. It is true you scarcely know me but it needs but a minute to love. One feels all at once the electric movement which strikes you at the same time. Tell me, do you love me a little?'

Georgina made the reply that must have been made by

ten million girls in similar situations. She said : 'I'm afraid of loving you too much.'

The following night whilst playing *Cinna* she glanced towards the Consul's box at the moment when she was beginning her monologue. The box was empty and the implication was so obvious that she almost faltered. At that moment, however, there was a vague disturbance in the house, followed by a burst of applause as the First Consul entered the theatre. As was usual the piece was broken off short and commenced all over again.

That night Georgina excelled herself. Her performance was a triumph and the curtain fell to a storm of applause. Constant was waiting below and off went Georgina for the third time along the road to Saint Cloud. That evening she capitulated.

Her account of the surrender loses the air of mockmodesty that clouds the earlier portion of her memoirs and Mlle Georges tells the story of the remaining years of their association with unusual frankness. In so doing she spares neither her own nor her reader's blushes, but throughout a story that is in some ways a sensual and sordid little intrigue there runs a thread of gaiety and simplicity. This strain does more to reveal the real Napoleon Bonaparte than a shelf of learned prose.

The relationship continued intermittently for several years, although once he had made himself Emperor and moved into the Tuileries it lost something of its initial sparkle.

For the first year or so, however, their love-affair was more in keeping with two adolescents than an association one might expect between a despot and a palace whore.

They romped and laughed together and she must have given him many hours of mental ease. The blight of sophistication never touched Georgina. She never learned how to use him, as Caroline Colombier had used him, and she never converted the money and gifts he gave her into a float for business ventures, as did 'La Bellilotte'. She did not even employ his patronage to further herself in her profession, and if any woman can be said to have loved Napoleon for the man he was at a given moment in his career then that woman is Marguerite-Joséphine Weimar.

Perhaps 'love' is the wrong word. Although she gave herself freely, and hurried to his side whenever he sent for her, she did not identify him as a lover but never ceased to regard him as a playful demigod. In the years to come, when his stock was low, she could never keep reverence from her voice when she spoke of him. She was honoured rather than flattered by his attentions and when describing the evenings they spent in one another's company she gives the impression that she has been singled out by an Immortal and can never do full justice to the occasion.

Of that first experience she writes :

'He undressed me little by little. He acted the lady's maid with such gaiety, with such grace and decency, that one had to yield in spite of oneself. How could one not be fascinated and attracted to such a man? He became small and childish to please me. He was no longer the Consul : he was, perhaps, a man in love, but whose love had neither violence nor roughness. He embraced you sweetly, and his words were tender and modest. Beside him it was impossible not to experience what he experienced himself.'

There was an amusing little scene when they parted at seven in the morning. Georgina, dismayed at the prospect of his servants seeing what she modestly describes as 'the charming disorder the night had caused', suggested that she be allowed to tidy the room. He pretended to share her embarrassment, so that we have a picture of the First Consul and his latest mistress remaking the bed before the door is opened to the staff ! This act on his part impressed the girl more deeply than any aspect of his behaviour.

The charade of pretending to remake the bed continued for the first fortnight of their association and never failed to delight her but he was gay and gallant in other ways. 'He dressed me,' she says, 'and put on my stockings, and as I had garters with buckles, which made him impatient, he had some round garters made for me, to be passed over the foot.'

In her scribbled notes to Madame Valmore (the woman who sorted and edited these curious memoirs) Georgina expresses some concern that they might be seen by her friend's son, but in spite of this she has no hesitation in setting down the most intimate details of the love-affair and her collaborator was not averse to passing them on to posterity. Thus: 'There was nothing shameless in the most intimate moments and no obscene words. He made charming remarks: "Do you love me, Georgina? Are you happy in my arms? I am going to sleep too." '

One day he expressed a desire to see her 'in sunlight' and sent Constant to fetch her at nine in the morning. He armed her openly through the autumn woods, clearing dead branches from the path, so that she might walk easier. He paid her the kind of attentions a young husband might pay his wife in the first weeks of marriage, expressing concern for her health and for the temperature of the rooms and she grew to love these manifestations of gentleness that she never afterwards found in the arms of lesser men.

In his company she met the great, men like Talleyrand, some of the famous Marshals and many of the dignitaries of the Empire. 'How bored these people were with their grandeur!' she observes; 'and how they take you up and drop you without a thought'.

Sometimes, when he was irritated with his associates, he was careless enough to criticize them to her. 'That devil Talleyrand wants everyone to limp like himself,' he blurted out on one occasion. 'He loves to upset all simple and quiet existence – he is a jobber, my dear Georgina!'

Another day, after commenting on her succession of maternal roles on the stage, he suggested that she should herself become a mother and when Georgina admitted that an event of this nature would make her 'completely happy' she was at once despatched to a woman in the *faubourg* Saint-

Antoine 'for instruction as to how maternity could be achieved'. To her lasting regret the visit proved fruitless.

He took no pains to conceal from her information that would have proved invaluable to enemy agents. He told her where he was going and how long he would be absent, grave risk on the part of a man who was a target for half the assassins of Europe.

One evening, after she had successfully dissuaded him from making her read aloud from a dull book, they both sat on the carpet and he told her he intended setting out for the camp at Boulogne at four o'clock in the morning and would be away for several days.

When she showed little or no concern he accused her of being unfeeling. The heat of the fire and the glittering fire-irons came to her rescue and her eyes began to water. Instantly he was delighted and to her secret embarrassment kissed what he felt sure were tears shed at the prospect of parting.

'I loved him so I did not deceive him really,' says Georgina half-apologetically. She does not seem to realize how much she had learned about him since the night she had laughed at him for kissing Prince Sapieha's veil.

This particular flow of tears showed an immediate and unexpected profit. Taking out a wallet he at once filled her lap with banknotes. In the morning, when he set off, she suddenly burst into tears that owed nothing to the sparkle of poker and tongs.

Tears did not figure in many of their meetings. More often there was laughter and the horseplay which is the key to his boyish delight in her company. She was an emotional safety-valve, used when the weight of his responsibilities threatened to crush him. One evening he hid from her and was at last discovered beneath a pile of cushions. On another occasion, amid peals of laughter, she summoned Constant and demanded a pair of scissors.

'What do you want to cut off?' he demanded with assumed alarm, and when she claimed a lock of his hair he ran away from her, protesting that he had far too little to spare.

They had one semi-serious quarrel when he urged her to marry one of his Generals. Here he touched her pride and she stormed at him but even this disagreement ended in laughter and no more was said about finding her a husband. There was, however, a somewhat more sinister incident, which came close to involving her in political events and would certainly have done so had she been more intelligent or less easy to please.

During the Consular period many English travellers had taken advantage of the Peace of Amiens to visit France, a country that had been cut off from foreign visitors by a decade of revolution and the resultant conflict between the Republic and the rest of Europe.

Among the spring visitors to Paris was a certain Captain Hill, an officer who was almost certainly in the employ of Pitt's secret service.

Captain Hill made contact with Georgina and tried hard to persuade her to emigrate. When she protested he told her that the Prince of Wales had been attracted by her and would give her anything she desired if she would come over to England.

The invitation was obviously a bait. The British espionage agents, certain as they must have been that a renewal of war was only a matter of months, would have found a renegade mistress of the Consul's extremely useful to them, particularly as the Paris underground was seething with Royalist and Jacobin plots aimed at assassinating Napoleon.

When Hill first tried to make contact with her she refused to see him but at length his persistence aroused her curiosity and she met him by appointment in the Bois de Boulogne.

She greeted his proposals with amusement and carried them straight to Napoleon. The First Consul also treated them as a joke, at least outwardly, but he passed the information on to Fouché, the Chief of Police, and we hear no more of the enterprising English Captain.

In November, 1804, Napoleon warned her that an event was approaching that would prevent him entertaining her for some considerable time. She took this as a hint that his elevation to the rank of Emperor would put an end to their friendship. The prospect of losing him depressed her so much that she could not bring herself to witness his coronation in Notre Dame.

She saw part of the procession from a house opposite the Pont Neuf and her essential amiability is revealed in her comments on Joséphine, the Empress, of whom she afterwards wrote: 'She was marvellous – she always had such perfect taste in dress and a benevolent glance which attracted you to her. On this occasion she looked simple and charming . . . grandeurs had not changed her! What a misfortune for France and the Emperor that he afterwards divorced her.'

Ten days after the coronation there was a command performance of *Cinna* attended by Emperor and Empress. The Imperial pair received a tumultuous reception when they entered the theatre but poor Georgina had to play through the piece without once looking towards the Imperial box. Had she done so, she says, and caught the Emperor's eye, she would have broken down altogether. As it was she had a struggle with her emotions and the kindly Talma, who knew what she was going through, went out of his way to help and encourage her.

When the curtain fell Georgina's dressing-room was packed with excited nobilities, among them Talleyrand, who limped up and teased her for being a flirt! Talleyrand was famous for his unpleasant sense of humour.

Five weeks after the coronation Constant surprised her by appearing suddenly with the customary summons.

Georgina spent hours at her toilette before leaving for the Tuileries. She gained the Emperor's apartments by a difficult, roundabout route and he did his best to restore their relationship to its gay, familiar footing.

He failed. Not even his charm could surmount the barrier that had now risen between them and Georgina, who was reluctantly growing up, resigned herself to a permanent change in their association. 'The Emperor has driven away the First Consul,' she says sadly.

It was not simply his new grandeur that had interposed between them. Some of Napoleon's simple tastes had been laid on the altar of Notre Dame and he was disposed to seek his relaxation in more sophisticated company, notably that of Madame Duchâtel, a slim and strikingly beautiful blonde in the service of Joséphine, and a contrast in every way to the plump little tragedienne.

Perhaps Georgina was changing too, for she began to take note of other men, Demidoff, a Russian financier, with huge interests in the Siberian iron mines, and Metternich, the Austrian diplomat, who in the stormy decade ahead was to do more than any one man to overthrow the Empire. Metternich already had a great reputation as a ladies' man and boasted that he never kept less than half-a-dozen mistresses at one time.

In the year before the new storm broke over Europe, however, Georgina did pay an occasional visit to the Tuileries by night. It is from someone else's pen that we hear how she was once discovered in the Emperor's rooms by Joséphine.

There seems no real proof that it was Georgina who played the leading role in this undignified incident but it might well have been her. If so, then it might account for the fact that her visits to the Tuileries soon ceased altogether and her association with Napoleon came to an end.

The story implies that, whilst Napoleon may have had no taste for farce on the stage, there was a strong farcical element in his private life at this time. No sooner had he installed himself in the Tuileries than there began a persistent prying campaign on the part of his wife and a clumsy and evasive counter-offensive on his part. Neither his own behaviour nor that of his wife add much dignity to the Imperial legend.

An active display of jealousy on the part of Joséphine was something new in Napoleon's married life.

Up to the moment of her coronation Joséphine had felt far too insecure to risk an open breach with him on the grounds of his taste for actresses and readers. His Egyptian idyll does not seem to have interested her much, for she only quoted Madame Fourès' name (and that almost in passing) when defending herself against Napoleon's reproaches.

As Emperor Napoleon bitterly resented her intrusion into what he considered was his personal life and over and over again he assured her that she had no need to concern herself over his relationships with other women. These, he declared, were purely physical demonstrations on his part and meant nothing whatever to a marriage now sanctified by Church and State.

Being the kind of woman she was, that is, one who was more interested in maintaining outward appearances than emotional ties between husband and wife, Joséphine would probably have continued to turn a blind eye on Constant's eight o'clock coach-service. What threatened to promote a dangerous rupture between them was not his infidelity but the unremitting spite of Napoleon's brothers and sisters, who continued to wage war on the marriage with an energy that would have been better directed towards the maintenance of their own dignity.

Their behaviour at this period was outrageous. In addition to launching an open campaign aimed at bringing about a divorce they conducted themselves like greedy peasants who have discovered that one among them owned a goose that laid golden eggs.

No act was too mean, too stupid or too vulgar that they failed to perform it with zest. Elise, the eldest daughter, partnered brother Lucien in an amateur theatrical show and appeared on the stage wearing revealing pink tights and nothing else. Lucien, as Ambassador to Spain, took to speculating in financial deals, forgetting that he already possessed as much money as he could conveniently spend.

Joseph and Lucien openly criticized the family breadwinner's foreign and domestic policies and went so far as to consort openly with his personal enemies and elect themselves joint mouthpiece of the Emperor.

Louis, for his part, did not meddle much in politics but contented himself with making the life of his wife Hortense a hell upon earth.

Pauline, the most fetching of the Bonaparte girls, indulged in one love affair after another, until her behaviour became a public scandal.

Caroline and her swaggering husband Murat continued to whine, wheedle and bluster for more money and greater honours, encouraging Marshal Bernadotte to hatch out one or two more half-baked plots against the man to whom all three owed position and income.

Jerome, Napoleon's youngest brother, was abroad with the navy at the time but this did not keep him out of mischief. He deserted his vessel, went off on an extended spree in America, lived extremely well on his brother's credit and finally contracted a stupid marriage with the daughter of a Baltimore merchant.

Napoleon, the long suffering, forgave all but Lucien, who finally exceeded his brother's patience and was kicked out of the country. Studying the antics of the Bonaparte clan at this period one cannot but think that France would have benefited greatly by an Imperial edict banishing the entire bunch to the Antipodes.

His family's ceaseless intrigues against Joséphine made no impression at all upon Napoleon. One of the ex-Consuls echoed their pleas to put Joséphine away and marry some-one who could provide the country with an heir. Napoleon reacted violently to this unsolicited advice. 'No,' he thundered, 'was my mother a tigress?' The time was to come when he would make up his own mind on the matter but that time was not yet.

Joséphine continued to worry and her uncertainty showed in the enrolment of a small army of household spies. The duties of this cohort were to report in detail upon her husband's nocturnal wanderings in the corridors of the Tuileries.

What ultimate benefit she hoped to gain by this stupid and ineffectual plan is difficult to guess. One might have supposed that she would have realized by this time that her real interest lay in continuing to exercise her matchless charm on useful people and to look fixedly in the wrong direction whenever her husband's attention was momentarily attracted by a pretty face or figure. It was not her prying, however, that resulted in a sensational exposure of the Georgina liaison. This came about as a direct result of a sudden illness on the part of the Emperor whilst he was closeted with the actress in his apartments at the palace.

It has been stated on good authority that Napoleon was an epileptic. There is not much reliable evidence of this during the period of thirty-five years that he led an active life in a variety of climates, but on two occasions his health did interfere with his direction of battles.

On the night of the palace débâcle he is reported to have fallen into a coma and Georgina, the sole person present when the illness occurred, lost her nerve and became semi-hysterical. It seemed to her that the Emperor was either dead or dying and she made such a commotion that servants converged on them from all directions.

In her haste to summon assistance she had overlooked the fact that she was naked except for a chemise and among those who answered the alarm bell was Joséphine. The interesting scene was cut short by Napoleon's sudden recovery. When he noticed that his room was half full of people, that Joséphine was among them, and that Georgina was dancing round the bed in her chemise he flew into a furious temper and bundled everybody outside. He then turned on the wretched Georgina and cursed her for her failure to keep her head, working himself up into such a frenzy that he came near to fainting for the second time.

Napoleon never really forgave Georgina for her share in

this bedroom comedy. After this no more was heard of her visits to the Tuileries. She continued, however, to play leading roles at the theatre and was still a popular star when, in May 1808, she committed the second great folly of her career by running out on a performance and crossing the frontier in the company of an opera dancer called Dupont.

Then, as now, it was an unforgiveable crime for an artiste to run out on an advertised performance and both Napoleon and the public were furious. It was at first supposed that she had eloped with Dupont but it later became known that she had fled to Russia in order to join a nobleman called Benckendorff whom she believed would marry her.

Benckendorff had been her lover whilst he was living in Paris, attached to the staff of the Russian Ambassador. The Russian diplomat had not decoyed her out of France for his own pleasure but merely to play the part of a pawn in a St Petersburg intrigue.

The Czar, at this time, was enslaved by a certain Madame Narishkine, whom the court party were extremely anxious to replace, and Benckendorff's party planned to use Georgina as a kind of decoy. By this means, they thought, the Little Father might be induced to return, by stages as it were, to the embrace of the disconsolate Czarina. It was a typical Russian manoeuvre, outwardly cunning but outrageously clumsy.

Georgina, of course, had no suspicion that she was to be embroiled in Russian politics and already considered herself as good as married. She wrote to her mother in France that month signing herself 'George Benckendorff'!

Somewhere along the line the tortuous plot wandered off course and although the Czar received her and gave her a handsome piece of jewellery she does not seem to have impressed him as much as the optimistic Benckendorff anticipated. In spite of this Georgina's arrival in St Petersburg caused a considerable stir, so much so that she decided to settle there and might well have done so, ultimately retiring from the stage and making a good marriage, had not war broken out between the two countries again in the early summer of 1812.

The war was more than an inconvenience. Georgina's position as a Frenchwoman and an ex-mistress of the French Emperor would have been a very difficult and dangerous one during the French invasion, had Alexander, the Czar, been a less amiable man. Certainly Georgina did not go out of her way to remain unnoticed amidst the frenzied demonstrations of patriotism that accompanied Napoleon's advance on Moscow.

The Battle of Borodino outside the capital was a hard-won victory for the invaders but at St Petersburg it was celebrated as a Russian triumph and there were junketings and illuminations. Georgina was far too French to make a show of taking part in them and kept her windows dark and tightly closed. They would have been smashed had not the Czar ordered that she was not to be molested and she was still there when the starving and frostbitten survivors of the Grand Army staggered back across the Niemen and word buzzed across Europe that Napoleon's star had fallen.

Only one person in Holy Russia was not taken in by these rumours and that person was Georgina. Unable to remain longer among her country's enemies, or witness their glee at the hideous disaster that had overtaken the French she somehow secured a passport, packed her trunks and gifts and went home via Sweden.

At Stockholm she ran into some old friends. In the interval between her flight from Paris and her return from Russia, the intrigues and flatteries of Désirée's husband had at last paid a dividend. Bernadotte was now Crown Prince of Sweden and about to lead an army of his adopted countrymen against the hard-pressed nation whose uniform he had worn for twenty years. His anti-Imperialism, however, did not extend to a discarded mistress of Napoleon. He and his wife received Georgina as a friend and facilitated her journey to Dresden, where the French armies were regrouping for their final challenge to a continent in arms.

It says much for Georgina's reputation among the troops that she was warmly welcomed after four years' stay among the toughest of their opponents. She was sent back to Paris and her former lover at once reinstated her at the Comédie Française. Before she left she played with the Comédie company in Dresden, and all her friends, including Talma, received her with pleasure, saying nothing of her madcap flight into Russia or her almost unforgivable action in running out on a billed performance.

By Imperial decree she was restored to all her rights as a member of the Society and Napoleon even instructed that she should be paid for her years of absence. In this instance, however, he did her a bad turn, for there was bitter resentment among the loyal members of the company when this fact became known.

Georgina remained in France during the allied invasion and Napoleon's absence on Elba. When the Emperor returned to fight Waterloo she came into brief prominence once more by performing a useful piece of service to the Imperial cause. In some way or other she had contrived to obtain possession of documents that compromised the Chief of Police, Fouché, and these she sent to Napoleon, without any thought of reward.

Napoleon was touched by this act of loyalty. With his customary address to detail he had discovered that she was very hard up.

'She didn't tell you she was in low water?' he asked of the messenger and when the man replied in the negative he added : 'Well, I happen to know that she is ! Give her twenty thousand francs from my private purse !'

Waterloo was fought and lost and the friends of Napoleon paid dearly for their loyalty. The Bourbons who had scuttled away into a second exile the night before Napoleon approached Paris, were again restored by allied bayonets. They at once celebrated their triumph by shooting Marshal Ney and hounding other prominent Bonapartists into exile and penury. The violet was the Imperial emblem and Georgina, showing her usual disregard for self-interest, outraged the Superintendent of Theatres by openly displaying a bouquet of violets in her corsage. This brave but foolhardy gesture led to her instant expulsion from Paris.

For the next five years she played the provinces and then, when the flames of hatred were dying down, she slipped back into Paris and made her peace with the Bourbons. She was still too popular to be openly persecuted and was given a benefit performance at the Opera, where she received a tremendous reception by the Parisians.

Firmly re-established she began starring in romantic dramas and scored a number of brilliant successes, later touring Italy, Austria and Russia in a number of successful plays.

It was flesh, not folly, that was to bring her down in the end.

As the years passed she began to put on weight at an alarming pace and soon she was so fat that she could only walk with difficulty. She hung on to the shreds of her professional reputation with a tenacity that is almost pitiful, attempting over and over again to overcome her terrible handicap and keep her place in the sun, but in May 1849, when she was sixty-two and almost elephantine, she gave up the struggle and retired.

Millions of francs and a king's ransom in jewels had slipped through her fingers during her long career but in her old age she was almost penniless and is believed to have subsisted on a small pension given her from a government fund.

After the establishment of the Second Empire she could probably have obtained all she needed from the new Emperor, Napoleon's nephew, but she hated cadging and preferred to make what she could by jotting down her amiable memories and getting them rewritten and issued by her friend, Valmore.

She died in 1867 at the age of eighty and was buried in the

famous cemetery of Père-la-Chaise, where so many of the famous Marshals now lay.

Before she died, and when she could still get about, she used to pass alongside the Tuileries and look up at the windows of the room where, more than sixty years before, she had been entertained by the man whose name was now a legend.

Old, shuffling and so fat that people exchanged ribald remarks about her as she passed, she nevertheless retained memories that her age and infirmities could not dim. While others in France could recall the Emperor as a proud conqueror on a white horse, surrounded by a glittering staff and dispensing favours from his throne, she knew him only as a tired and harassed young man, who had welcomed her company and her silly chatter and the comfort they brought out of the night. Perhaps her memories evoked a sense of fulfilment that she had never achieved during her long career on the stage.

CHAPTER XII

Stage and Salon

One of the manifold duties of Napoleon's Postmaster General was to keep a wary eye on the incoming letters written in a feminine hand. Occasionally this watch yielded interesting results.

One morning a letter addressed to a certain Mademoiselle Guillebeau, one of Joséphine's readers, was fished from the bag and opened by the painstaking official. It was from the young lady's Irish mother and the Postmaster must have knitted his brows at the maternal advice contained therein. Madame Guillebeau's instructions to her promising daughter might be paraphrased as follows :

'Get hold of facts that might prove useful in keeping a hold on the Emperor and either improve your position with him or make sure you abandon it to your advantage !'

The Postmaster General, feeling, no doubt, that he might save mother and daughter a good deal of unnecessary spade work, sent the letter on to Napoleon. An hour or so later there was a vacancy on Joséphine's household staff.

This incident is a good illustration of the frame of mind prevailing among the attractive young women surrounding Napoleon during the brief period between his ascension to the throne, in 1804, and his departure for the new theatre of war in Bohemia and Moravia, in 1805.

Prior to his coronation he was far too busy to offer himself as a target to designing mothers and daughters. Subsequently he spent most of his time in the field and continued to do so right up to the time of his second marriage, in 1810.

The creation of an Imperial court and the golden opportunities it offered the astute young women who surrounded

Joséphine tempted many mothers (and a number of equally alert husbands) to bait toothsome traps for the susceptible monarch. Once such a trap was sprung the young woman concerned was in a strong position. Either she acquired money and social influence or, if she failed to improve her position with the Emperor, she could always retire gracefully and take her pick from the covey of husbands the Imperial match-maker kept waiting in the wings.

Some of these hopeful young ladies dreamed of acquiring real political power, such as had been wielded by the mistresses of the Bourbon kings, but these were woefully disappointed. The Emperor was no Bourbon and the only woman in his life who was ever allowed to exercise the slightest influence on the conduct of the realm was his second wife, Marie Louise, herself the daughter of an Emperor.

No conqueror in history was more vulnerable to feminine charm than was Napoleon Bonaparte; no monarch was less disposed to mingle business with pleasure.

These would-be Pompadours were often an intolerable nuisance to him for by no means all were unmasked as quickly as the luckless Mlle Guillebeau.

From December 1804 onwards the Tuileries teemed with pretty women and every single one of them was on the look-out for a meaning glance from Napoleon or, if that was not forthcoming, a wealthy and distinguished husband with prospects of becoming wealthier and more distinguished under Imperial patronage.

The renewal of the war against the European coalition did more for Napoleon than consolidate his fame as a military genius of the highest order. It almost certainly saved him from leaving his reputation on the bonestrewn beach of the Sirens. Signs were not lacking during the eighteen months preceding his great victory at Austerlitz that the brilliant young man of the Army of Italy was on the way to becoming a cynical voluptuary.

This period is the high noon of his philandering, the time when his amours come nearest to dominating his personality to the exclusion of everything else and blunting the fine edge of his superbly efficient brain. There was not the slightest danger of this happening whilst he was under the spell of the empty-headed Georgina, but Georgina was not the only attractive tragedienne in Paris and neither were all the beauties of the capital actresses by profession.

Far more subtle women than plump little Georgina were lying in wait for the big prize and their lairs were the salons of the newly-created duchesses of the Empire. Other calculating coquettes thronged the card-tables of sister Elise and sister Caroline, still more the household of the easygoing Joséphine, who was ready to enrol any pretty girl as a Lady-in-Waiting on the strength of a plausible hard-luck story.

It was in these salons that Napoleon almost came to grief. Apart from his association with Georgina, whose story has been told, his affairs with actresses were casual, light-hearted and purely transitory, some of them almost brutally so, as in the case of the hapless Mlle Duchesnois.

Catherine-Joséphine Duchesnois is the saddest of all Napoleon's conquests.

She was twenty-five when she made her début at Versailles and although her face has the pensive beauty of a wounded doe, with huge, haunting eyes and a pretty, submissive mouth, she lacked the vivacity of a woman who can help a busy man forget the cares of high office.

It is impossible to shed responsibilities in the company of women who look like Catherine Duchesnois. One is more likely to become involved in their tragic acceptance of heavy burdens. Berthon painted her in the role of Joan of Arc and she looks like Joan of Arc, an hour or so before they led her to the stake. How a man of Napoleon's experience could have imagined that she would be capable of introducing the Georgina atmosphere into his apartment is just one more enigma attaching itself to this prince of enigmas. It was, perhaps, the same kind of error as that which induced him to select the blundering, conscientious Grouchy as the right man to pursue the beaten Prussians after the battle of Ligny and to get himself and his army thoroughly lost in the process.

At all events, on at least one occasion he did summon sad-eyed Catherine to his room and Constant escorted her to the Tuileries by the same route as that used for Georgina and other favourites.

It happened, however, that Catherine called on a particularly busy evening and when Constant informed the Emperor that the lady had arrived Napoleon sent word to say that he would join her very soon but in the meantime she was to get undressed!

What the solemn Catherine thought of this indelicate command is not recorded but an acquaintance of Catherine's once described her as 'a person who never fails to grasp one's meaning'. It is therefore not surprising to learn that she obeyed with resignation, noting sadly that the hour was late, the season early autumn and the room fireless.

Napoleon must have been very busy indeed that evening. Half an hour ticked away but he showed no signs of appearing. This was particularly unfeeling of him for he was fond of a blazing hearth and the patient Duchesnois, standing in her chemise, was soon chilled to the bone.

At length she concluded that he must have forgotten her and after wrapping herself in some discarded garments she summoned a servant and sent a message reminding him of her presence.

It was an act of folly. To interrupt Napoleon when he was hard at work was to court an explosion of wrath. Timidly reminded of the fact that Mlle Duchesnois still awaited him he spun round on the luckless messenger and barked : 'Indeed? Then tell her to go away again !'

It is a pity that Catherine Duchesnois did not write her memoirs. Had she done so we might have had a particularly vivid pen-picture of Napoleon as she thought of him during her cheerless journey home that evening.

Napoleon Bonaparte, *from a lithograph by Delpech*

Joséphine, Empress of the French, *from a lithograph by Delpech*

Mademoiselle Mars, *by Gérard*

Hortense de Beauharnais, daughter of Joséphine

Countess Walewska, *by Robert Lefebre*

Marie Louise, *after a drawing by Durand-Duclos*

Désirée, Queen of Sweden, *by Gérard*

The Emperor Napoleon I in his coronation robes

One other lady of the theatre who had cause to complain of Napoleon's behaviour at this time was Thérèse Bourgoin, also a tragedienne and a keen rival of both Georgina and Catherine Duchesnois.

In the case of Thérèse it was not pride that suffered but pocket. To her dying day she was to harbour implacable resentment against her Imperial lover.

Thérèse Bourgoin differed very materially from her fellow-victim, Duchesnois. She was pert, pretty, independent and a past-mistress of the art of backstage repartee. She had sparkling, insolent eyes, a laughing mouth, and the type of round cherubic face that sometimes advertises mischief in the features of an intelligent child.

Nobody, least of all the Paris theatre-goer, was ever fooled by this air of innocence. She was eighteen when she made her début and twenty-one when, as a member of the Society, she attracted Napoleon's notice. Long before this she had learned how many beans made five.

At the turn of the century Thérèse was a rich man's mistress and her protector happened to be Chaptal, Napoleon's fifty-year-old Minister of the Interior. The Emperor, of course, was well aware of this, as indeed was everyone else in Paris society, for Chaptal was so proud of possessing a pretty and distinguished mistress that he paraded her everywhere and it was known that he could refuse her nothing

Madame Bourgoin, an adventuress from choice, made the most of this indulgence but was nevertheless ready and eager to improve her position on the social ladder. When at last she was invited to pay a call on the Tuileries she said nothing about it to Chaptal, being resolved, no doubt, to make the most of her opportunities with the eagle and keep the old buzzard in reserve.

Unwittingly she overplayed her hand and became involved in an unpleasant political intrigue. She emerged from it bruised, breathless and very bitter.

Napoleon, at this time, was anxious to replace Chaptal by his brother Lucien and he did not feel disposed to sacrifice the chance of achieving this at the expense of Thérèse. He therefore summoned her to his apartments one evening whilst he was actually in conference with his Minister of the Interior and he saw to it that the unfortunate Chaptal overheard the name of his pretty visitor the moment it was announced.

The Minister must have found it very difficult to conceal his surprise and fury. He did so, however, and hastily excused himself, leaving the Tuileries seething with rage. The moment he arrived home he sat down and wrote out his resignation, which was precisely what Napoleon had intended he should do.

This little comedy proved very expensive, not only for Thérèse, who lost a wealthy lover on the spot, but for Napoleon, who thus made himself two lifelong enemies.

Up to that moment Chaptal had been an enthusiastic Bonapartist. He had played an important backstage part in preparing the country for Napoleon's assumption of power and during the Consulate he had entertained two of his master's most important guests, the King and Queen of Etruria, at a spectacular fête staged in his own garden.

After abandoning the fair Thérèse he continued to serve the Empire but did so sullenly, watching his rival like a savage old hawk. When cracks began to appear in the Imperial façade he was not slow to add his voice to those of the critics. On the Emperor's return from the disastrous Russian campaign it was Chaptal who passed the word that 'half the fibres of Napoleon's brain are no longer sound !'

Thérèse's own revenge was equally characteristic and much more immediate. Her witty, sarcastic tongue was an ideal weapon of offence and year after year she wagged it, cheerfully and mercilessly, in the cause of belittling and mocking the man who had cost her the patronage of her indulgent lover.

When peace was signed between Napoleon and the Czar, at Tilsit, in 1807, she anticipated her colleague Georgina's escapade by slipping away to St Petersburg. Here she amused Russian society by recounting all the latest Paris jokes about the Emperor. She was a great social success and many were the titters she earned from the Russian aristocrats at Napoleon's expense.

He, for his part, kept a wary eye on her for he was well aware that she was slandering him. On the next occasion that he met the Czar, at Erfurt, he counter-attacked by recounting some equally spicy stories about Mademoiselle Bourgoin, after which he warned the Czar that she was a dangerous and unreliable woman.

When Napoleon fell, Thérèse openly rejoiced and made a great display of loyalty to the Bourbons, continuing to do so when Napoleon escaped from Elba and came home for the Hundred Days.

She did not gain very much by this ostentatious display, for the Bourbons were not distinguished for their gratitude. In the years that followed Napoleon's exile we hear far less of her as an actress than we hear, for instance, of that unrepentant Bonapartist, Mlle Georges.

She retired from the stage when she was forty-eight and died four years later. Like a number of the men and women who had achieved fame under the Empire, she was buried at Père-la-Chaise, close to the spot where her former rivals, Mlle Georges and Catherine Duchesnois, were to lie. Other distinguished Imperialists were close at hand. In the same cemetery lay buried several of the famous Marshals, including Davout, Masséna and Ney, men who had quarrelled as continuously and acrimoniously as had the gay ladies of the Comédie Française.

Père-la-Chaise will not be the most tranquil of cemeteries of Judgement Day.

The story of Napoleon's association with ladies of the theatre would be incomplete without a reference to the most accomplished actress of them all. She is the one whose intimacy with the Emperor is based more upon hearsay and speculation than upon recorded fact.

This charming woman was the famous Mademoiselle Mars, who played a wide variety of parts at the Comédie Française in the early years of the century and lived on to play in Victor Hugo's dramas long after the death of Napoleon.

Accounts of Mlle Mars' appearance vary. One contemporary declares her to have been 'painfully thin', but the fair-minded Mlle Georges, who associated with her over a long period, describes her figure as 'the most ravishing one could possibly see'.

There is no dispute, however, as regards the loveliness of her face. Madame Junot, who took theatrical lessons from her, goes into rhapsodies about her eyes, her beautiful teeth and what must have been a bewitching range of expression 'that could reveal a sentiment before it was uttered'.

Her disposition was equally attractive. She possessed the mental agility of Thérèse Bourgoin, the amiability of Marguerite Georges and the powerful intensity, when on stage, of the gloomy Catherine Duchesnois.

Napoleon himself shows proof of her artistic superiority in a letter dashed off to the Superintendent of Theatres in the summer of 1813, when the Comédie Française company had come to Dresden to amuse the doomed army.

The letter is an instruction to pay gratuities to the various artistes, and the errant Georgina, who had just rejoined her countrymen after her protracted Russian adventure, received eight thousand francs. Thérèse Bourgoin, in spite of her non-stop slander campaign against Napoleon, was awarded six thousand. Mlle Mars was given ten thousand. Catherine Duchesnois evidently missed her cue again for her name does not appear at all.

The story of how Mlle Mars came to attract Napoleon's attention is unusual. Although he must have seen her play many parts at the theatre she does not seem to have impressed him until he caught a glimpse of her watching a military review, in the courtyard of the Tuileries.

There were occasions, even on parade, when Napoleon could act with pleasing informality. He often interrupted these reviews to hold little conversations with his bearded grenadiers and when this happened Emperor and private soldier would reminisce for a moment or two over past campaigns.

These encounters usually ended by Napoleon pinching the veteran's ear (his invariable gesture of affection) and awarding him a decoration for distinguished conduct.

At this particular review the Emperor was rather less familiar and the ear-pinching was reserved for a more intimate occasion. On seeing Mlle Mars he spurred his horse through the cordon of guards and addressed the pretty spectator directly. 'So you are returning the visits which it gives us so much pleasure to pay you at the Théatre-Française?'

Mlle Mars was so dumbfounded by this display of informality that for once in her life she could think of nothing to reply.

It was probably this encounter that led to closer acquaintance, although it is strange that no gossip of the period seems to have written of the association with the attention to detail shown in respect of Mlles Georges, Duchesnois or even Bourgoin.

Madame Junot is the authority for what little we know about this woman and she pays a very high tribute to her both as an actress and an individual.

The story of how the two women established a friendship is an illustration of what came to be known as the 'Troubadour Movement' that flourished in the First Empire.

The Troubadour Movement was a latter-day revival of twelfth-century chivalry, when every knight rode out to battle with a lady's glove or favour attached to his helm, and a resolve to conquer or die in her honour.

Napoleon, an incurable romantic, encouraged this cult and all through Napoleonic literature we find instances of dying men sending romantically-worded last messages to their loved ones at home or entrusting a comrade with the delivery of a lock of hair or a portrait.

Colonel Marbot, himself a nineteenth-century knight-errant, promised to perform such a mission on the field of Pultusk and this kind of thing was by no means confined to the officers of the Grand Army. Sergeant Bourgoyne, trudging along the endless road from Moscow during the great retreat, was constantly turning aside to collect souvenirs and last words from dying guardsmen and soldiers of the line.

Whilst their men were in the field the women at home amused themselves in various ways and one of their most popular pastimes was that of organizing amateur theatricals.

In the winter of 1806–7, when the Emperor and his Marshals were groping through the Polish bogs and snow-drifts in pursuit of the Russian Army, the court was busily engaged in rehearsing a specially-written play for a forthcoming fête.

The leading spirits of this entertainment were Napoleon's sisters, Pauline and Caroline, of whom an observer says: 'They may have been the two prettiest women in the world but they were certainly two of the worst actresses that ever trod the boards of a theatre!'

Madame Junot, who also had a leading part, was most anxious to perform well, if only to prevent the audience from screaming with laughter at the antics of the two over-confident Princesses. She, therefore, engaged Mlle Mars to coach her and it would appear that her choice was a good one, for the entertainment went off to everyone's satisfaction. There is no reason why it should not have done, with or without the professional attendance of Mlle Mars. Its preparation had occupied the Imperial court the entire winter!

As in the case of the majority of amateur entertainments there was a grave shortage of men in the company. Whilst the women were play-acting, a drama of a very different kind was being played out several hundreds of leagues to the east, where the Grand Army had received its first major check at the bloody battle of Eylau.

Could anything be more illustrative of the first Empire's Troubadour Movement – men charging an army in a snowstorm and their wives and sweethearts bickering about the allocation of roles on the amateur stage?

CHAPTER XIII

'The everlasting "I"'

Embroiled in transitory love-affairs as he was during the pre-Austerlitz lull in his career as world conqueror, Napoleon did not cut such a ridiculous figure with the actresses as he did with the more designing and infinitely more unscrupulous women of Joséphine's suite.

It was in this circle that he came near to advertising himself as the laughing-stock of Europe.

The first and least serious of these encounters was his affair with Madame de Vaudey, a reader, who first attracted him in the early summer of 1804.

Madame de Vaudey is the most vicious and unforgiving of all the women who schemed to enslave him and her bitterness against him, when he finally came to his senses and expelled her from court, was to cross the borderline of sanity.

Madame de Vaudey came from an aristocratic family and survived the Revolution to find favour with the new régime. Her father, Michaud D'Arçon, had been a distinguished military engineer under the Bourbons and as a young woman she had married another aristocrat, de Vaudey, who was a Captain in the Royal Army and later a Senator under Napoleon.

She was a tall, attractive young woman, well schooled in the formalities of court life but now that the days of hereditary privilege were gone unable to adjust herself to a reasonable standard of living.

In her extravagance and passion for trivial amusements she rivalled Joséphine but in addition to being a reckless spender she was an inveterate gambler.

She was so addicted to card-playing that she carried a

pack of cards with her wherever she went and was not averse to inviting idle aides-de-camp and court officials to play a few hands in odd corners of the Imperial establishments. If a card-table was handy so much the better. When it was not she was always happy to oblige with her lap.

Napoleon got to hear about these hole-in-corner games and at once put a stop to them but he was much attracted to the instigator and she became his mistress during a state visit to Aix-la-Chapelle.

Later that summer the Imperialist train set out on a journey to the Rhine and Madame de Vaudey, as one of Joséphine's Ladies-in-Waiting, accompanied the progress.

What happened concerning her on the journey is not known but it is established that de Vaudey returned to Paris convinced that she held Napoleon in the hollow of her hand. She accordingly proceeded to run up debts to the tune of hundreds of thousands of francs. Dunned by tradesmen, dressmakers and jewellers, she blithely collected their bills and sent them along to her lover, pointing out that prompt settlement would relieve her of tiresome petitioning by creditors.

Nobody could be more indulgent with a silly, pretty woman than the master of France. He paid the debts and when she appealed to him a second time he paid them once again. For a man already saddled with the most expensive wife in Europe he behaved with commendable reserve.

There was, however, a limit to the Imperial patience and when the saucy little gambler presented him with a third set of bills he lost his temper. 'Why should I pay so dearly for what I can obtain so cheaply elsewhere?' was his surly but logical comment.

Madame de Vaudey was somewhat alarmed by this unreasonable attitude but she did not let it depress her. After a brief interval she wrote him a pitiful letter, explaining that she was now faced with 'debts of honour' and that if she failed to find the money within twenty-four hours she would be obliged to make an end to her life.

It is strange to learn that the greatest military bluffer of all time was wholly taken in by such a letter but he undoubtedly was and at once despatched General Rapp, his swaggering German aide-de-camp, to de Vaudey's charming house in Auteuil. Rapp arrived with the money in his saddle-bag.

The aide-de-camp expected to find the lady in hysterics, with a bottle of laudanum in her hand and a pocket-pistol at her bedside. He was understandably bewildered when he broke in upon the merriest of card parties, with Madame de Vaudey holding court over a roomful of excited gamblers. His sudden arrival threw the hostess into a flurry of dismay but she was a cool hand and had survived worse scrapes. Gaily and plausibly she pocketed the money and began to explain the party away.

Rapp, however, was a man of the world and was not fooled for an instant. He reported the circumstances in detail to Napoleon, who at once wrote to his mistress instructing her to resign from her position at Court. This time he was genuinely outraged. In spite of tears and a string of fertile fabrications he held firmly to his resolve and from that hour would have nothing further to do with her.

When it was plain to her that he would never relent she took her last shot from the locker. Dipping her pen in vitriol she sat down to write her memoirs, outdoing the actress Thérèse Bourgoin in defamation of character. She did not like many others, wait until Napoleon was a discredited exile, but went to work right away and the memoirs she wrote soon came to Napoleon's notice. He took no retaliative action beyond refusing to allow her to show her face at court.

As the years slipped by, Madame de Vaudey became more and more hysterical in her rage against him. When he abdicated in 1814, she joined the shrill chorus of critics, exulting in his overthrow and licking the elegant shoes of all the implacable *émigrés* who came creeping back to Paris at the tail of the Russian, Prussian, Austrian, British and Swedish armies.

Even then the tide of her hatred for the man who had treated her so generously did not reach its highwater mark. In March the following year, when she learned that Napoleon had escaped from Elba and was advancing triumphantly on Grenoble, she fought her way through the confusion of the Bourbon exodus and offered to travel south and assassinate the Ogre. She needed, she declared, neither pistol nor dagger, simply a post-chaise and, of course, a good supply of funds.

The official to whom she appealed did not take her offer very seriously. He probably had a good inkling of what was likely to happen to any funds advanced to her for the crazy project. We later hear of her as a penniless, half-blind and half-paralyzed beggar, using her dog-eared memories as a means of subsistence. It is a fitting epilogue for such a pitiless harpy.

The story of Napoleon's second infatuation among the ladies of his wife's household lacks the dramatic 'shape' of the de Vaudey episode. It does not even boast a climax and has, for one reason or another, been shielded by a veil of secrecy such as surrounds no other love affair of the Emperor.

Even now, after the passage of more than a century and a half, the main facts of this brief, passionate attachment between Napoleon and his wife's most enchanting Lady-in-Waiting are in doubt but in spite of this the affair was one of the most important in his life.

The Consular and Imperial courts contained more beautiful women than a Sultan's harem. At least half those who attended Joséphine or, as brides of the Marshals and court dignitaries, attended the card parties and fêtes of the Empire, were extremely attractive women. We have the evidence of male and female diarists for this and on this fact alone they all agree.

Two of Napoleon's sisters possessed striking good looks and when young men made up their minds to marry almost every high-ranking officer in the Imperial army chose grace, charm and a pretty face rather than wealth or family background.

Marriage for love was not confined to the hundreds of dashing young officers who thronged the Imperial court during the intervals between campaigns. Civil servants in their late forties and fifties married pretty but penniless girls in their teens, caring not a rap whether their brides came to them with or without dowries. Dowries in any case were often hard to come by for the majority of the best families had been ruined by the Revolution.

The social upheaval, however, had paid the women of the French middle-class a casual dividend. Just as the two world wars of the twentieth-century freed women from the stupid and stuffy conventions of the Victorian age, so the French Revolution opened up new vistas to girls of intelligence and adaptability.

Oddly old-fashioned in these matters. Napoleon did his utmost to apply a brake to the new freedoms but he did not succeed in preserving the conventional barriers. He sometimes pontificated about the New Woman and all his life he had a horror of the blue-stocking and the woman who meddled in politics. For all his psychological insight and authority he was no match for the nimble-witted young beauties of the salons. They paid lip-service to his opinions but they laughed at him behind his back and their demureness evaporated like sun-drenched dew the moment his attention was engaged in the field. Shamelessly they continued to employ their physical attractions to achieve material ends and almost all of them proved far more adroit than he at riding out the political storms ahead. He died in lonely exile. They, with few exceptions, died in an atmosphere of wealth and respectability.

The Queen of this troupe, the shrewdest Circe of them all, was young Madame Duchâtel, a woman who caused Joséphine more tears and wretchedness than all the actresses on the Paris stage.

In a court renowned all over Europe for exquisite feminine charm Duchâtel outshone her competitors.

She was blonde, with cornflower-blue eyes, a perfectly-shaped aquiline nose, lovely teeth and a slender figure, as supple and lissom as had been Joséphine's in her youth. She had, in addition, poise, winning manners (when she cared to display them) and a good singing voice. She was also an accomplished harpist.

Duchâtel had the same range of facial expression as the man whom she set out to capture. Naturally haughty and over-confident, she could, in a mere second, soften her lovely features by a bewitching smile and it was a smile that seemed to promise the submissive tenderness that Napoleon had been searching for since his lonely youth. Madame Duchâtel's instincts undoubtedly made her aware of his pursuit of this particular rainbow and the moment she took up her post as Joséphine's Lady-in-Waiting she went to work with a single-mindedness rarely seen in a woman of twenty.

Her husband was thirty years her senior and they met but seldom, for whilst she spent most of her time at Court he held a responsible post in the civil administration of the Empire. Responsibility did not usually preclude the Empire's politicians from enjoying plenty of leisure but Duchâtel was a hard-working man with a high sense of honour. He was also a tolerant soul and gave his wife all the personal freedom she desired and she took full advantage of his trust. Among her ardent admirers were Marshal Murat, Napoleon's brother-in-law, and his stepson, young Eugène. It is doubtful whether Monsieur Duchâtel ever learned of his wife's infidelity and perhaps this is one of the reasons why secrecy still surrounds an attachment that was common knowledge among all the women of Joséphine's household at the time.

The affair between them was no uninhibited, boisterous association, such as Napoleon had formed with Georgina, and it had little in common with his studied infidelities of the past, like the brief and brazen affair with Marguerite Fourès, in Egypt. This time Napoleon was deeply in love, with the enthusiasm, as well as the fatuity, of a sixteen-year-old schoolboy. The very intensity of his feelings masked the object of his admiration for he was very susceptible towards the lady's position at court and went to great pains to avoid the risk of a scandal that would lead to Duchâtel's removal for reasons of state.

For once Joséphine was thoroughly foxed. She had no doubt whatever that her husband was indulging in a high-powered love-affair and it was plain that her rival could be numbered among the young women of her household. The problem was, which one? When she set out to determine this she was required to match the deep, Italianate cunning of a man whose business it was to confuse all the politicians.

For several weeks Napoleon had the better of the exchanges. He began to spend more and more time in his wife's drawing-room, where he made a practice of speaking to every young woman at the whist tables. He flirted, openly but lightly, with most of the young wives and often left them blushing when he passed to converse with others. He chided them gently about eating olives at night. He asked them if and when they expected to present their husbands with an heir. He commented upon the size of their hands and feet and sometimes his bluntly expressed pleasantries occasioned acute embarrassment, for nobody could ever be sure what he was going to say next.

Joséphine watched him narrowly, less than half her mind upon the cards she held. Napoleon sometimes took a hand or two, but he never played the game seriously and would cheat outrageously. Then, as suddenly as he had appeared, he would leave and Joséphine was obliged to maintain a polite conversation while endeavouring to recall the names of women who left the salon about the same time.

Her first guess was woefully inaccurate. She got it firmly into her head that the Emperor's new fancy was little Aglaé Ney, the charming wife of the already famous Marshal and a protégée of Joséphine's.

Poor Madame Ney, recently married and deliriously in love with her gallant, hot-tempered husband, was distressed beyond words when Joséphine's manner towards her began to cool. The little Maréchale, who was yet another of Madame Campan's young ladies, turned appealingly to her school-fellow, Queen Hortense, declaring her innocence and complaining of gross injustice on the part of the Empress. Hortense, realizing that Aglaé was blameless, soothed her outraged modesty and finally persuaded her mother that she was in error.

Junot's young wife, who was to become the famous Duchess d'Abrantès, was another suspect and not perhaps without cause, for Madame Junot herself recounts a delightful story of the Emperor's habit of walking into her bedroom early in the mornings and commenting to her on his mail, which he opened and studied at her bedside table! She was, however, entirely innocent and the utmost familiarity Napoleon attempted in Madame Junot's bedroom was a sly pinching of her foot through the bedclothes.

At last Joséphine was lucky or unlucky enough to spot the real culprit and from then on set herself the disagreeable task of catching husband and mistress in circumstances that would make denial impossible.

It was a foolish decision. There are some husbands who cannot bear to be made to justify themselves and Napoleon Bonaparte was such a man. Interference into what he selfishly regarded as his private life infuriated him and he had long ago ceased to look upon himself as an ordinary individual, bound to observe the ordinary rules of conduct.

In matters such as this – indeed, in almost every matter – he considered himself far above law and if Joséphine did not wish to be reminded of her own indiscretions in the past her safest course would have been to do what so many wives do in similar circumstances – look the other way and wait until the affair died a natural death. She had plenty of grounds for believing this would happen sooner or later. Every other love-affair on his part had been comparatively short-lived and in her case there was a particular need for caution, for his family were still anxiously seeking an opportunity to accomplish a final rupture of the marriage. There are, in fact, strong grounds for believing that his sister Caroline had sponsored Madame Duchâtel's bid in the first instance. Such was her jealousy of Joséphine that she never ceased to introduce him to beautiful women in the hope that he would form a permanent attachment with one or other of them.

In this case, however, Joséphine was determined to play the role of a jealous wife in search of irrefutable evidence of infidelity. She badly overplayed the part, so badly that it is no fault of hers that the matter did not end in a triumph for the Bonapartes and utter disaster for her.

During her careful watch of her husband's movements she discovered that he had a small private apartment over his rooms adjoining the orangery at St Cloud, the rooms where he had first entertained Georgina when the valet Constant brought her to the palace.

One day she noticed that both Napoleon and Madame Duchâtel left the salon together. She not only decided to hurry in pursuit but made the unpardonable error of confiding in Madame Rémusat, a member of her household.

Madame Rémusat, who probably knew a good deal more than Joséphine of the Emperor's latest infatuation, attempted to dissuade her mistress on grounds of maintaining the Imperial dignity but Joséphine was in a sullen, bitter mood and refused to listen. After exploring Napoleon's offices on the first floor and drawing a blank there she made her way up to the little apartment above the orangery. Here, at long last, she ran her quarries to earth.

The door was locked and when she listened at the keyhole she distinctly heard the voices of both her husband and his mistress. Losing all sense of restraint she cried out and began to rattle the door-handle.

There is something pitiful in this spectacle of a woman renowned throughout Europe for her poise, tact and dignity, standing helplessly outside a bedroom door, rattling the handle and wailing protests like a wronged woman in an improbable stage play.

The voices inside the room ceased and after a long pause Napoleon emerged, his brow as black as Lucifer's. Even then Joséphine clung to her determination to make the most of the opportunity. 'I know I ought to have controlled myself,' she admitted later, to Madame Rémusat, 'but I simply could not do it. I broke out into a torrent of reproaches!'

The limpid blue eye of Madame Duchâtel filled with tears. They were not tears of shame but tears of dismay at being discovered with the Emperor in a disordered room. Napoleon, however, shed no tears. Instead he launched a terrifying offensive, showing far more indignation than he had shown on the occasion when poor Georgina had lost her head at the Tuileries and tugged the bell-rope. He foamed with rage, reiterating his private declaration of independence at the top of his voice. He was, he declared, a man apart and utterly refused to be bound by any man's rules of conduct! 'You ought', he raved, 'to agree to anything I take into my head! I have the right to answer all your complaints by an everlasting *I*!'

He had, of course, no such right and well he knew it. His hysterical rage on such occasions is that of a wilful child, claiming self-justification where none exists. He succeeded, however, in convincing Joséphine that she was somehow in the wrong and when the wretched scene had played itself out she fled back to the drawing-room and re-entered it a much-chastened woman.

Madame Duchâtel soon joined her there but the moment the distant rumble of Napoleon's voice, accompanied by the crash of overturned furniture, began to penetrate the apartments below Duchâtel fled, leaving Rémusat and others to do what they could to soothe the outraged dignity of the guilty party.

He soon simmered down and from then on Joséphine wisely fell back on her familiar line of defence, the steady and silent flow of aggrieved tears. She ought never to have abandoned this position and after the St Cloud episode she occupied it for the duration of the affair. Napoleon must have found Madame Duchâtel very engaging for the undignified scene outside the upstairs apartment did nothing to bring him to his senses.

Soon the entire court, notwithstanding the bitter winter season, was hustled off to Malmaison, where no preparations had been made for its reception and everyone except the unrepentant Napoleon and the cool-headed Madame Duchâtel suffered extremely from the cold.

Emperor and mistress now took no pains to hide their attachment and even walked together along the bare chestnut avenues. Joséphine watched them from the windows, waiting and waiting for the flame to burn down under the steady drip of her tears.

The end came suddenly. Whether Napoleon simply tired of Duchâtel's blonde loveliness or whether, as seems more likely, she made the same old mistake of over-reaching herself and began to meddle with state affairs, we shall never know. Towards the spring, however, Napoleon suddenly presented himself to Joséphine, admitting whole-heartedly that he had been deeply in love but that now it was all over. 'Don't weep about it,' he said blandly, 'it was nothing at all!'

According to Madame Rémusat, our principal informant on this incident, he added : 'Did I cause you pain? Come then, forgive me and I will tell you all about it!'

Joséphine was only too ready to forgive but her patience must have been sorely tried when he asked her to extricate him from an affair that was now distasteful to him! She had not, however, acquired a European reputation for tact without possessing limitless reserves of it and at once set about the business, beginning by reading Madame Duchâtel a long and gentle lecture on 'the unwisdom of appearing too familiar with the Emperor!' '*Other people*', she told her, '*have a tendency to put a wrong interpretation on such familiarities!*'

Even the self-possessed Madame Duchâtel must have gasped at hearing this from the lips of a wife who had come within throwing distance of catching her in bed with her husband.

Duchâtel had more common sense than most women of her age and station. She accepted her defeat with good grace and was not, in fact, dismissed from her post in the household. She was no outraged spendthrift, like de Vaudey, and no high-spirited artiste, like Thérèse Bourgoin. She settled cheerfully enough for the half-loaf of a permanent position at court and both she and her ageing husband reaped the full benefits of her restraint. She bore Napoleon no secret ill-will in after years and we hear of her presence at fêtes given during the Hundred Days, when loyalty was in short supply.

One more mark can be added to her credit column. When the Napoleonic legend had grown to marketable proportions she never attempted to cash in on her past by writing her memoirs.

Perhaps she had plenty of money and was under no necessity to resort to journalism, or possibly she lacked the literary flair of Madame Junot and others. There might even be another reason for her commendable silence. She might have preferred her husband to keep his illusions.

CHAPTER XIV

'Father absent and unknown'

On 13 December 1806, when the Emperor and the Grand
Army, having crushed the Prussians at a blow, were floun-
dering through Polish mud and coming to grips with the
Czar's hordes, a male child was born at Number 29 Rue de
la Victoire, the street in which Napoleon had spent his brief
honeymoon with Joséphine.

The child was registered as 'the son of Eléonor Denuelle,
a spinster, of independent means, its father absent and unknown'.

There were certain inaccuracies about this simple entry.
The mother was not a spinster in the accepted sense of the
word. A mere eight months previous to the event she had
been the wife of a Captain of dragoons. The father was certainly absent but he was not unknown; he was the most
celebrated man in the world.

Eighteen days later, on the last night of the year, a courier
clattered into Imperial headquarters in Poland and Napoleon was informed of the birth. He not only acknowledged
the child as his own but at once settled upon it a very considerable sum of money.

He had reason to be delighted. Illegitimate though Léon
Denuelle was, he was living proof of Napoleon's capacity to
father a child.

Napoleon was thirty-seven when Léon Denuelle was born.
Supremely self-confident in every other sphere he had nonetheless entertained grave doubts for several years regarding
his ability to procreate. It was something that profoundly
disturbed him for it must have seemed strange to him that

not one of his affairs with young, healthy women had resulted in the conception of a child. He had grumbled, good-naturedly, of Madame Fourès' shortcomings in this respect. He had also encouraged Mademoiselle Georges to take certain steps in order that she might present him with a child but she, too, had failed him. There had been no tangible proof of his affection from Grassini, Duchâtel or any of the actresses who had slipped into St Cloud and the Tuileries by night. Could it be possible that his lack of a legitimate heir was due entirely to the ageing Joséphine? After all, she had presented her first husband with two children?

All these doubts were to be resolved by an eighteen-year-old school-friend of his sister Caroline. From the moment the muddied courier delivered the Paris despatches at Pultusk on that December night Napoleon's mind began to formulate plans for divorce and remarrage but these plans were to remain in abeyance for another two and a half years.

Napoleon did almost everything in a tearing hurry, but the setting aside of Joséphine and the choice of her successor were not matters that called for a snap judgement.

It is ironical that the woman who sparked off such a train of events should have been Louise-Catherine-Eléonore Denuelle de la Plaigne, the most casual of Napoleon's entanglements with self-seeking women.

There had not been and there was never to be the smallest emotional ingredient in their association. From first to last (and its duration was measured in weeks) the association was purely physical. There was no element of warmth or even friendship in the liaison, no light-heartedness, as in the case of the little Bellilotte, no midnight romps, as in the case of Mademoiselle Georges, no exchange of passionate letters, no protestations, no tears, evasions and stormy scenes, such as those accompanying his pursuit of Madame Duchâtel. The affair began offhandedly within a month of the victor's triumphant return from Austerlitz. It ended abruptly with news of the birth of Léon. He never entertained Eléonore again and it is doubtful whether he ever set eyes on her after the early autumn of 1806, when he left Paris to humble the legacy of Frederick the Great on the field of Jena and disappear into the northern fogs at the head of his victorious legions.

The story of Eléonore Denuelle illustrates Parisian society as it existed up to the time of Napoleon's marriage to an Arch-duchess and his subsequent spring-clean of the court.

Eléonore's full name has a sonorous ring but her family background is not nearly so impressive.

She was the daughter of a speculator and an exceptionally pretty adventuress. Father and mother had dubious reputations and despite their pretensions to be gentlefolk they lived on their wits, like a couple of confidence-tricksters. They maintained a luxurious establishment designed, no doubt, to inspire confidence in their clients, and Eléonore, who at seventeen was already a striking beauty, was their trump card. They determined to use her to stabilize their fluctuating fortunes.

Man and wife made considerable sacrifices to this end. At a time when money must have been hard to find they managed to scrape together sufficient to send their daughter to the famous Campan school for the daughters of the ambitious rich. During the period when Eléonore was growing up in this establishment in St Germain-en-Laye, it was at the pinnacle of its fame. Joséphine's daughter was a pupil and so were her neices and cousins. Caroline Bonaparte, youngest and most vivacious of the First Consul's sisters, was the star boarder, and the daughters of some of the soldiers whose names were already renowned throughout Europe were receiving their education at the feet of the wily Madame Campan. Where better could the pretty daughter of a seedy speculator hope to meet influential friends, girls who would grow up to make splendid marriages and be certain of places at court?

The money paid in school fees came near to being thrown into the Paris sewers. The Denuelles were an impatient couple and when Eléonore was seventeen, and had yet to attract a rich husband, her parents suddenly lost their nerve and fell into the neatly-baited trap of a scoundrel one degree more astute than themselves.

Forbidden entry to the best drawing-rooms on account of her shady reputation, Madame Denuelle de la Plaigne made the stupid mistake of displaying her daughter at the theatre. Progress, or apparent progress, was instantaneous. A handsome dragoon Captain named Revel presented himself and was soon hard at work wooing Eléonore and flattering her parents.

Revel was an extremely plausible scoundrel. He not only convinced parents and bride that he was a wealthy man, possessing brilliant prospects in the cavalry, but successfully resisted his future father-in-law's premature attempts to borrow money!

The couple were married in January 1805, eight months before Eléonore's eighteenth birthday.

By March, just two months later, the Denuelles, father, mother and daughter, were aware of their collective blunder. Revel, who had lived on credit throughout the honeymoon, was arrested on a charge of forgery and the department of Seine-et-Oise sentenced him to a term of two years in gaol! He now disappears from the story but only for a time. He was to prove an Old Man of the Sea to the hapless Eléonore for much of her harassed life.

The Denuelle family did its utmost to repair this disastrous situation. Eléonore was at once despatched to Madame Campan for advice and the good lady passed her on to the most celebrated of all her pupils, Eléonore's school-friend, Caroline Murat, now the wife of the Emperor's most distinguished cavalry leader.

Caroline's initial response to her school-friend's plea was lukewarm. She placed Eléonore in an establishment for gentlewomen of distressed circumstances and the girl's circumstances certainly qualified her for such a retreat. This was not, however, the kind of help that she and her parents were seeking. They wanted something much more tangible and they importuned until they got it – a post for Eléonore in Caroline's household, first as a humble usherette, later as a reader.

Once on the establishment of so powerful a patron Eléonore settled down to make the most of her opportunities.

She was a tall, graceful girl, a brunette with exceptionally dark eyes. Her brief experience with Revel had taught her a good deal about the art of attracting men, and her mistress Caroline, herself quite an expert in these matters, soon noticed and assessed the girl's possibilities. Always on the look-out for someone to break down her brother's obstinate affection for the despised Joséphine, Caroline so arranged matters that Napoleon was made aware of the lovely reader the moment he returned from his greatest triumph at Austerlitz.

In January 1806, Eléonore received the Imperial summons, remaining in the Tuileries for two or three hours and repeating the visits throughout the late winter and early spring of that year.

Having gained the prize for which hundreds of young Parisians were competing she then took what steps she could to ensure her future. On 13 February, that is, within a fortnight of meeting the Emperor, she sought and obtained a divorce from Revel, the decree being made absolute in April. By that time she was pregnant and installed in the house in Rue de la Victoire where her child was born the same year.

There is no doubt whatever that Léon Denuelle was Napoleon's child. Never, at any time, did he fail to acknowledge the boy and additional proof is available in Léon's striking facial resemblance to his famous father.

Napoleon displayed his customary generosity in providing for mother and child. Léon was placed in the care of the same nurse as little Achille Murat, Caroline's son, and when he reached the age of seven some distinguished guardians were appointed to watch over him and superintend his education. One of his mentors was Napoleon's former secretary, Baron de Méneval.

Two years later, when Napoleon was fighting for his throne inside the frontiers of France, he made arrangements amid the press of terrible events to increase the boy's allowance by twelve thousand francs. Three days after his final defeat at Waterloo he again remembered him, giving him ten shares in a company, valued at a hundred thousand francs. He further remembered him in his will at St Helena, assigning him a large sum for the purchase of an estate.

And Eléonore? He made material provision for her but beyond this he would have nothing further to do with her. On one occasion, when Léon was a baby in arms, she called uninvited at Fontainebleau but was sent away unseen after being soundly rated for her temerity in paying an uninvited call upon the head of the State.

His coldness to the mother did not extend to the child. He invariably sent for the boy when he was visiting his sister Caroline, and sometimes he would dandle him at the breakfast table, giving him sweets and toys. Always he seemed grateful for the boy's existence, as though he could never fully repay him for having resolved his gloomy doubts regarding paternity.

The mother's bad luck dogged her subsequent marriages. As in the case of Madame Fourès, Napoleon arranged that an obliging husband should be found for her and in February 1808, she married a Monsieur Augier, then an infantryman, later a cuirassier.

On the day of Eléonore's second marriage she was given an annual settlement of twenty-two thousand francs, then worth something like a thousand pounds. Augier took her with him to the war in Spain, which he survived, but during the Russian campaign he was taken prisoner and died as a result of privations suffered during the great retreat.

Less than two years later the dogged Eléonore took a third husband, yet another soldier, this time in the service of the King of Bavaria, but the fall of Napoleon, in 1814, gave her first husband Revel the chance he had been awaiting. Representing himself as a cuckolded victim of 'The Tyrant' he settled down to blackmail his former wife. When his early endeavours failed he filed further suits against her but either Eléonore was too astute for him or the petitioner's reputation was too much for the courts. Revel came away empty-handed and consoled himself by writing a pamphlet setting forth his wrongs.

Better fortune awaited a younger blackmailer who materialized in time to sour Eléonore's middle age. Her son Léon proved an even more persistent scoundrel than Revel. He was also more successful in the line of business he selected as a means of livelihood.

In the will dictated shortly before his death at St Helena Napoleon expressed a mild wish that little Léon would become a magistrate 'providing he has an inclination that way'. Léon did not become a magistrate but he did show a marked inclination for litigation. The whole of his life was spent in filing suits and writing memorials aimed at providing him with sums of money to squander at the gaming tables.

There is, in fact, nothing to record about him apart from this lifelong recourse to law. Year after year, decade after decade, he sued and sued and sued for cash, making the wildest claims against his wretched mother and importuning government departments for credit and recognition. There was no end to his claims, some of which were so improbable that one suspects he was mentally deranged. Every now and again Léon's efforts met with limited success but the money he was awarded was always dissipated overnight, after which he at once returned to his desk to make new and even more extravagant demands upon someone.

Napoleon III, his father's nephew, found him an infernal nuisance. At one stage in his career Léon forsook law and challenged the Man of December to a duel. Notwithstanding this Napoleon III granted the monumental pest a pension of six thousand francs and the payment of Napoleon's legacy, about a quarter million francs in all.

The Civil List paid his debts half a dozen times but still he went on spending and sueing, spending and sueing, using his famous father's name to promote all manner of hare-brained schemes each aimed at establishing the fame and fortune of Léon Denuelle.

It is to be hoped that Eléonore grew accustomed to the persecutions of her ex-husband and her half-crazy son, and that the latter part of her life offered compensations for the ill-luck that dogged her youth and young womanhood. She never emerged as a public figure but she must have learned how to handle money, for in spite of Léon's ceaseless dunning she managed to keep the bulk of her fortune intact. This was made possible by Léon's eventual emigration to the United States and here, at long last, he found a humble substitute for his mother, for it is recorded that he married a cook.

Eléonore died in comfortable circumstances on 30 January 1868, when the Second Empire had but two years to endure before it was swept away by Bismarck's Prussians. She was then a woman of eighty and had survived the father of her child by nearly forty-seven years. Nobody of the period seems to have written anything about her later life. She did not remain in the public eye, like some of the actresses whose favours she had so briefly shared. Her sole claim to fame is that she supplied proof of Napoleon's capacity to father a child, but this, as events proved, was no small achievement, for it set in motion the machinery of statecraft that led directly to the Austrian marriage. This, in turn, was to have an important effect upon the break-up and redistribution of Empires.

In this respect Eléonore Denuelle de la Plaigne earned her niche in history, a wider niche perhaps than some of the more spectacular courtesans who responded eagerly to the summons of Constant, the palace valet, and followed him through back doors and winding passages into the Emperor's private apartments.

CHAPTER XV

'How long the winter nights . . . !'

In December 1806, Napoleon was writing letters to Joséphine that were couched in terms of longing and fond affection. He had not written to her in this strain since the occasions he had turned aside on the road to Italy and dashed-off avowals that have since found a place among the most passionate love-letters of history.

For the greater part of 1806 man and wife had been separated by great distances and now he was missing her sorely. Obsessed by the management of a huge army and the intricate problems of state he was working at a pace that would have broken most men; he began to yearn for the solace and companionship that only Joséphine could dispense.

His associations with other women afforded him momentary relief from the demands his expanding genius made upon him but the new relationship existing between Napoleon and Joséphine was immune from spoliation by women like Duchâtel, and Eléonore Denuelle. The partnership had taken them a long way. It dated from the days when neither of them could expect much of Fortune. It rested upon the solid foundations of shared poverty. It reached back into experiences that were remote from courts and kings and related to the workaday tasks of coaxing a simple livelihood from the trade of soldiering. Their marriage had proved a sound investment, the soundest that either of them had made. The greatest tragedy in Napoleon's life was that both he and his wife consistently undervalued this investment. In the end he was to cash it for a worthless pedigree.

Preoccupied with the fall of Prussia and the train of new problems that followed this country's collapse, worried by the presence of an unbeaten Russian army on his flank and the certainty of England exploiting its recent triumph at Trafalgar, his private thoughts turned more and more frequently to Joséphine.

'I lack only the pleasure of your company . . .,' he wrote in November and again, a fortnight later, '. . . if the journey were not so long you could come as far as this (Berlin) . . .' Later still, when his armies had surged into Poland and were heading for Warsaw, '. . . one thinks little of beauties in these Polish deserts . . . they are not at all what you suppose . . . there is no other woman for me . . . how long are the winter nights. . . .'

The sentiments expressed in these affectionate letters were not insincere. They were the sighs of a lonely man, isolated on a self-made mountain of grandeur, a man weary to death of casual encounters. They were the outpourings of a man who yearned for the tried and deep-rooted comfort of a woman who knew him not as an Emperor and a Kingmaker, but simply as a husband, harrassed beyond belief.

Then, quite suddenly, the mood changes. Letters continue to reach Joséphine, who was eagerly awaiting her summons to travel east from Mayence, but the tender strain disappears and is replaced by a jocular, half-mocking note, still friendly and still genuine but aimed now at keeping her at a distance.

There were two reasons for this sudden about-face. One was the despatch informing him of the birth of Léon Denuelle, the other a chance encounter with an eighteen-year-old Polish Countess, the woman who was destined to share with Joséphine the distinction of being the only person with whom Napoleon found it possible to throw aside the mask of patronage for more than an hour or so.

It is remarkable that these two events, both of which had a great effect on his future, occurred within a period of twenty-four hours.

On the last night of the old year he learned that he had fathered a child. On the first day of the new year he met and was enchanted by Marie Walewice-Walewska, the wife of a seventy-year-old Polish patriot, a man whose eldest grand-child was eight years older than Marie when she had married him at the age of sixteen.

The circumstances in which they met are such as would be rejected by a conscientious writer of a magazine serial – he, a conquering hero, hurrying through snowdrifts to liberate her country, she, the flaxen-haired, blue-eyed heroine, fighting her way through hysterical crowds in order to be among the first to greet him as deliverer.

The meeting, which lasted less than a minute, took place in the drab little town of Bronia, between his Headquarters, at Pultusk, and the capital city of Warsaw. She was almost the first of the delirious Poles now gathering in thousands to hail the demigod who promised to restore their dismembered state to its ancient dignity.

Dashing through the snow Napoleon's carriage stopped at a posting-house and Duroc, the Grand Marshal of the Palace, hurried inside to make arrangements for fresh horses.

He was met by two well-dressed women, hemmed in by a mob of shouting peasants, and the younger woman at once addressed him in broken French, begging to be presented to Napoleon and extricated from what looked like becoming a dangerous situation.

Duroc, struck by the strangeness of the encounter, at once conducted the two ladies to the Emperor. Greetings were exchanged and the Poles withdrew, perhaps with an escort to help them fight free of the cheering mob.

That was all. The carriage swept on to the capital, where Napoleon at once established his Headquarters in the ancient palace of Poland's kings.

It could have ended there and might well have done so had not Napoleon possessed the kind of memory for faces that he exercised over terrain and the habitual errors of his opponents. In any case, Marie Walewska's face was not easy to forget, neither was her sylphlike daintiness and low-pitched voice. Thus he recognized her instantly when, at the insistence of her elderly husband, she attended the grand ball at the palace shortly after Napoleon's arrival. The Emperor at once sent Duroc to her with an invitation to dance but the Grand Marshal returned crestfallen. The lady, he reported, did not dance and begged to be excused.

Napoleon was not unduly put out. It must have occurred to him that a woman who would wear a simple white dress without jewellery, when every other woman in the room had prepared an elaborate toilet, was an exceptionally shy and retiring person. Her refusal only made him more eager to pursue the acquaintance and he toured every reception-room, speaking a few words to every woman in the room simply in order to come face to face with her.

When Marie's turn came she blushed and stammered. He passed on without pressing the point but it was not lost on the assembled patriots. Here, they reasoned, was a woman who could bring more benefits to Poland than ten divisions of cavalry. Here was a chance to exploit the liberator's well-known susceptibility for pretty women.

Prince Poniatowski, the leader of the Polish liberation movement, was instantly informed and he and his intimates began to cast about for a method of employing the trump card that had fallen on to the ballroom floor.

There were no prudes among the Polish nobility. The fact that Marie Walewska was married to one of their supporters did not cost them a moment's hesitation. Each of them maintained a mistress and one at least kept three in his country-house. They considered Napoleon exceptional in that he had not brought along a company of Imperial concubines in the train of his army. If he was eccentric in this respect, and preferred to devote himself to one, then they were only too anxious to accommodate him and further the cause of Polish independence on a four-poster.

In the meantime Napoleon opened his own campaign, employing his usual tactics, a bold attack on the weakest point – in this case a woman's vanity. First, however, the field had to be cleared of rival skirmishers, for the breathtaking beauty of the young Countess was already attracting them by the dozen.

Power has privilege. Every time a starry-eyed French staff officer stepped forward with an invitation to dance he was summoned to the Presence and packed off on some fool's errand into the depth of the winter night! Young Bertrand was one of the first victims and he does not seem to have resented this unfair exercise of authority for years later he accompanied his master into exile. Louis de Périgord was another and it soon became clear to the boldest among them that they must look elsewhere for partners if they relished their stay in the capital. Having thus summarily disposed of the opposition Napoleon left the ball and went back to his apartments to write a note.

In the circumstances it was a remarkable note for an Emperor to write to a young married woman, a girl he had seen but twice. Napoleon was almost always direct in these matters but the following message, taken to Marie's lodging by the faithful Duroc, was classically forthright. It read:

'I saw but you. I admired but you. I desire but you. Answer at once and calm the impatient ardour of – N.'

It was almost an edict but it produced no reply beyond the spoken words: 'There is no answer.'

Puzzled and irritated but still unable to believe that his advances were being flatly rejected, Napoleon tried once more.

This time he introduced an air of injured innocence into his letter: 'Have I displeased you? I hope the opposite. Or has your first feeling vanished? My passion grows. You rob me of my rest. Vouchsafe a little joy, a little happiness, to the poor heart that would fain worship you! Is it so hard to give me an answer?' Then, with a trace of Imperial petulance, 'You now owe me two!'

Duroc, who had broken a collar bone in a carriage accident that week and was not enjoying this particular siege, hurried off with the letter but again he returned dismayed and empty-handed. The lady, it seemed, was not to be won by conventional means.

Prince Poniatowski was called in, not directly by the Emperor but probably by the unhappy Marshal of the Palace. The Polish patriot was only too eager to help but notwithstanding long, persuasive conversations, that ended in his being locked out of Marie's suite, he made no deeper impression than had the French Marshal. Marie's door remained double-locked. She had not the slightest desire to bring the potential liberator of Poland a little happiness, nor yet a little joy.

Napoleon now called up his heavy artillery and it took the form of a formidable battery of half-promises. Combining blandishments with a number of broad hints of a political nature he ended his third letter with the phrase : 'All your wishes will be fulfilled ... your country will be even dearer to me if you have compassion on my heart !'

Meantime pressure other than Napoleon's had been building up outside the bedroom door. Poniatowski and his aides raved and pleaded. Soldiers and sister Poles cajoled, argued and persuaded. Even old Walewska himself (the only patriot who was not in the secret) did his utmost to persuade Marie to 'show a little more enthusiasm for the cause'.

At last, half-distracted by this cacophony, she yielded to their pleas and was conducted to the Emperor's quarters by Duroc late in the evening. She remained there three hours and left as chaste as she had entered.

This is not surprising. She had spent the entire three hours in tears !

Marie Walewska's sturdy resistance to Napoleon was not the opening performance of a coquette. She was an exceptionally modest woman, entirely without guile. She was genuinely devoted to her religious faith and entertained a deep respect for her marriage vows. Unfortunately for her she also possessed a Pole's selfless devotion to Poland and was as eager as Poniatowski himself to see it escape the embrace of the Russian bear and take its rightful place among the family of nations.

Had she been less of a patriot it is extremely doubtful whether she could have been persuaded to yield to the enormous pressures put upon her by her fellow-countrymen and by the most powerful will in the world. Having surrendered, however, having once spent a few hours alone with a man whom she later came to know as no other human being, including Joséphine, was to know him, she yielded to his charm and gentleness and became his in a way no other mistress had succeeded in doing in the past.

For Marie Walewska there was always something pathetic about a man who had chosen to follow a lonely, tempestuous path and fulfil such a sterile destiny. Perhaps his loneliness and his strange helplessness made a strong maternal appeal to her. Perhaps her loveless marriage had stirred in her a physical yearning to be desired and needed, as other young wives are desired by their husbands. Or perhaps she, too, was touched by a star-born ray of destiny and saw herself, now or ultimately, sharing his path of loneliness as far as the grave.

These are questions that can never be answered. They remained for ever in the heart of the little Polish blonde who captured his imagination so quickly and for so long a period and who was to go down in history as 'the only woman Napoleon ever loved', or 'the only woman who really loved Napoleon'.

Like Duchâtel, Marie Walewska had dignity. She did not rush to her writing bureau and begin scribbling her memoirs the moment the Titan tumbled from his throne. What little we know of her true feelings for him are deduced from the story of their widely-spaced meetings over the few years that were left to them. There is evidence enough to suggest that, for a time at least, this man relived his youthful idyll in the cherry-orchard at Valence and found something of the fulfilment he had been pursuing through battle smoke for twenty-one years and was to pursue for eight years more.

Marie Walewska was born Marie Laczinska. Her family ranked as nobility but her father died when she was a child and her mother had a hard struggle to maintain and educate six children on the resources of their small estate.

At fifteen and a half Marie left school, where she had been moderately well educated, and was at once offered a choice of two bridegrooms, both powerful and both wealthy. One, the son of a Russian General, was personable and of a suitable age. The other was Anastase Colonna de Walewice-Walewska, then aged seventy.

She chose the grandfather. He at least was Polish.

Her life, up to this time of the meeting at Bronia, had not been a happy one. Count Walewska was kind but dull. The life of a young, eager girl, endowed with exceptional charm and beauty, sharing a gloomy country house with an old man, could not have been much to her taste but she found some sort of consolation in the practice of her religion and soon acquired a reputation for being exceptionally devout.

Within a week of their first meeting alone Marie Walewska was Napoleon's mistress and during the remainder of his stay in Warsaw she visited him every night and was present at all receptions. If she was not there he refused to make an appearance and soon even the old Count, her husband, began to realize what was taking place.

Napoleon showed the same boyish delight in her as he had displayed during his affair with Madame Duchâtel, yet it is certain that in the company of the young Pole he found more disinterested companionship and far more genuine affection. She wanted, it seemed, no rewards for her sacrifice and even the independence of Poland was shelved. She demanded neither jewels, honours nor political influence in return for the hours she spent with him.

His letters home continued in jocular vein, almost as though he was secretly laughing at himself, until Joséphine, now very impatient to join him, resorted once more to terms of tearful reproach. Then he suddenly became snappish : '. . . I insist on you having more courage ! I hear that you are always weeping ... be worthy of me ... show more character !'

Poor Joséphine ! She possessed no shred of the kind of character that he demanded of her and by this time she had heard all about the pretty little Countess. It was not that she minded an occasional peccadillo on his part, a mere turning aside from the savage business of killing. She was resigned to this kind of thing and had come to take it for granted, as indeed had most of the wives of his Marshals and staff officers. What worried her was the disturbing report that Napoleon was madly in love and that this Polish affair did not promise to burn itself out brightly but speedily, as in the case of actresses at the Comédie Française. He was behaving once more like a romantic schoolboy and she remembered with bitterness the ridiculous Duchâtel episode, when he had waltzed them all out to Malmaison in the depths of winter, simply in order to provide a more intimate setting for his adolescent love-affair.

She had need to worry. Not all the affairs of state, not the presence of a large Russian Army ready to do battle for the domination of Eastern Europe, could cause him to forsake his second mistress in the field. Berthier and his staff officers grumbled that the Emperor was neglecting his business and should face the stern tasks ahead.

They soon had their wish. In early February the Grand Army moved across the snow towards the bloody field of Eylau and received, in addition to terrible casualties, the first major check an army led by Napoleon had ever received.

In a blinding snowstorm the massed squadrons of the dashing Murat, Caroline's husband, partially retrieved the day, but there could be no more fighting until the ground hardened and the French sullenly withdrew, the shattered divisions to cantonments, their Commander-in-Chief to the castle of Finckenstein, in Prussia. Here his interrupted idyll was resumed and Napoleon took his meals alone with Marie. She had burned her boats. Her aged husband had now turned his back upon her.

For weeks they dallied here while little Berthier bent over his maps and planned the approaching campaign.

Napoleon, it seemed, was sick and tired of statecraft and of the business of making war. He still worked hard enough to kill two men but by his standards the pace had slowed to a shuffle and there were long intervals when nobody but Marie saw him.

Finckenstein, a huge, fortified castle, was large enough to house the entire staff. Ambassadors came and went, among them the emissary of the Persian Shah. The Emperor toyed with the idea of fomenting trouble for the British in India, then passed on to dictate a letter to the Sultan of Turkey, promising him the earth if he would harass Southern Russia in the Czar's absence.

All this time Marie Walewska lived upstairs in a room adjoining his own and whenever he could spare a moment he hastened to her and closed the door on the Shah, the Sultan, on waiting Europe and the bugle calls of his cavalry picquets.

Here, alone with her, there was beauty, peace and warmth. Here he could discuss with a true friend the shattering news from Paris that his brother's son, Napoleon-Charles, the spoiled child of Joséphine's daughter, Hortense, whom he would have made his heir, had died after a two-day illness. Marie Walewska had never seen the boy but she knew how to soothe a man experiencing real grief. One day, but not yet, they would have a child of their own, a boy destined to grow up to be a credit to his memory and to France, but at Finckenstein that was away in the future, like the approaching battle that was to establish a balance of power for the next five years.

The ground had hardened now. After ten weeks at Finckenstein the glittering divisions of the army moved out, the gaps of Eylau filled and its invincible commander once more with his mind firmly fixed upon the business in hand.

On 14 June, anniversary of another great triumph in the field, the Russians were totally defeated at Friedland and Czar and conqueror met on a raft to discuss spheres of influence.

On 27 July Napoleon made a triumphal re-entry of Paris and six months later Marie, too, travelled west, to see Paris for the first time.

No open association followed their reunion. A long time was to elapse before another Finckenstein offered itself and when it did weightier matters were looming, more campaigns, more battles, a divorce and another marriage that brought him what Marie could never hope to bring him, a legitimate heir to his vast, sprawling conquests.

An indication that Marie Walewska's quiet, tenacious charm had made a permanent impression upon Napoleon's heart is found in the curious gap that exists in the record of Napoleon's personal life following his triumphant return to Paris after the victory at Friedland.

Apart from the six years he spent on St Helena, the period that followed, from the late summer of 1807 to the autumn of 1808, was in some ways the most uneventful of his life.

He did not install Marie as an acknowledged mistress. There is no doubt but that she followed him to Paris within six months of their parting or that she was there during the greater part of the remaining years of his reign, living, of all places, in Rue de la Victoire.

He seems to have had some special preference for this particular street. It was here, when it was known as the Rue Chantereine, that he had first called upon Joséphine and it was to her house in this same street that the couple had repaired after their casual wedding in '96. It was here, at No. 29, that Eléonore Denuelle was installed and Léon was born, in December 1806. It was at No. 48 in the same street that Marie Walewska established herself, when she settled in Paris after the birth of her own son, Alexander-Florian.

For a brief spell after his resounding victory over the Russians Europe was at peace but in the autumn of that year the long Spanish nightmare commenced with the invasion of Portugal, Britain's oldest ally.

Napoleon did not go to the Peninsula for another year. Instead he sent his old friend Junot, the gay young hussar who had shared so many of his early adventures and was now married and longing for his Marshal's baton.

Junot had come a long way since he had attracted Napoleon's notice at Toulon. Recently he had been enjoying a spectacular flirtation with Napoleon's youngest sister, Caroline, during his governorship of Paris, when the veterans were roughing it in Poland. Napoleon, who was far less tolerant of others' indiscretions than he liked to be with his own, reproached him severely when he learned that Junot's carriage, complete with servants in livery, had been seen outside Caroline's house at two o'clock in the morning!

'You were very much in error to compromise the Emperor's sister in this manner,' he admonished and Junot, who must have wondered how it was possible for any man on earth to compromise Caroline, begged forgiveness and was packed off to Lisbon, with orders to capture the Portuguese Royal Family and win glory!

He failed in both endeavours. The King and court escaped to Brazil and Junot was soundly beaten by a dour, long-nosed British General who was still unknown on European battle-fields.

In the interval between arriving home from Eastern Europe and rushing down to Spain to prosecute the new war with a burst of his former energy, Napoleon settled down to rule. In general he was extremely busy, even for him, and he had very little time to cultivate the society of women.

One or two flit across his path at this time and are seen for a brief instant or so. The first was Madame Gazzani, a beautiful Genoese, concerning whom there were rumours of an affair whilst the Emperor was recuperating from his exertions at the Palace of Fontainebleau. Madame de Barral (of whom it was said that she could manage a court train with more elegance and skill than anyone at court) was another with whom his name was linked.

It is of Madame de Barral that Constant tells an amusing story involving himself.

The valet, charged with delivering an Imperial message to the lady's bedroom, missed his footing on the sill of her conveniently open window and fell with a loud crash, disturbing everybody and severely bruising his knee, elbow and head.

The message was undelivered and Constant returned to his master expecting sympathy. He received little enough. After listening to the valet's story and laughing heartily at his fall, Napoleon suggested that they should give Madame de Barral an hour or so to recover from her fright and then try again. Constant attended to his hurts during the interval and inside the hour he was guiding his master back to the window and assisting him to enter it. The lady could not have been so alarmed as Napoleon supposed, for the window was still open and this time there was no stumble. Napoleon remained inside for the remainder of the night.

Madame Junot goes out of her way to defend Madame de Barral's virtue and we have only the valet's word to the contrary. Nevertheless, the episode rings true. It was in keeping with Napoleon's puckish behaviour at this period and he would have thoroughly enjoyed a midnight prowl in the company of his valet.

Another pretty woman said to have attracted him at this time was Madame Savary, the wife of his Chief of Police.

Madame Savary's figure, according to Madame Junot, was the most marvellous she had ever seen. It is said that Napoleon discussed this lady's virtue, or lack of it, with her husband and advised him to ignore her shortcomings. Savary, being Savary, did so. Apparently he shared his master's trivial views on infidelity. 'It is a trifling thing when we know of it and nothing at all when we don't!' the

Emperor once said to a young woman with whom he was discussing the subject.

Mesdames Gazzani, de Barral and Savary are mere shadows in his life. If Napoleon did show them any special favours, then he acted with discretion and neither one of them came near to replacing Joséphine, Marie Walewska or even Georgina in his affections.

In 1808 war broke out with Spain and the entire Peninsula began to blaze. He dropped everything and hastened into the south-west, scattering the wretched Spanish armies before him and bundling Sir John Moore, and his rashly-handled British Expeditionary Force, out of the country by January 1809. Then he turned his back on Spain, leaving it to be conquered, administered and finally lost by a random assortment of bickering Marshals. His attention was once more needed in central Europe, where Austria had climbed to her feet and was once again challenging Long-boots.

Marie Walewska followed him down to the Danube. She was installed in a large house, close to the Habsburgs' Palace of Schönbrunn, which had been emptied of its royal occupants for the third time in the last few years.

Among the important personages who fled at the terrible man's approach was the eighteen-year-old daughter of Emperor Francis, a girl who had never been left alone with a man other than her father. She thought of the French Emperor as The Ogre. She was to change her mind in the near future.

Something of the old Finckenstein relationship was resumed with Marie Walewska during the brief Austrian campaign. Napoleon, Heaven alone knew, had sufficient worries and distractions throughout that sultry summer. His army was obliged to cross the swollen Danube in order to attack the Austrian forces and at Aspern-Essling it received an even more severe check than it had suffered at Eylau, two years before. For five stifling weeks it was cooped up in the island of Lobau and it needed the old-style victory at Wagram, in July, to steady the rocking of the Imperial throne.

There was a by-product of the campaign. In the spring of 1810, when the peace treaties with Austria had been signed, Marie Walewska grew homesick for her beloved Poland. It was here, at Walewice, that she determined her son should be born. It was a conqueror's son, a symbol perhaps of Poland's determination to be free when rival kings had ceased to question the overlordship of the child's father.

Alexander-Florian-Joseph-Colonna Walewska was born on 4 May 1810, and later in the year Marie, accompanied by the child and her sister-in-law, set out for the capital of Europe once more.

Nobody remarked on her arrival or on the paternity of the child. Parisians were already looking for the arrival of another child, fathered by the same man. During Marie's absence there had been a gorgeous wedding at Notre Dame, with the bride's train carried by four Queens! Napoleon, it was said, was now learning to dance in order to please his young Austrian wife, the girl who could wiggle her ears without disturbing the pleasant vacuity of her face.

It is not recorded what Marie Walewska said or thought about these spectacular developments. Austria continued to lay claim to a slice of Poland, the Poland that Napoleon had once promised should be free.

CHAPTER XVI

The Emperor's best friend

A formidable amount of nonsense is still spoken of Napoleon's allegedly rigid adherence to what he called his 'star', or 'destiny'.

That he was sometimes influenced to a degree by a semi-mystical conception of personal ambition there is no doubt, but in his years of maturity he did not allow personal ambition to obscure his main object in life. His 'star' – that is, his conception of destiny – was no longer a pursuit of merely personal aggrandizement but a much wider and deeper interpretation of what he genuinely believed to be his purpose on earth. It was a ready acceptance of enormous responsibility.

By midsummer 1809, when he was nearing his fortieth birthday, he considered himself more of a force than a man. He had certain broad ideas (and most of them, in retrospect, have proved extremely sound ones) of how mankind in the West should develop. Loathing muddle and disorder, he bent his entire will to the creation of a new society in Europe and he had hopes of extending the authority of this society all over the world.

Primarily he was not a conqueror but a superb organizer. He took little pride in victory on the field and certain of his wars were forced upon him by monarchs and governments, who still thought in terms of mediaeval statecraft. Whenever his arms were crowned with success he at once made peace, usually on very generous terms. Egocentric he certainly was but his egoism, unlike that of his opponents, had a purpose that reached out beyond personal elevation. Whilst the dictum of the English squires, the Bourbons, the Romanovs, and Hohenzollerns was 'What we have we hold!' Napoleon's aims might be summarized in the phrase 'What I have I develop!'

For his main purpose he was ready to sacrifice time, energy, health, happiness and certainly peace of mind. In the main history has vindicated his dream of federalism. The course of the nineteenth and twentieth centuries has shown that western man cannot survive, much less progress, if he continues to reject the idea of federalization. It was federalization, not naked dictatorship, that lay at the back of all Napoleon's strivings and trapesings up and down.

His determination to sacrifice tranquillity of spirit on the altar of his grand purpose is nowhere more clearly demonstrated than in his reluctant divorce of Joséphine, in the winter of 1809.

This decision was the hardest he was ever called upon to make and it cost him endless wretchedness. Once it was made he was never afterwards the same man, for the effort of will demanded of him was so immense that he lost something of the power of making decisions. In the six years that stretched ahead indecision was to play a large part in his fall. Ultimately it was to lead him into a situation where all the decisions were made by his gaolers.

For years now he had been contemplating divorce, not because his wife had lost the allure she had held for him but because it was essential for him to have a legitimate heir. He knew that without an heir time would render his life's work meaningless, at least as far as he saw it, and as we are dealing with his personal affairs it is from this standpoint that we must view the divorce.

Several factors delayed his decision to put Joséphine aside and seek a new wife who could stabilize his Empire, giving it a sense of permanency that all European governments had lost since the Paris mob stormed the Bastille.

One such factor had been his doubts regarding his own fertility and these had been resolved, first by the birth of

Eléonore's son, Léon, finally by news of Marie Walewska's pregnancy in the autumn of 1809.

Secondly, the problem of whom he should marry was surmounted by every kind of difficulty.

Finally, and this is undoubtedly the major reason for his prolonged hesitation, there remained his deep affection for Joséphine and the profound despondency that he knew would follow his decision to separate from her.

His love-affairs (with the possible exception of that with Marie Walewska) had nothing to do with the deep affection he now entertained for his wife.

The passionate adoration of his Italian days had long since spent itself but the stresses of the fantastic journey they had made together had forged a bond between them that made the sexual tie insignificant. Such physical satisfaction as he derived from women like the actress Georges, or the bewitching Duchâtel, were of small importance when balanced against the mental relief of an hour in the company of the forty-six-year-old Joséphine. All the other women, Walewska excepted, had his vigour, his fierce and possessive joy in the physical domination of a woman, and his occasional playfulness when his nervous tensions were relaxed. Joséphine had his respect, his admiration and the inner core of his boyish affection. To put her away, to exchange her cold-bloodedly for some stranger lacking that fund of shared experience, was a sacrifice that even a will such as his found almost impossible to make.

Yet he made it, inflicting upon himself the long-drawn-out agony of renunciation and self-doubt. Absurd, ruthless and unnecessary such a sacrifice might have been but it was not, by any standards, made lightly or cynically. It was to cost him more misery than the ultimate renunciation of his throne.

The event that finally enabled him to make up his mind was dramatic.

Whilst at Vienna, during the Austrian campaign, a young fanatic attempted to assassinate him. It was a botched, half-hearted attempt, easily thwarted by his aide-de-camp, Rapp, but it made a profound impression on him; so did the stolid resolution and contempt for death displayed by the would-be assassin, a young man called Staps.

Just prior to this attempt Napoleon had received his second wound in battle, his first being a bayonet thrust in the thigh, at Toulon, at the very outset of his career.

A spent musket-ball struck his foot as he witnessed the storming of the town of Ratisbon, and whilst neither of these incidents came close to ending his life they nonetheless gave point to the forebodings of his advisers. One and all began to speculate on what might happen to the Empire should he lose his life before he had named a successor, a successor, moreover, who could command the unquestioned allegiance of state, army and allies.

Walewska's condition dissolved the last lingering doubts he entertained that Eléonore Denuelle's child might not have been his own. Added to this, both he and Imperial France were now at the summit of their fortunes and it was time, if at all, to consider the future.

Slowly and dismally he made up his mind and once having done so he set about implementing his decision in a dreary, half-hearted and utterly uncharacteristic manner.

He began by informing Eugène, Joséphine's son, and it was from this young man Joséphine had her first real intimation that the long-anticipated blow could not be delayed.

He then took the astonishing step of instructing the palace architect at Fontainebleau to seal up the communications between his own and Joséphine's apartments. Finally he sent word that he was returning from Vienna and expected her to meet him at Fontainebleau on 26 October, or at latest, the 27th.

Joséphine received these broad hints in uneasy silence. Ever since her indiscretion of ten years ago, when she had played the fool with Hippolyte Charles at Malmaison, she had known that a divorce was a probability rather than a possibility. She had weathered the first terrible storm on his return from Egypt, dissolving his resolution in a steady flood of tears and the earnest pleas of her son and daughter. She had had many anxious moments during the preliminaries of the coronation, when the entire Bonaparte clan was actively intriguing against her and threatening to break up the marriage. There had been fresh anxieties on each of the occasions when Napoleon was reported to have fallen in love, first with Duchâtel, later with Marie Walewska. Finally, a little over a year before, Fouché, then Minister of Police, had had the temerity to approach her and hint that she should sacrifice herself for France.

Each time, however, the threatened eclipse had passed and the old relationship between them had not only survived but flowered as the years went by.

Fouché, the handsome, icy-hearted policeman, had been very sternly handled for daring to approach her on the subject of divorce and Napoleon, to everyone's amazement, had feigned surprise that such a project should have entered the statesman's mind. She could not have been entirely fooled by this demonstration of innocence but she had been immensely cheered by the events that followed it, for that summer, the summer of 1808, the Emperor had taken her down to Bayonne to meet (and help to kidnap) the Spanish Royal Family.

The months they shared during this expedition proved to be among the happiest of their marriage. All his old playfulness towards her had returned. They had stayed at the Castle of Marrac near the shore and had sometimes picnicked on the beach. Laughingly he had dragged her into the water and stolen her silk beach slippers, throwing them into the water and compelling her to enter the carriage barefoot 'in order that he might see her pretty feet'. She had been of immense use to him in the difficult business of handling the enraged Spanish Bourbons and their return to Paris together was a triumph.

It was the last moment of happiness they were to know

as man and wife and almost the last that she was to know on earth.

Even when he rushed off to settle the Austrian threat the skies remained clear for a few more months.

As recently as the summer of 1809 he was writing fond letters to her from the battlefield, signing them 'Adieu dear – I send you a kiss,' or 'Yours ever'. She must, nevertheless, have known that there could only be one end to this agony of doubt, for she, beyond all others, knew how much his purpose meant to him.

Fundamentally she had changed little since the days when she sat waiting for the tumbril rattle in Les Carmes prison. She was still a past-mistress of the art of self-deception and could not bring herself to believe that, when it came to a trial of wills, he would be proof against tears and protestations. When the courier brought her the coldly expressed message to meet him at Fontainebleau she panicked and made a half-hearted attempt to flee but this only exacerbated matters. He was the first to arrive and found the palace unprepared for him. He was furious but there had been many such storms in the past and somehow she had always managed to outride them and win him over. She succeeded again, or appeared to succeed, on this occasion. After grumbling and rumbling a little he said nothing about a divorce and nothing to explain the partition between their suites. They spent a quiet if slightly uneasy period together before packing up and leaving for Paris.

Then, on the night of 30 November, the sword fell, descending with such suddenness that it gave her no chance to rally for a final counter-attack upon his susceptibilities.

That night they had dinner alone together and it was a silent, gloomy meal. She was watching him, speculating on his thoughts, when suddenly he got up and led her into the adjoining salon. She knew then that he meant to pronounce the dread decision and in spite of the months of suppressed foreboding it must have come as a terrible shock to her.

He told her in gentle, halting terms, speaking of 'over-mastering destiny' and of their joint duty, to 'sacrifice personal happiness in the interests of France'.

Without any real hope she threw down her final hand. It consisted of two shrieks, a long wail and a desperate fainting fit.

Now it was his turn to panic. Utterly distraught and inarticulate with dismay, he summoned Bausset, the Prefect of the palace. Bausset rushed in to find Joséphine 'insensible' at his feet.

The Emperor found his voice.

'Are you strong enough to carry the Empress to her apartments?' he demanded and when the Prefect said he was: 'Take her down the staircase, whilst I hold the light!'

Bausset did his best but the staircase was very narrow and at the bend Napoleon was obliged to summon another attendant to hold the candlestick. He was then able to take her feet and blunder forward, himself on the edge of hysteria. At the final turn of the stairs Bausset's worst anxieties were relieved. Joséphine opened her eyes and in a whisper that Napoleon did not hear said: 'You are holding me too tight!'

The Prefect was wise in the duties of a palace servant. He held his peace until the time came to write his memoirs. Reading his account one is inclined to suspect that something akin to a wink passed between them.

After that events moved forward if not swiftly, then at least with the measured rhythm of a funeral march.

On 15 December the Bonapartes and the Beauharnais met in solemn conclave at the Tuileries. If the former family was cockahoop over their long-delayed triumph its members did not dare to show elation. The Emperor's expression was excessively solemn and Joséphine's daughter, Hortense, wept throughout the entire proceedings.

Joséphine herself was calm for already some of the worst of her fears had been allayed. Preoccupied to the very end by material considerations of dress and income she had been immensely relieved to hear that she was to lose none of the outward trappings of her position. Her debts, as mountainous as ever, were to be paid. Her income was fixed at three million francs per annum. She was given Malmaison, a town residence and a hunting box. She was to retain her title and all its trimmings – armorial bearings, military escorts and carriages. Nevertheless the conference must have been a terrible ordeal for her.

King Joseph was not present at the conference. He had troubles enough of his own, in Spain. Madame Mère, Napoleon's mother, looked on with a peasant's phlegm but sisters Pauline and Caroline sniffed a few dutiful tears into expensive handkerchiefs when their brother rose to read his prepared speech, setting out in detail the reasons for the gathering.

Eugène, Joséphine's gallant son, maintained a wooden expression. Hortense, his sister, contributed nothing but sobs and tears. Every now and again Napoleon's voice faltered and then, summoning reserves of courage she had never thought she possessed, Joséphine rose to read her own speech, managing to get through most of it without breaking down.

'... it is my duty to declare that, as I can no longer hope to bear children and thus satisfy his political needs and the interests of France, I am happy to be able to give him the greatest proof of attachment and devotion which has ever been given to anyone on this earth ... I owe everything to his kindness : it was his hand which crowned me. ... I shall still be the Emperor's best friend ...'

And so on, until the speeches were done and the deed of divorce was signed. Eugène, who a few months before had led an army in battle, found the ordeal insupportable and collapsed. The conference broke up and all was over, or nearly all.

That night, at two o'clock, Napoleon's bedroom door opened and he glanced over the edge of the coverlet to see the figure of Joséphine standing at the foot of the bed. There was no calmness or dignity about her now. Her hair was loose, her face stiff and her eyes empty and staring.

Napoleon scrambled out of bed as she fell on her knees beside him. He threw his arms round her shoulders and at his touch she began to sob.

'Be brave,' he urged, 'you know I will always be your friend!'

They remained together another hour and in the end it was he who needed comforting.

There remained the final exit and she graced it with something more than her customary dignity. Her quitting of the Tuileries had about it the tragic grandeur of Marie Antoinette's journey to the guillotine.

In the early afternoon she came down the grand staircase for the last time. Her household women and all the palace servants crowded round to see her go and say their farewells. Everyone, says an eyewitness, was in tears, but on this occasion the Empress, who had so often resorted to tears in the past, shed none. On the tide of others' tears she passed out of the Tuileries, never to set foot in it again. Outside, as though Paris, too, wept to see her pass, the rain fell steadily.

In the streets and boulevard cafés Parisians discussed the news. Everyone loved Joséphine but many felt that an alliance between the Emperor and his oldest rival would mean permanent peace, something that France had but briefly experienced since the day Danton had roared: 'The Kings of Europe advance against us! We throw at their feet, as gage of battle, the head of a King!' Frenchmen recalling Henri IV might have reasoned that if Paris was worth a Mass then peace was worth an Empress.

The fighting men thought otherwise. For the veterans who had now marched into most of the capitals of Europe this woman had become a talisman, a guarantee of their victory under the eye of the man she loved. They remembered her in the old days, following her husband from triumph to triumph in Italy, and they were not to know that it had required scores of passionate letters to get her there. They associated her with the Pyramids, Marengo, Austerlitz, Jena, Friedland and Wagram and they were to remember all this when the shadows stole over the Empire. As they trudged through the mud on the final retreat into France four years later they were to say to dying conscripts: 'It wasn't always like this, we've never had a day's luck since we lost the old lady!'

CHAPTER XVII

The princess who wiggled her ears

'The brilliant and lofty qualities of the Archduchess Marie Louise, of which I have been specially informed, have enabled me to act in conformity with my policy ...,' wrote Napoleon, in what would now be referred to as an official handout to state departments, on 26 February 1810.

Even allowing for the conventional wording of such correspondence this pronouncement arched the eyebrows of the Minister for Foreign Affairs, who was the first recipient of the high toned announcement. He must have spared a passing thought for the true nature of the eighteen-year-old girl who was on the point of replacing Joséphine as Empress of France.

Lofty she certainly was in the hierarchy of European aristocracy. Her lineage went back over seven centuries and somewhere along its course was a drop of blood from every reigning house in the Western world. Brilliant, however, was an adjective that could hardly be applied to her. Her accomplishments to date added up to a little music, some half-hearted painting, some skill at embroidery, a working knowledge of several foreign languages and, above all, a diverting ability to wiggle her ears without disturbing her face.

Even for a girl reared in the convent-like atmosphere of an Austrian palace, Marie Louise was regarded as dull and complaisant to the point of stupidity. Hedged around with idiotic protocol and mentally walled up by Spanish etiquette that even in those days was regarded as monstrous by less formal royal families, she had not yet learned the fundamental difference between the sexes. She had never, for a single instant, been left alone with any man other than her father. In the courtyard of her apartments at Schönbrunn and the Hofburg were hens but not a single cock. All her pets were female and the vaguest reference to the part played in the act of procreation by the male animal was extracted from her carefully supervised books with a pair of scissors!

She had never been to a theatre. Her jewellery, in the much-harassed and poverty-stricken court of her father Francis, was limited to some hair-rings, a few seed pearls and a necklace of corals. Day and night she was guarded by a succession of hawk-eyed governesses and waiting-women. Her very thoughts were extracted, scrutinized and fed back to her by her gaolers. She had, in fact, been subjected to a non-stop brainwash since the day she emerged from the cradle.

There never was a bride who went more innocently to her marriage-bed. Yet there had never existed a girl whose ultimate arrival there was less of a certainty. In short, her preparation for an event which she, her parents and the lowliest among her attendants recognized as inevitable, constituted a gross assault upon human dignity. Only a girl as bovine as Marie Louise could have survived it without suffering permanent damage to her nervous system and general health.

The divorce of Joséphine and choice of another wife presented Napoleon and his advisers with one of the most ticklish political problems ever posed.

It was one thing to read a sheaf of declarations to a sombre gathering of relations but quite another to select a bride from a ruling house. Having accomplished this, the greatest labour remained. Napoleon was required to beat down the legal and religious obstacles that interposed between the liquidation of one marriage, blessed by Church and State, and the consummation of a new one into the most hidebound royal house in Europe.

The last-minute decision of Napoleon to accede to José-

phine's request and be married by the Church on the very
eve of the coronation cost him a vast expenditure of time,
trouble and exasperation.

It would have been simple enough to discount the casual
ceremony performed by the sleepy Paris official, in March
1796. Marriages during the Revolution were never taken
seriously and the entire ceremony in this particular case had
lacked the air of finality that usually surrounds any marriage,
even one between a half-willing adventuress and a penniless
artilleryman.

There were, however, two further obstacles to the can-
cellation of this marriage and one had been created by
Napoleon himself. It was he who, in 1806, had issued an
edict to the effect that no member of the Imperial Family
was to indulge in the luxury of a divorce! In addition, there
existed a special article in the French Civil Code under
which no woman of forty-five or over could legally be set
aside on the demand of her husband.

This last hitch did not amount to much. Joséphine had
unwittingly put herself outside its protection when she had
lied so cheerfully about her age at the drawing up of the
original marriage contract. Officially she was still only
forty-two.

There was, however, the attitude of the bride's father to
be considered. Francis was the principal advocate of Rome
among the crowned heads of Europe and it was imperative
that he should be satisfied that the marriage between his
daughter and his late enemy was binding as far as the
Church was concerned. The union could not have been more
badly timed for Napoleon. At the moment of sueing for the
Pope's blessing he had confiscated the Papal Estates, virtu-
ally imprisoned His Holiness and drawn upon himself a Bull
of Excommunication!

Having finally turned his back on the prospect of a Russian alliance, however, and countered the Czar's endless pro-
crastinations by announcing that the Russian Grand Duchess
Anne was too young at fifteen to become the mother of an

heir to the Empire, Napoleon set about slashing through his jungle of difficulties with the thoroughness of an Imperial cavalry squadron dispersing a body of Austrian infantry.

On the day following the distressing family scene at the Tuileries and the spectacular exit of Joséphine from his life he requested the French Senate to ratify the divorce. The Senators lost no time in doing exactly as they were bid. They were probably hastened in their work by the memory of what had happened to an august assembly of legislators some ten years before, when Napoleon's grenadiers had ejected them from the assembly at the point of a bayonet. Having disposed of the political problem, the Emperor then gave his full attention to the religious side of the matter.

There is a Gilbert and Sullivan air about his approach to the last-minute religious ceremony, the one that had immediately preceded his coronation in 1804. Unable to cancel it out he fell back on pretending that it had never really existed. The church marriage, he declared, was null and void, simply because he, the bridegroom, had been a disgruntled and unwilling partner to it! As further prooof to its worthlessness as a binding, religious contract he cited the fact that no witnesses had been present. This was quite true – he had made sure of that at the time – so that one way and another he enabled his advocates to convince the Ecclesiastical body in Paris that the whole affair was a farce unworthy of their attention.

Even then, however, it was not all plain sailing. It was necessary for all the documents of the case to be rushed to Vienna, where they were to be inspected by the Austrian Ecclesiastics. When the time arrived for the official scrutiny the correct papers were found to be in Paris! There was a frightful to-do. Couriers galloped to and fro along the muddy roads, ambassadors and secretaries scurried in and out of the embassies and the Hofburg, frenzied messages and notes were exchanged, weighty opinions sought and a torrent of legal jargon poured out to support and uphold such opinions.

In the end everybody except the Pope was satisfied and in

early March arrangements were made for a proxy wedding.

The bride's uncle, Charles (who, less than a year before, had almost defeated the bridegroom on the banks of the Danube), consented to stand in for Napoleon. The Emperor's official representative at the ceremony was his Chief of Staff, Berthier. He could hardly have chosen a better man. Berthier, whose latest title had been chosen from an Austrian defeat, was himself something of an expert in complicated matrimonial affairs. Compelled by Napoleon to marry a Princess he was still sharing a house with his wife and his adored mistress, the lady whose portrait he had worshipped so devoutly in the deserts of Egypt.

Such a farce, of course, could never have been played out had the bride's family been less anxious to conclude the alliance. Four times in recent years Austria had been humbled by the French legions yet somehow Austria had survived and was still France's most dangerous rival in the West.

On the basis of the modern adage Francis came to the conclusion that, having failed to defeat his terrible opponent, the simplest course was to join him. Everyone who mattered in Vienna was wholly in favour of the marriage and even His Holiness admitted, though glumly, that it was a good stroke of policy for the Austrian court. The sole objector, the one person who flatly refused to give ground, was the bride's stepmother. Her hatred for Napoleon was so intense that nothing whatever could induce her to conceal her rage and dismay.

The bride had no say in the matter whatever. All her life she had been taught that her father's will was law and nobody seems to have recalled that her childhood and adolescence had been chequered with flights from the man who was now to become her husband. Similarly, nobody seemed to remember that Marie Louise had formed a habit of crossing herself whenever his name was mentioned. Papa said that she must marry an Ogre and so she would marry an Ogre. Such was her nature and training that, had Papa decreed it,

she would have drifted meekly into the embrace of Beel-
zebub himself.

She did, however, make one feeble protest and set it down
in a letter written to her father from Ofen, shortly before the
proxy wedding. On receiving his terse reply, however, she
expressed herself perfectly satisfied with his reasoning and
set about preparing for the sacrifice without more ado. Who
was she to question Papa and his advisers? The people of
Vienna were greeting the news with shouts of joy and the
Stock Exchange was so certain of a prolonged peace that
nobody wanted to dispose of a single share and business was
at a standstill.

Napoleon did nothing half-heartedly.

When he made war he was not content until opposing
armies were broken and scattered. When he concluded that
the French educational system was in need of a little attention he reorganized it from primary to university level.
When he was dissatisfied with a group of public buildings he
not only pulled them down but rebuilt all the thoroughfares
that surrounded them.

Thus, having made up his mind to marry into an hereditary house, he displayed the prodigality of a prince in a fairy
tale.

No sooner had the preliminary arrangements for the
match been signed and sanded than a convoy of wagons set
out on the long journey between Paris and Vienna. It re-
sembled the caravan of a fabulous Eastern potentate.

The freight included twelve dozen assorted chemises of
the finest cambric trimmed with lace and embroidery, each
costing something like five pounds sterling; twenty-four
dozen handkerchiefs; twenty-four bed-jackets; thirty-six pet-
ticoats; eighty night-caps and scores of dressing gowns,
towels, dresses and pieces of chamber linen, all of the finest
quality.

And this was just a beginning. Day after day further con-
tributions towards the most elaborate and expensive trous-

seau in the history of marriage flowed south-east in a never-ending stream. Nobody in Vienna had ever seen anything like it and even the prosperous Parisians were awed by the immensity of the Emperor's bounty. The lace alone cost over eighty thousand francs and a single embroidered gown five thousand. There was a shawl valued at three thousand two hundred, three dresses valued at seventeen thousand three hundred francs, Cashmere shawls at some two thousand pounds sterling and twelve dozen pairs of assorted stockings, the price of which ranged from one pound to three pounds ten shillings a pair.

There were shoes, slippers, trinkets, ornaments, buckles, girdles and every conceivable item of dress that a bride was likely to need. Then, when every bottom drawer in the Hofburg was full to overflowing, a stream of special couriers cantered into Vienna bearing caskets of jewellery, valued at four hundred thousand pounds.

The personal adornments laid at the feet of Marie Louise before she had so much as set eyes on the man she was to marry would have filled the display stands of the largest shop in Vienna. They included, for instance, a miniature of her Imperial fairy-godmother, set in diamonds and costing thirty thousand pounds and a necklace and two pendants valued at a total of one and a half million francs, besides tiaras, toiletsets, rings and brooches almost without number.

Well might the poverty-stricken court party at Vienna congratulate itself on the fruits of its policy, for Napoleon did not stop at sending gifts to the bride. All cooperative members of his bride's household were handsomely rewarded for the part they had played in forwarding the match. In addition Marie Louise, almost buried under his rain of gifts, distributed rewards to all who helped her unpack.

Having exhausted the resources of Paris salons and goldsmiths the Emperor now switched his energies towards the apartments in which he intended his bride to live.

Suites at all the principal royal residences were renovated and redecorated throughout and everything likely to remind

Marie Louise of her predecessor was removed and replaced.

Then, in a further furious effort to combat his gnawing impatience, Napoleon looked to his own wardrobe, ordering a new suit that was so stiff with embroidery that it enclosed its wearer like a suit of plate armour and had to be sent back to the tailor. All manner of diversions were tried to make the time pass more quickly. He went hunting and even learned to waltz but no matter how desperately he burned up his energy he remained as restless and turbulent as a child awaiting his first visit to a pantomime.

All the visitors in the Tuileries and to St Cloud were dragged round the premises to inspect the apartments that he had prepared for his bride and there was an embarrassing moment when one portly notable became tightly wedged in the narrow staircase connecting Napoleon's study with the rooms of the Empress-to-be.

As the weeks passed the bridegroom's impatience became the joke of Paris but Napoleon did not care a fig if his subjects laughed at him. His despondency had evaporated and although he showed an eager interest in Joséphine, and even visited her at Malmaison, he was very careful never to be left alone with her and contented himself with affable enquiries regarding her wants.

Writing home to her father and giving him the latest gossip from Paris, brother Jerome's wife, Catherine of Westphalia, filled pages with a lively description of Napoleon's impatience to be married. 'Nobody has ever seen him like this,' she wrote and indeed, nobody ever had, not even his valet, or his Marshal of the Palace, Duroc. He was in wonderful health, keyed-up, nervously jocular and as ebullient as a schoolboy. He was young again and the future stretched before him like a highway paved with gold and lined with flowers.

At last word reached him that Marshal Berthier was escorting the bride across the frontier.

The meeting between them was to be at Soissons, on the

28th of March, and at the towns through which the bridal party was to pass triumphal arches had been erected and all the streets garlanded. Nervous mayors and bevies of schoolgirls stood by grasping speeches of welcome and posies.

As the bride's cavalcade entered France and rumbled westward a stream of Imperial couriers galloped up with messages (often illegibly written apart from the final 'N') and a supply of fresh gifts but there came a time when the Imperial impatience burst the dam of commonsense. Napoleon found that he could wait no longer. Not an hour. Not a second.

She was due at Soissons on the 27th and on that date Napoleon thundered into the town accompanied by his brother-in-law, hard-riding Murat, King of Naples and most dandified of all the Marshals.

The dismayed reception committee stood by whilst Napoleon flung himself out of his new clothes and donned the simple uniform of an artillery Captain. Then, without a word to anyone and with only Murat as escort, he spurred through pelting rain along the road to Vitry, where they informed him Marie Louise had slept on the night of the 26th.

At Courcelles, between Soissons and Vitry, he took shelter in the church porch and it was here, at long last, that he had his first glimpse of the heavy coach, rolling along through the sleet, surrounded by a drenched escort of outriders and cavalry.

The great moment had arrived. Shaking his rein he galloped forward, bent on surprising the occupants, but the Master of Horse, Audenarde, was on the alert. Reining in his horse he rose in his stirrups and shouted 'The Emperor!'

The coach stopped and Napoleon, dripping wet, flung himself from his horse, pulled upon the door and scrambled inside, planting a kiss on the cheek of the astonished, travel-weary girl, who sat demurely beside her new sister-in-law, Caroline.

Caroline, more accustomed to her unpredictable brother than the bride, promptly introduced him to the speechless Louise.

Horses were changed and the coach set off again at a spanking pace, dashing through towns where welcome committees hunched under dripping decorations and open mouthed mayors stood waiting with sodden speeches in their hands. It drove on without pause until nine o'clock in the evening, when Compiègne was reached and the royal party entered the apartments prepared for them.

Salutes of cannon thundered out over the town and surprised servants ran nervously in all directions. Napoleon strode into the palace calling harshly for supper and no speeches.

Supper proved a very trying meal for the tired, damp company.

No one had expected them and the palace was thrown into an uproar by their sudden arrival. Caroline was there and on her best behaviour, for this was surely a great personal triumph for a woman who had been scheming to replace the hated Beauharnais for the better part of a decade.

Murat, her husband, was there, having changed his dripping uniform for something more comfortable. Cardinal Fesch was at table, 'Uncle' Fesch, whose elevation, like that of everyone else present, was due to the energy of his dynamic nephew. He was the same uncle who, more than five years before, had obligingly added the blessing of the Church to a previous Imperial marriage and in a manner of speaking it was Uncle Fesch's moment. Turning to him shortly before the meal was over Napoleon asked a sudden embarrassing question : 'Is it not true that we are legally married?'

'Why yes,' replied the startled Cardinal, 'according to civil law you are married, sire !'

The answer satisfied Napoleon, even if it failed to satisfy some of the others, including the Austrian envoy. Sharply he bade the assembled company goodnight and whisked his wordless bride to her quarters. He remained there all night and breakfasted at her bedside in the morning.

'My friend,' he is reported to have said to an intimate, when he was back in his own quarters, 'marry a German! They are the best of all women, sweet, gentle, fresh and innocent as roses!'

CHAPTER XVIII

'Did she laugh or cry?'

Not long after Marie Louise had settled in the Tuileries Napoleon allowed his wife to have a private interview with Metternich, her fellow-countryman.

His action astonished the court for he had laid down the strictest rules regarding his wife's accessibility to men. So strict was this supervision that he would allow no man to approach her. A distinguished member of her staff who called in a cabinet-maker to explain the working of an intricately designed piece of furniture was scolded like a naughty schoolgirl.

He was very anxious, however, that the Austrian diplomat Metternich should take home to her father a favourable report of the Empress's state of mind and he was, moreover, confident that anything she said about him in his absence would be to his credit.

'Well,' he demanded of the Austrian, when they were alone after the interview, 'has the Empress abused me much? Did she laugh or cry?'

He was aware, of course, that she had done neither. The girl who could wiggle her ears was not given to emotional displays. Nevertheless, laughter would have been the more likely reaction, for there is not the slightest doubt that the Habsburg bride had soon come to terms with her situation and was far happier than she had ever expected to be this side of Jordan.

Not only was she overjoyed by the prodigality of her husband – she had been assured of that weeks before he had scrambled into her coach at Courcelles – she was convinced by this time that Napoleon as a man had been badly misrepresented to her in the past. She found herself very agreeably surprised by his unruffled affability, his gay and immediate response to every demand she made upon him and by his acts of thoughtfulness, such as installing her favourite little bitch in her rooms before their arrival in Paris. Above all, she was stirred by his attentions as a lover.

Ignorant of the art of courtship as Marie Louise undoubtedly was when she arrived at Compiègne after her tiring drive through the rain, she was far from being so when she arrived in the capital a few days later.

Her father and governesses had shielded her from all knowledge of sex during her upbringing at Vienna, but they had married her off to a man who knew all there was to be known about love, who could be as tender and winning with a young girl as he was fierce and overriding with an obstinate Ambassador, a man who, at a moment's notice, could touch any chord of a woman's emotions and produce therefrom a harmony of accord that he was unable to extract from grim-faced statesmen and hard-fighting Generals of Division.

Few men had had more experience with women, and now that he was over forty he did not make the mistake of demanding ardour in his partner. What he wanted and what he desperately needed from her was gentleness, complaisance and an end to scenes of jealousy and reproach.

In Marie Louise he found exactly what he was seeking.

At eighteen she was a robust, fully-matured woman. When demanding a physical description of her from one of his old campaigners shortly before they had met Napoleon had nudged the soldier and asked : 'Has she got plenty of this and that?' It is not known exactly what General Lejeune, his messenger, said in reply to this camp-fire query but he was probably reassuring. Marie Louise had indeed 'plenty of this and that' and is reported as possessing 'a very fine bust and a pleasing if unremarkable figure'.

She had, in addition, an abundance of fair hair, a fresh (some say 'florid') complexion, only slightly marred by small-pox, tiny but well-shaped hands and feet and an excellent constitution.

One of the reasons that had led Napoleon to select her was a report he had heard of the astonishing fertility among the women of her family. Her mother, poor soul, had borne thirteen children before passing to her rest and making way for a second wife. Her great-grandmother broke all Habsburg records. She produced twenty-six!

What Napoleon did not know and what he was gratified to discover was that Marie Louise, for all the sternly repressive measures exerted over her throughout her adolescence, was a very sensual young woman, possessing that degree of sensuality often found in heavy, dullish women of her type. Surprised, and disconcerted as she doubtless was by the unceremonial speed he had shown in consummating the proxy wedding, she was greatly flattered by her husband's ardour.

In the few years they were to remain together she never lost this need of him, or ceased to find him anything but pleasing as a lover and husband. This fact is established in her diaries and in the letters she wrote home to her anxious father in Vienna.

Only a month after their first meeting she was writing: 'Heaven has answered the prayers you uttered on my wedding-day. May it soon be yours to be as happy as I am now.'

As early as 16 April, that is, less than three weeks after her impatient husband had carried her off from the supper table at Compiègne, Count Metternich, the Austrian witness was reporting:

'He is so obviously in love that he cannot conceal his feelings ... her slightest wish is invariably anticipated and their intimate relations are perfectly happy. What pleases me most is that she feels this completely!'

It was a fairly accurate estimate of the situation and yet, was he 'so obviously in love' with her? Was it possible that he, who had enjoyed the favours of some of the most experienced and beautiful women in Europe, could find much more than a humdrum satisfaction in the responses of a stolid and rather stupid girl of eighteen?

The answer to these questions is that he had changed. In

the last year or so he had changed very much, both as a lover and as soldier and ruler. He was wearing down far more rapidly than those about him realized. He had crammed into his forty years more mental and physical experiences than any two men of his generation. He was getting stout, despite a sparse diet and plenty of exercise. He was still fit and active but he was aware, even at this stage, of the disease that was to kill him in less than eleven years, a cancer that had already accounted for his father and was to kill one sister and one brother. He wanted peace and a chance to enjoy an Indian summer of domesticity. He left the war in Spain to his Marshals and a sorry job they made of it in his absence. His personal tastes, always simple, now became those of a bourgeois. Immediately after his second marriage he entered what might be described as his slipper and fireside phase and this phase was to endure for another year. Even then he did not turn his back on it from choice and always he was to recall it with pleasure. Not once was he to refer in terms other than those of tenderness and gratitude to the woman who made this interlude possible.

Certainly no young wife was ever fussed over or cossetted more than was Marie Louise. He gave her riding lessons. He played parlour games – blind man's buff and forfeits! He took her with him on state progresses. He embraced her every time he entered her room. He, who loved warmth and insisted on huge fires, now sat shivering in her apartments because she preferred plenty of fresh air and had fires extinguished. He even toyed with her glove when she left one on his desk and was once seen lifting it to his lips, like a youth of seventeen, sad in the absence of his adored.

It makes a strange picture, this man in whose presence kings trembled and armed hosts fled, seated at his desk and kissing a glove in the momentary absence of a wife of eighteen. Had he discarded his twenty-five-year-old dream of romantic fulfilment? Or had he, as he approached his forty-first birthday, found peace in the acceptance of a good second-best?

There was a fulfilment of a sort ahead, fulfilment and nerve-wracking anxiety.

Within a few months of marriage he learned that his young wife was pregnant and that the long-awaited heir to the Empire could be expected in March. Joyfully the news was broadcast throughout France and her dependant states. In Moscow and Spain there was despondency. In England the exiled Bourbons cursed aloud. In Paris and Vienna there was public delight.

In June, barely three months after the wedding, Marie Louise's stepmother had written to her husband of the girl's distress occasioned by the lack of symptoms of pregnancy but by August these doubts were seen to be premature. In late summer Marie Louise was writing home : 'I am feeling well but take care of myself as much as my horror of medical orders permit,' and later, 'I still feel pretty well ... and am trying to arm myself with courage and resolution for the moment of my confinement. ...'

That same summer another Marie drifted into Paris, accompanied by a child, a few months old.

The baby, a Pole, was already a Count and his mother took him out to Malmaison, where he was much admired by yet another woman who had mothered Napoleon when he needed mothering.

What did these two women, one a discarded wife, the other a half-forgotten mistress, have to say to one another on this strange occasion? Did they discuss the forthcoming event that was already the talking point of every Chancellery in Europe and every fashionable salon between Moscow and Lisbon?

It is probable that they did, speculating upon the sex of the child who was to be known as the King of Rome. Even poets were hard at work versifying the topic and one at least was writing of the father *'Faire toujours ce qu'il voulait'* – he usually gets what he wants.

CHAPTER XIX

'The summit of my happiness'

At ten o'clock on the morning of 20 March 1811, the city of Paris erupted.

A balloon, manned by the pioneer Blanchard, rose over the city, its occupants showering printed bulletins on the people below. The city was full of gallopers as couriers sped out of every gate, spurring north, south, east and west on the first stage of journeys that were to end as far away as Moscow and the embattled Spanish peninsula. Excited crowds converged on the Tuileries as guns began to thunder from the artillery park, the first report silencing the chatter of Parisians as they began to count – one, two, three, up to twenty-one.

On the twenty-first shot there was a sudden hush, lasting hardly more than a couple of seconds. Then, as the twenty-second report echoed over the forecourt, the city rocked with cheers, the prolonged mighty roar reaching out into the uttermost suburbs of the capital.

The scene in front of the Tuileries reminded an eye-witness of that he had seen there one stifling August day, nineteen years before, when the Paris mob had stormed the palace and massacred its garrison, but the people gathered there now were displaying a vastly different public sentiment. They were throwing their hats into the air and embracing one another, exclaiming that this was the greatest day for France since 4 July 1789. At the age of forty-one years and seven months the Emperor Napoleon had a male heir at last.

It had been an anxious time inside the Tuileries.

At six o'clock in the morning Napoleon took a bath, re-flecting that this was the third day of his wife's labour. In the Empress's apartment stood twenty-two witnesses, each a notable, and every man and woman among them tired and strained to the point of collapse.

Four doctors, the most distinguished in the land, stood beside the great bed. A Norman peasant girl, engaged as a wet-nurse, sat close by, her hands in her lap. Like the dukes and the counts, the Marshals and the Senators she was wait-ing. Everybody in Paris was waiting.

For hours the tension inside the palace had been almost unbearable and it did not ease when Dubois, one of the doc-tors, hastened into Napoleon's presence and whispered that the situation was critical and would require the use of in-struments.

Napoleon mastered his terror and spoke calmly, as though issuing an order for the advance of his final reserve in the course of a critical battle.

'What would you do in a normal case such as this?' he wanted to know.

Dubois gave him an honest answer. He would use instru-ments.

'Then use them now,' Napoleon told him shortly. 'Treat my wife as though she was the wife of a tradesman in the Rue Saint-Denis!'

It was a pretty speech but it meant less than nothing. How could it, when so much depended on the well-being of that morsel of humanity struggling to emerge from the womb of the wife of this man?

Fifty-three million subjects throughout France and her dependant states had been awaiting this event for nearly seven years and beyond France it was a matter of vital im-portance to a ring of enemies and would-be enemies. The sex and survival of the child were important to men in cruisers in the Channel and to autocrats in Muscovy. It meant as much to Poles awaiting the rebirth of their nation and to

Spanish mountain fighters, planning fresh descents on French convoys.

Time passed slowly, the minutes dragging by in endless suspense.

Napoleon entered the room and took his wife's hand but he had no stomach for this kind of battle and his nerves could not sustain him there for more than a moment or two. He drifted back to his own rooms and presently they came to tell him that it was now a choice between the survival of mother or child.

Impassively he gave his orders. The mother's life was to be saved at all costs; the child's was of secondary importance.

Two more agonizing hours elapsed before they came to him with somewhat better news. Marie Louise had rallied but the child appeared to be still-born. He sighed but his relief was evident to everyone present.

Another ten minutes passed before they came again and this time he read joy in the doctor's face. The child was alive and had responded to a massage of warm napkins, a gentle smacking and a few drops of brandy blown into its mouth by a surgeon. The news was even more sensational. It was a boy, a King of Rome!

His apathy dropped from him before they had finished speaking. Eyes alight with joy he snapped into his customary briskness, becoming on the instant the Napoleon of Arcola, Rivoli and Austerlitz.

'My pages and the salute!' he roared and without another word strode out on to the balcony to acknowledge the tumultuous cheers of his subjects.

Three days later the news was received in Vienna and because the French alliance still meant peace it was greeted with equal delight. Not universally so, however, for at least one disgruntled Austrian made a prophecy. 'In a few years we shall have this King of Rome here as a beggar-student.'

It is to be doubted whether even the prophet took his prediction very seriously. For all that it was an astonishingly accurate statement. Twenty-one years later the prisoner-Prince was to die in this city, a King of Rome in legend only.

Slowly the tempo of the Tuileries returned to normal.

There was a private christening that same evening, when Napoleon, the child in his arms, advanced triumphantly upon the font. Marie Louise, utterly exhausted but more than satisfied with her achievement, received a suitable fairy-tale reward, an eight-row necklace of magnificent pearls, eight hundred and sixteen of them in all and costing the Privy Purse a total of half-a-million francs.

When she was stronger she wrote gleefully to her father in Vienna, and Francis, the Prince of Snobs, at once set his savants searching for the ancient lineage of his formidable son-in-law. Francis did not like to reflect that his grandson was also the grandson of a penniless Corsican lawyer.

The savants dug deeply into the registers and archives of ancient towns and sun-baked villages, but they were only partially successful. Francis was able to inform Napoleon that his special research team had finally unearthed traces of the original Buonapartes in Treviso. Napoleon was not impressed. Reflecting that the House of Habsburg had been founded some six centuries before by a man such as he, a soldier who had also carved out an Empire with his sword, he said : 'I prefer to be the Rudolph of my race !' The proud Habsburg never forgave the taunt.

Napoleon sat down to write to Joséphine, still living at Malmaison, the pretty country home where she had once considered exchanging her husband for Hippolyte Charles and where she was swimming in yet another lake of debt. Her ex-husband knew all about her post-divorce bills but in his hour of triumph Napoleon did not let them worry him. He wanted Joséphine to learn the momentous news from his own hand. 'I am at the summit of my happiness,' he wrote.

Joséphine was generous enough to share something of his joy. She interpreted his act in writing to her as a proof of his continuing affection.

For weeks there were fêtes and celebrations. Even the

poorest slum-dweller put out his decorations and illuminated his attic window. The watermen of the Seine staged a spectacular carnival and every Parisian of note put on his best clothes and trooped off to Notre Dame to witness the public baptism, on 9 June.

For the father the novelty of possessing a healthy and attractive son never grew stale. In the wake of Napoleon, the solicitous bourgeois husband, came Napoleon, the proud and playful parent. Never in the past had any one person, or any one triumph brought him so much solace and joy. Every hour that he could spare from desk and audience chamber was devoted to the child and as soon as the boy could toddle he was given the run of the Imperial study.

Sometimes the father's teasing and playfulness verged on the grotesque. One day he would place his famous black hat on the baby's head and gird his ceremonial sword around the tiny waist, another he would hold the child before a mirror and make hideous faces, so hideous that the King of Rome would squeal with delight or terror, nobody was ever quite sure which. He would seat the boy next to him at meals and dip his fingers in claret, allowing the child to suck the wine, or smear the baby's lips with gravy and shout with laughter as his tongue curved out to lick it.

Statesmen and governesses looked on gravely at these antics and several began to remark on the Emperor's growing lack of dignity, on the bad influence that this sort of behaviour would have upon a Prince. Napoleon laughed at them. Napoleon did not consult them on their views of how the future master of fifty-three millions should be reared. Instead, as though foreseeing a future when he had nothing but the child's portrait to comfort him, he squeezed every ounce of pleasure from his greatest triumph of all.

It was not so with the boy's mother. Not even motherhood could animate the vacuity of Marie Louise's peasant brain. She did her bare duty, no more and no less.

In the morning she would have the child brought to her and watch it grow bored and restless as her calm blue eyes regarded it over the top of a newspaper. Later in the day she sometimes spent ten or fifteen minutes beside the cradle but she was not liberal with caresses and never went into the nursery without a tapestry to occupy her hands. She was always relieved when one of her waiting-women summoned her for her music practice, or her painting lesson with Isabey. Perhaps, at the back of her slow-moving mind, she sometimes wondered what all the fuss was about. The child was there, the child was healthy and that was surely that.

Probably she was right and Napoleon was wrong. His judgements were not as sound as they once had been. He took less and less interest in the undercurrents of the many rivers he had crossed and the tireless intrigues of his sycophants were beginning to bore him. As for the never-ending war in Spain, he often forgot about it for days at a stretch. Marshal Masséna had come limping back from Portugal with an army of mutinous skeletons. Soult, one day to be cheered by Britons in the streets of London, was being soundly beaten by them at Albuera. A minority party in Austria was doing everything possible to poison the mind of the Imperial father-in-law against his daughter's realm. Britannia continued to rule the waves and frigate Captains thumbed their noses at Napoleon outside his own harbours.

For a year or more he ignored all this, or largely so, that he might watch his child grow sturdy and ride about the palace grounds in a carriage fashioned like a shell and drawn by goats.

At length, however, a cloud-bank loomed from the east that he could not ignore. His five-year-old friendship with Czar Alexander foundered on the Imperial edict to boycott British trade. Reluctantly the Emperor shut the nursery door and summoned his legions.

His army, the largest since Persian Darius had invaded Europe, surged across Europe, groping its way across the endless plains and forests to Moscow. It was essential to the dynasty that he should lead it but in assuming this new responsibility he paid his wife a compliment that he never paid Joséphine. He made her virtual Regent of France, his sole overlord during his absence, with power to sign important documents and power to take political decisions such as he had never granted to a living soul, not even the faithful Berthier or his revered mother.

He set off in May 1812, and Marie Louise watched him prepare to go, her face as blank and amiable as it had been the day they told her that she must submit to the embraces of an Ogre.

CHAPTER XX

Snow Scene

They were not, as it happened, to part so soon.

Since they had met they had shared the excitement and fatigue of five Imperial progresses and this, their journey into central Europe in the late spring of the year of 1812, was to be their last and most spectacular progress. It was also their final interval of serenity. From henceforth all their meetings were to take place against a background of chaos and the crash of a ruined Empire.

All spring troops were moving eastward, men of every nation wearing every variety of uniform and livery. Three hundred and twenty-five thousand soldiers crossed the Niemen into Russia and of these only a third were French. The others were a motley, half-unwilling legion of Poles, Bavarians, Saxons, Italians, Badeners, Westphalians, Dutchmen and Austrians.

In the centre of this cavalcade, fêted by petty kings and fawned upon by civil authorities, rode Emperor and Empress, he still at the pinnacle of his success, she enjoying the reverent prodigality of this tender, corpulent husband and the astonishing deference his presence guaranteed among all who came to pay their respects at each stage of the journey across Germany.

There was an additional reason for happiness on the part of Marie Louise during the triumphant journey to Dresden. He had promised her that she should meet her family at the journey's end and that once he had left for Russia she would be free to take a holiday with her father, in Prague.

For Francis was now an ally and his daughter, simple soul

that she was, had no inkling that his minister Metternich, the man who had urged this marriage upon her, was already insuring himself and his master against a defeat of Napoleon in the vast plains that lay between Dresden and the Muscovy capital.

Years later Napoleon was to describe his Austrian marriage as 'an abyss covered with flowers'. So far Marie Louise's elegant feet had trodden nothing but flowers strewn upon firm ground. She had no means of knowing that an abyss was there and neither, it seemed, had her father. He and his son-in-law exchanged friendly greetings at Dresden and even Marie Louise's stepmother, whose hatred of Napoleon had in no way abated, was shrewd enough to pretend to affability. She had no reason to behave otherwise. During the visit she emptied her stepdaughter's wardrobe and arrayed herself in gowns provided by the man she loathed.

If Napoleon was aware of his mother-in-law's raid on the Imperial wardrobe it stirred no resentment in him. Instead he made haste to increase her loot by a lavish distribution of dressing-cases, shawls, gold watches, dresses, hats and turbans, to the value of hundreds of thousands of francs. His ultimate reward for this liberality was treachery within one year and active connivance at his wife's adultery within two.

On 24 June the French army crossed the frontier and began its interminable advance into Russia. It disappeared so completely that it took fast-riding couriers twenty-eight days to convey Paris despatches to the Emperor's tent. There was not much hard fighting, for the Czar's armies steadily withdrew before the advance, setting a precedent that was to bring disaster to a feeble imitator of Napoleon one hundred and thirty-two years later.

Marie Louise, refreshed by her holiday in Prague, returned to Paris on the 8th of July and at once assumed her pleasant round of music lessons, painting lessons and tapestry weaving. Nobody took her state appointment very seriously and a bizarre conspiracy, aimed at spreading false news that her husband had been killed in battle, and declaring her marriage invalid and her son illegitimate, did not even reach her ears until it was suppressed and the badly-scared administration had arrested the conspirators.

There was plenty to occupy her mind during that summer, so much indeed that she spent very little time with her child and was only moved to display a maternal interest when she heard that the King of Rome's governess, the beloved 'Mama 'Quiou', had had the boy's likeness painted in miniature and despatched to his father in the field.

The picture, which depicted the child riding on a lamb, delighted his father, who unpacked it in his bivouac before burning Smolensk. Napoleon already thought very highly of 'Mama 'Quiou' as a governess and this act of thoughtfulness on her part greatly increased his regard for her. 'I am glad of this opportunity of expressing my great satisfaction in all your care of him,' he wrote, after expressing his thanks for such a welcome gift.

Marie Louise, learning in due course of the miniature's despatch, thought that perhaps it was time she, too, displayed a little devotion. Since marrying the most famous man in the world she had enlarged her ideas somewhat and this was evident when she ordered Gérard, one of her famous painting-tutors, to execute a full-sized portrait. Gérard must have worked very quickly for this second likeness arrived in Napoleon's camp on the eve of the battle of Borodino, the bloodiest and most costly engagement of all Napoleonic battles up to that time.

The troops had arrived in front of Moscow after a long and exhausting march and their Commander-in-Chief decided to use the portrait of his heir as a fillip to morale. He therefore issued orders that it should be placed on a chair outside his headquarters where it proved an object of considerable interest among the men, thousands of whom were to leave their bones on this ground the following day.

There is an ironical twist in the fate of these two portraits. The miniature sent by the governess remained in Napoleon's possession for the remainder of his life and his eyes were fixed upon it when he lay dying at St Helena, nine years later. The larger and more cumbersome portrait was abandoned during the great retreat and probably fell as loot into the hands of some Cossack troop-leader. Gérard, however, had had the forethought to make a copy and this copy was willed by the Emperor to the governess he so much admired!

The Grand Army entered deserted Moscow unopposed on 15 September. In the city were a few stragglers and hundreds of brutish incendiaries.

By 18 September four-fifths of Moscow was a smouldering ruin, by mid-October the French battalions were in full retreat, hurrying westward in the vain hope of finding winter quarters before the Russian winter engulfed them.

The high tide of French triumphs had already begun to ebb. It had, in fact, been ebbing for months, although scarcely anyone realized as much.

Company by company and squadron by squadron, the instrument that had held Europe in thrall for sixteen years disintegrated in blinding snowstorms along the road to Smolensk, Vilna and Orcha. Bands of cautious Cossacks harried the tortured columns by day and night but their presence was a mere irritant compared with the devastating assault of the north wind.

Guns and baggage were abandoned, starving men were burned to death in frantic efforts to warm themselves and stragglers fell out by the thousand, combing the squalid villages on each side of the route for a few dozen potatoes or a sip of Danzig gin.

At the crossing of the Beresina sixty thousand camp-followers were abandoned and only Marshal Ney, with a few hundred indestructibles, stood between the Grand Army and total extinction.

In late November despatches reached the half-frozen staff officers, acquainting them with Malet's conspiracy to seize power. The margin by which this crazy coup had missed success persuaded Napoleon that his only chance of survival was to get home as soon as possible.

He handed over the 'command' to the bleating Murat and set off from Smorgoni, travelling by sledge with two companions and risking capture in an unescorted journey through plains infested with Cossacks, partisans and brigands.

His luck held. By 10 December he was in Warsaw, where the Poles were still patiently awaiting the restitution of their kingdom and the nationalists continued to talk hopefully of the Emperor's obsession with a Polish countess, also called Marie.

There was little room for hope, despite Napoleon's studied optimism. He had travelled incognito, under the name of Monsieur Reynival and on arrival in the Polish capital he waited, stamping his numbed feet, at the Hotel d'Angleterre, whilst his envoy, Caulaincourt, went to the embassy for help. 'The more I bustle the better I am!' he told the astonished Abbé de Pradt, who could hardly believe his eyes when he was summoned into the presence of this haggard, hooded figure who claimed to be the Emperor of France.

Help was found and the journey continued, the Emperor's route passing within miles of Walewska's castle, a circumstance that prompted Napoleon to suggest a halt. He was dissuaded by Caulaincourt and the fugitives rushed on, from Warsaw to Dresden and then, in a carriage loaned by the distraught King of Saxony, to Erfurt, Maintz and finally Paris, which he reached late at night on 18 December. It was thirteen days since he had left the army at Smorgoni.

Not a soul in sleeping Paris expected him. How should they when they had only just received his famous 29th bulletin, telling them, in the frankest possible terms, of the chain of disasters that had overtaken the army.

He had difficulty in getting past the Tuileries guard and when a member of the Empress's staff encountered two exhausted, befurred figures on the point of stamping into her mistress's apartments she shouted loudly for help and flung herself in front of the bedroom door.

There were hurried explanations as the startled attendants knuckled the sleep from their eyes. The Empress hurried to embrace him and at once he was talkative and wildly optimistic. What had happened was due to the climate. He would raise another army and defeat his enemies in Germany. He would avenge himself for the miseries of the retreat.

He would do this and that, at once! Confidence crept back into the capital. Men and women, Marie Louise among them, who had been half resigned to watching a curtain fall upon the Empire, quickly rallied to him and forgot how easily that mountebank conspirator Malet had gulled the administration into believing that the Emperor was dead.

A new conscription was anticipated and seventeen-year-old conscripts began to shuffle into the depots. 'Marie Louises' they were called by the cynical veterans who doubted whether the beardless recruits had sufficient stamina to sustain them throughout a week's active service.

Marie Louise now found herself invested with the full power and responsibilities of Regent. She was given the power of life and death over her husband's friends and enemies, the right to sign pardons and warrants of execution, the task of watching over the seat of government and defending with her life the rights of her three-year-old son.

Garrisons were called in, new guns were forged, cavalry regiments were remounted and the Emperor rode out at the head of a new army. It was almost as large an army as the one that had disappeared into the snowdrifts along the road from Moscow.

At first it looked as though the veterans were wrong.

The conscript armies of 1813 stood fire as well and better than the men of Egypt and Austerlitz. There were even a few victories before an armed ring closed on the French and the Prince of Sweden, whose wife Désirée Napoleon had once wooed, declared against his countrymen.

Then the Austrian marriage was seen to be worthless after all, for Francis, father of the girl-Regent in Paris, declared against the man who had married his daughter and a hundred thousand Austrians came in on the side of the Czar.

Napoleon's enemies now included the Russians, the Prussian nationalists, the English, who were busy herding Brother Joseph across Spain, the Swedes, led by a renegade French Marshal, the Spaniards, who were merrily boiling their French captives in oil and crucifying stragglers to convent walls, and finally every disgruntled aristocrat whom Napoleon's amnesties had failed to tempt back to Paris.

It was only a matter of time, time and awareness on the part of cautious autocrats that they now had this demon by the tail.

In January 1814, he was still whirling his little army about the fields and villages of north-eastern France; by April it was all but over, with Ney himself demanding an abdication and declaring, gravely, that 'the army would obey its chiefs before the Emperor!'

What had happened to Marie Louise?

During the brief season of barren, summer victories she had joined her husband at Mayence and they had found time to take a few drives together. In August, when her father joined his enemies, she returned to Paris and there, on the brink of his campaign to defend France, he was able to rejoin her for a brief spell.

He rolled the King of Rome on the floor, romping with him for the last time before hurrying back to all that remained of his army, fifty thousand exhausted, frostbitten men, who were still able to tumble the dispersed allies out of many of the positions they occupied.

In mid-March Napoleon inadvertently sealed his own doom. In a letter written to his wife he confided to her a plan to strike at the allied communications. The vital despatch fell into the enemy's hands and Czar Alexander at last decided to call Napoleon's bluff.

Ignoring the squirming French army he marched round

it and attacked Paris, a Paris with more traitors in its councils than there were honest defenders up on the walls.

Poor silly Marie Louise was quite distracted. She had never expected to face a crisis of this nature. Talleyrand urged her to stay and defend the capital, others urged flight with the government to Rambouillet and this was the course she followed, leaving Paris to be surrendered without a fight.

She can hardly be blamed. The city was given up to the conquerors by Marshal Marmont, Napoleon's oldest friend, and among his advisers was harassed brother Joseph, who had just abandoned an empty throne in Spain. Even the Emperor himself had written urging her to take precautions not to let herself and the King of Rome fall into the enemy's power.

At eleven o'clock on the night of the 29th March, after endless orders, counter-orders and delays, Marie Louise and her train set out for Rambouillet. Two days later Paris was occupied and Napoleon, who had been on his way to defend it, turned back to Fontainebleau.

He was never again to set eyes on his son or the woman whom he had chosen to found his dynasty.

CHAPTER XXI

The Chaperon

She did not remain at Rambouillet. Hopeless panic had now overtaken the relatives and adherents of Napoleon and with the exit of the Empress and her son from Paris the entire edifice began to crumble.

Under weeping skies the Bonapartists scuttled in every direction, hardly one of them sparing a thought for anything but their own personal futures. There had never been a betrayal on this scale. In Paris of 1814 loyalty was not worth a sou.

The cataract of fear carried the Imperial train through Rambouillet, through Chartres (where breathless Brother Joseph overtook it) and down to Blois on the Loire. Here the dripping courtiers stayed to catch their second wind and there was even talk of crossing the Loire and raising the countryside in defence of the eagles.

It was not to be. Couriers arrived with worse news from Fontainebleau. Joseph, and his brother Jerome, tried to eject Marie Louise from her temporary sanctuary by main force but other advisers offered conflicting plans and she refused to move deeper into the provinces. Secretary Méneval, fearing for the famous Regent diamond which was attached to a sword, broke the weapon in half and concealed the diamond in the Empress's workbag!

After a few days' lull roving bands of Cossacks began to appear and Marie Louise, pale, tired and hopelessly adrift on a seat of doubt, fancied that she would be taken prisoner by these shaggy horsemen. She therefore accepted a plan to move back to Rambouillet and throw herself on her father's mercy. Even this scheme was only half implemented. The royal refugees, taking with them all the Imperial plate, a fortune in diamonds and twelve million francs, trailed off to Orleans, where they hung about waiting for hard news to emerge from the whirlpools of rumour.

Already, whilst still at Blois, the Empress had received more or less official news of her husband's abdication.

She had also been informed of his half-hearted attempt to commit suicide by taking a non-lethal dose of poison. This shocking intelligence harassed but by no means overwhelmed her. It was, in fact, quite impossible to overwhelm Marie Louise. The messenger is said to have conveyed the news to her whilst she was in bed 'with her naked feet protruding from the coverlet'. Instead of bewailing the moral collapse of her husband and the material collapse of the Empire, the Empress, according to the chronicler, coyly noted the direction of the messenger's gaze and remarked : 'Aha ! I see you are looking at my pretty feet !'

Such was the woman the Victor of Austerlitz had chosen for a mate. Even Joséphine could have improved on her conduct under fire.

At Orleans a commissioner of the new Paris government arrived with a somewhat more sinister purpose than that of circulating the latest news from the capital. He had been sent, he declared, to make a clean sweep of Napoleon's money and jewellery, now regarded as the property of the State !

Glumly the Imperialists handed over all that was available and the licensed thief went off with the loot. There was nobody to argue the legal aspect of the demand and the man seems to have known his business, for he not only emptied the workbag and found the diamond, but appropriated all the Imperial plate, leaving the Empress without so much as a drinking-cup !

Marie Louise, pushed this way and that by biased and conflicting counsels, began to question her child-like faith in Papa. 'How is it my father allows this?' she wailed. 'When I was married he promised faithfully to uphold my rights !'

Francis, even had he been so inclined, was not in a position to uphold anybody's rights at that moment in history. He had been a latecomer to the wake and the Czar of Russia, who had chased Napoleon all the way from Moscow, regarded him as a very junior partner in the enterprise.

Left to himself the Czar, an incurable romantic, would probably have confirmed Marie Louise as Regent during her son's minority. 'I don't know these Bourbons,' he remarked, when the legitimists were pressing their claims for reinstatement, but the Bourbons lost no time in introducing themselves to the victor and the slender opportunity of safeguarding the King of Rome's heritage was lost.

The Czar then had a madcap notion of making Bernadotte, traitor French Marshal, Crown Prince of Sweden and arch-trimmer of Europe, a King in Napoleon's place. Had he done so little Désirée would have at last won the crown she missed by a hairsbreadth in 1796, when her father, the soap manufacturer, was reported to have remarked, 'One Bonaparte in the family is enough!'

Such an idea, however, was quite unacceptable to the French soldiers. Some of them might be disposed to shout a casual 'Vive le Roi!' instead of a 'Vive l'Empereur!' and many civilians were already sporting the white cockade of the Bourbons, but soldiers and civilians stopped short of enthroning a man who had led an army of Swedes against his fellow countrymen and had cantered into Paris in the company of Cossacks and Prussian hussars.

By mid-April the situation had sorted itself out.

Napoleon wrote to his wife in a more optimistic vein, explaining that he was being exiled to the isle of Elba and was due to leave Fontainebleau for the Mediterranean immediately. He wrote to her in affectionate terms. 'A kiss for the little King,' he concluded.

This news seemed conclusive enough and Marie Louise at once left Orleans for Rambouillet, where she was informed that she was to become the Duchess of Parma and that her son would inherit the Duchy on her death.

At Fontainebleau Napoleon resigned himself to not seeing his wife and child again until he was established in his island kingdom and on 30 April he set out on his long journey.

It was to prove one of the most terrible experiences in his life.

As he progressed south the cries of 'Vive l'Empereur' grew noticeably fainter and when he entered Provence he was greeted by jeers and violence.

He had always hated mobs and the experience unnerved him, so much so that he disguised himself as an Austrian officer and rode ahead of his carriage. He even had the interesting experience of hearing himself described as a tyrannical monster by a serving girl at an inn.

The journey occupied a week, during which time he had ample opportunity to assess the real value of popular acclaim.

At one town he saw himself burned and shot in effigy. At Valence, the scene of his first romance, he was met and reviled by his old companion-in-arms, Marshal Augereau. The Marshal had followed the example of practically all the men and women who owed their titles and fortunes to this pale, morose traveller.

The conquerors had now agreed among themselves what should be done with Empress and child.

First it was unanimously decided that both should be prevented from joining with the fallen Emperor. Then it seemed necessary to the peace of Europe that the young Napoleon should be kept separated from his mother and isolated from any Frenchman who entertained strange ideas of loyalty to his father. In accordance with these decisions Marie Louise was persuaded to set out for Vienna and she and her son travelled via Dresden, where they were met by Marie's stepmother. The latter was enjoying to the full the overthrow of the man she hated.

It was a very different meeting from the Dresden encounter of two years before, when the Austrian Empress had pounced on her stepdaughter's magnificent wardrobe. Now it was Marie Louise who came as a pensioner and the party travelled down to the Austrian capital with the ex-Empress still in doubt as to what kind of future was in store for her.

Dull and unimaginative she undoubtedly was but she was not without some misgivings as to how her behaviour would strike the exile. Thus far she can be excused her blunders and confusion. In the space of four years she had been rocketed from the mental isolation of an impoverished court to a seat beside the most dominant man in the world. Thence she had been reduced almost overnight to the position of borrowing cups and plates.

She did not worry overmuch about her son's future. His governess, 'Mama 'Quiou', was still in nominal charge of the boy and the conquerors told Marie Louise that she might, if she wished, obey her physician's instructions and take the waters at Aix, in Savoy; on condition, of course, that she left her boy behind in Vienna.

She drifted away happily enough and fugitive Bonapartists told themselves that she was only pretending to be complaisant and that Aix was not very distant from the Eagle's new cage, at Elba.

Perhaps she did have some vague idea of using the pretext of a medical cure to flee the mainland and join her husband, or perhaps she still believed those who told her that such an action would jeopardize her own future and that of her son. No one will ever really know for whilst, in certain circumstances, it is possible to read the mind of an intelligent person it is impossible to read a mind that barely exists.

She set out for Aix in June and at a stage outside Geneva she met a horseman, sent by her father to act as her equerry. Rightly she supposed him to be a spy in Austrian pay.

She did not take very kindly to this gentleman at first. His appearance was grave and dignified, without being in any way impressive. He wore the uniform of an Austrian hussar and a black patch obscured his right eye. He looked somewhat older than thirty-nine, his correct age so they told her. From the outset he treated her with elaborate courtesy and respect.

Later on, at Aix, she came to know him rather better and her attitude to him gradually changed.

He had, it seemed, the complete confidence of her father, of Schwarzenberg, the Austrian Commander-in-Chief, and of Metternich. He was an accomplished musician, a married man with a family and something of a dandy in appearance and deportment. Above all, he possessed, in her estimation at least, a store of profound wisdom and a very pleasant way of imparting it to her.

His name was Neipperg, Count Adam Neipperg, and he had a curious duty to fulfil.

Count Neipperg had been very carefully selected for the post of equerry to the ex-Empress but his qualifications were not the kind that are set down on paper, not even in secret correspondence between professional diplomats.

It has never been established who actually selected him in the first place, or who gave him his detailed instructions, but whoever it was was an excellent judge of character. In Neipperg the Habsburgs found an ace of trumps.

Marie Louise took the waters of Aix very seriously. She was there practically the whole summer and Napoleon, who had learned of her whereabouts, heartily approved the idea in spite of the fact that he was now desperately anxious that his wife and child should join him in exile.

Spies on both sides came and went. One agent carried a lock of Marie's hair across to Elba, and during the early part of her stay at the spa the ex-Empress seems almost to have made up her mind that her duty lay in complying with her exiled husband's wishes.

This was Neipperg's cue. Fervently he explained to his ward how dangerous it would be to join him and how surely it would bring down upon her the wrath of her father and all his powerful friends. Steadily he kept up the pressure, hinting, explaining, reasoning, pleading, and each night he sent off a despatch reporting his progress to the anxious statesmen gathered at Vienna.

His reports were carefully scrutinized. Engaged as they were in the task of repartitioning Europe, the Captains and Kings in Vienna could still spare an hour or two to speculate on what might happen if Napoleon succeeded in enlisting world sympathy on account of his forcible separation from wife and child. It was essential, therefore, that the rupture should appear to originate from Marie Louise and demonstrate to all that it was she, the wife and mother, who had deliberately ranged herself with her husband's enemies. To compel her to quit Savoy and move to somewhere far removed from Elba, would lay the victors open to a charge of inhumanity towards a beaten foe.

By midsummer the signs were encouraging. In issuing orders to Neipperg to go to Aix the Emperor Francis had written : 'Help my daughter with advice' and in a month or so a letter arrived in Vienna from Marie Louise herself, referring in glowing terms to Neipperg's expert chaperonage and admitting : 'His manner pleases me !'

How well it pleased her the world was soon to discover. Shortly before Napoleon embarked upon his last throw and escaped from Elba to tumble the Bourbons out of France, Marie Louise, who had never been permitted to own a male animal but now had one in permanent attendance upon her, was expecting another child. Its father was a one-eyed equerry, noted for his persuasive manners.

The Princes of Europe, who were in the habit of describing Napoleon as the Beast of the Apocalypse, looked on and applauded.

CHAPTER XXII

Joséphine Entertains

Another woman who had been wife to Napoleon did some entertaining that summer, but it was conducted more openly than her successor's had been.

When news reached Malmaison that Cossacks were prancing round the half-finished Arc-de-Triomphe, Joséphine had a conviction that the wheel of fortune had now turned a full circle and that she might at any moment be thrust back into the equivalent of the little cell at Les Carmes, there to await the dread summons.

She shared her former husband's fastidious horror of mobs and she reflected that the hordes now advancing on the capital were not expected to remember her with affection. She was not a good-luck talisman to Russians and Prussians but simply the ex-wife of their arch enemy. She may also have recalled the fate of Dubarry, the mistress of a long-dead King who was hauled to the guillotine in the name of her royal lover.

Joséphine's daughter, Hortense, was one of the very few who kept her nerve during that terrible spring and Hortense advised her mother to take refuge at her hunting-box, in Navarre. Whither she fled, in a coach crammed with gowns and gold trinkets, a tempting windfall to deserters and marauders who had already pillaged their way across Europe in the wake of the armies.

It proved an exciting journey. When a few horsemen appeared on the skyline Joséphine's nerve gave way altogether. Instead of waiting to identify the strangers she leaped from the coach and fled madly across open fields, followed by a breathless footman.

The servant was not quite so distraught as his mistress and soon persuaded her that the horsemen were French. Fearfully she returned to the coach and continued her journey. At Navarre she was joined by a calm and resigned Hortense, who told her the news. Napoleon was down but she had nothing whatever to fear from his enemies, particularly the handsome and romantic Czar.

She had her customary weep and swift, inevitable recovery. She was even able to spare a sympathetic thought for the loneliness and despair of the man who had once written to her – 'Joséphine, be vigilant! One fine night the doors will be broken in and I shall be before you!'

There was not the slightest prospect of this happening now. A million armed men interposed between them and soon he would be even farther off than he was when he wrote her that wonderful letter from Milan.

It was time to consider her future and make her own dispositions and being Joséphine she was able to consider and dispose without finding it necessary to slander the man who had once worshipped her. A fortnight after her arrival in Navarre the Czar's aide-de-camp called and she found that she was in luck. The visitor happened to be an old friend and spoke up for her to his master.

Czar Alexander reacted to this appeal as a man of his temperament was certain to react. He despatched a courier with reassuring and flattering messages and as a result of these there was a hurried repacking and a prompt return to Malmaison.

Hortense, who took her official duties very seriously, left her mother for a time in order to remain at the side of the distracted Empress but the moment Marie Louise made up her mind to bow to her father's wishes she returned to Malmaison and took part in the social activities that were beginning to centre round Joséphine.

Hortense reached Malmaison on 16 April, just ten days after the conditional abdication of Napoleon. She found the garden full of Cossacks. Expressing surprise she was told that 'her mother was out walking with the Czar'.

Joséphine was a very fast worker when her dress allowance was threatened.

Alexander was the kind of man whom Joséphine was born to manage. Vain, mystical and generous, he saw himself as a latter-day Sir Galahad engaged upon knightly ventures. Joséphine, an ageing woman who had been set aside for a younger wife, appealed to his sense of chivalry and he went out of his way to be kind to her.

He became protector, friend and confidant, at once guaranteeing the payment of her French pension and doing as much for that of Hortense.

Paris settled down. More and more notabilities posted off to Malmaison. A visit to Joséphine became *de rigueur* for all the Princes and Princelings who had contributed to Napoleon's downfall. An extraordinary air of prosperity graced the lawns and terraces of the home that her taste had made so beautiful. The King of Prussia called and then the Crown Prince of Sweden, whose wife had once been cheated of a diadem by this slim, engaging woman. The Czar himself was often there, playing hide-and-seek with Hortense's children, and there was even a whisper that Joséphine's son, the redoubtable Eugène, might still be chosen Emperor of the French.

Nothing came of this, Joséphine's fondest hope. There were too many turbulent allies to be consulted and conciliated and in the end it was their arguments, and the tortuous policy of Talleyrand that prevailed. The Bourbon, fat and gouty, waddled back to the Tuileries after his interminable exile and Hortense, gibbering with rage, learned that Louis XVIII, brother to the King who had perished on the scaffold twenty-one years ago, regarded the year 1814 as the *nineteenth of his reign*!

Even the Czar was unable to digest this morsel and almost choked when he was told about it.

Joséphine, however, who had done plenty of date-juggling

herself, made the best of a bad job. She sent for Eugène and soon persuaded him to ingratiate himself with the new King.

There had been a time when Napoleon had begged her to face facts and he could have had no cause for complaint in this respect now. She had learned the art of fact-facing from a man who had neglected his own rules about how to behave realistically. Ultimately he had pursued so many shadows that he was now living in a house smaller than the one in which he had been born.

In May 1814, Joséphine was fifty years of age and this was her final season as a hostess.

On 23 May she was entertaining the King of Prussia. That same evening Hortense was entertaining the Czar, in Paris.

Late at night Hortense was summoned by her brother with news that their mother was seriously ill. The Czar at once despatched his own doctor to the patient and son and daughter hurried off to Malmaison.

On the 25th Joséphine was to have received yet another visit from the Czar but when he came she was too ill to receive him. By midday on the 29th she was dead.

Even her sudden death was made the excuse for another Bourbon slander against Napoleon. In the official announcement it was stated : '... extremely unhappy during her husband's reign, she sought refuge from his roughness and neglect in the study of botany' !

The charge was trebly false, Joséphine had thoroughly enjoyed the greater part of her life with Napoleon and she had commenced her study of botany in Martinique, when she was barefoot queen of the piccaninnies. During their long association as man and wife Napoleon had been ardent, deceitful, cynical, forgiving, casual and often exasperating in his treatment of Joséphine. Never once had he shown her roughness or neglect.

Sentimentalists in Paris – and there were still some to be found even in that dizzy season – put it about that the ex-Empress had died of grief. They were exaggerating; she died of diphtheria.

CHAPTER XXIII

'Master of the situation!'

Measuring only eighteen miles from east to west, the sun-drenched, sea-girt island of Elba had been by-passed by the worst storms of the last twenty years. It was inhabited by peasants and iron-workers, the former engaged in raising crops of fruit, the latter in extracting ore from profitable mines that had been worked since Roman times. There were also a few fishermen earning a meagre living from their saltpans and the sale of tunny-fish.

Elba is a beautiful place, with landlocked bays, deep woods and a ridge as high as Snowdon in the interior, but the new master of the island was not concerned with its natural beauties, except in so far as they might be coaxed to increase its revenue.

His furious mental activity, compressed into a small pond after having had oceans in which to wallow, at once began to thrust out in all directions, building, reorganizing, exploiting, calculating. The nervous force that, for nearly two decades, had been directed upon wide continents was now concentrated on a single, populated rock. Its effect upon the inhabitants was salutary.

The revenues were itemized, a navy consisting of 'a rotten old brig' and a few feluccas was organized, an Elban flag was designed complete with Napoleon's heraldic bees, and all the toy 'palaces' were given over to an assault column of builders and decorators.

Even an army was enrolled and probably no army in the world ever possessed such a preponderance of hard-fighting veterans, for the Great Powers, in their unwisdom, had allowed Napoleon to enrol six hundred of his guard as protector of his tiny kingdom. The allies would have done much better to have banned the guardsmen and let him take his wife and child.

For a bare month or so Napoleon was deeply absorbed in his little game of state-building, but after all it was a game and soon his main occupation on the island switched to entertaining his occasional visitors and pumping them for news from the mainland.

His first visitor was sister Pauline, favourite among his brothers and sisters, the beautiful, sensual woman whose love affairs had scandalized Europe.

Pauline was by far the most amiable of the Bonaparte clan and was also the prettiest and wittiest. Having once posed in the nude for the famous sculptor Canova she remarked, when asked if the pose had not made her 'a little uncomfortable?' – 'But of course not! There was a fire in the room!'

She remained on the island for two days and then left, returning to make her home there in October. Her giddy round of balls, fêtes and theatrical displays dumbfounded the the simple Elbans, who were beginning to wonder if a genie had transformed their little island into a setting for Arabian nights.

In August his mother arrived, also with every intention of remaining.

The grave, hard-fisted old Corsican was far more to the Elbans' taste than her son and daughter. She at once cut through the tinsel trimmings and set about doing everything possible to improve the islanders' standard of living.

She did not go to work in a grandiose, spectacular way or match her daughter's glittering behaviour but moved quietly round the island doing good in the style of a great lady, conscious of responsibilities towards the poor and lowly.

Sane, sensible Madame Mère! She had never been dazzled by the pomp and circumstance of the Empire and had made no secret of her misgivings. 'One day it will all disappear,' she had warned them, when they laughed at her peasant's parsimony and chided her for refusing to spend the money they lavished upon her. Events had now proved her right. Empire and incomes had disappeared overnight and here she was, doling out millions of francs to her head-strong son whose annual allowance, promised so readily by the Bourbons when he was still resisting an unconditional abdication, was being withheld month after month and causing him considerable financial embarrassment.

As the summer wore on and blazing sunshine beat down on the busy little kingdom the curious, globetrotting English began to appear, sailors and noblemen, some of whom had been fighting this man for more than twenty-one years.

They found him talkative and affable. They listened politely when he told them that an invasion of England would have succeeded and that the world could only be made safe for the middle classes by a concordat between the British navy and the French Army.

Then it became too hot to remain at sea-level and the exile and his small suite moved up into the mountains, occupying a four-roomed Hermitage, the Hermitage of Our Lady of Marciana, a building set in a beautiful forest of chestnuts and surrounded by banks of wild flowers.

It was here, on 1 September, that he received the most distinguished visitor of all, the woman with whom he had sat before blazing, open fires in the gloomy castle of Fincken-stein, during the winter lull between the desperate fighting at Eylau and the triumphs at Friedland and Tilsit.

She was a little stouter than she had been in the days and nights when he had found solace and ecstasy in her company but she was still very beautiful and so was her four-year-old son, the fruit of their renewed association during the see-saw Austrian campaign of 1809.

Walewska's visit was shrouded in secrecy and there were sound reasons for this. Behind a façade of furious outward activity Napoleon had had one primary objective through-out spring and summer – to entice his wife and the King of Rome to Elba and demonstrate to the world that his marriage into the oldest royal house of Europe was still acknowledged in the chancelleries of the world.

Plea after plea, letter after letter, gushed from his pen and was conveyed, openly or secretly, to the mainland. Each urged Marie Louise to pack up and join him, to occupy rooms that he had prepared for her in all his residences on the island. One such letter told how the ceiling in one boudoir now bore the device of two doves, tied together with a cord. The idea behind this motif was that lovers only increased the strength of their bonds by attempting to fly in different directions!

No wonder Walewska's visit was hushed up and even disguised as a visit by the Empress and the King of Rome. No breath of scandal must add to her difficulties in bringing about this reunion. No tittle-tattle of a renewed association with a mistress was to tempt her to think twice of bringing the King of Rome into his miniature realm.

There was no point in all the elaborate precautions he took to make the visit of Walewska and her child secret. His siege of Marie Louise was a dismal failure. His literary bombardment made no impression at all on a wife who was already betraying him, not only actively but in the more important and less defensible sense, for all his letters were laid dutifully before his father-in-law's counsellors and it was not until New Year's Day, 1815, that she at last sent a vague reply to his appeals.

Napoleon met Marie Walewska and her son within riding distance of his Hermitage. Because her carriage was unable to negotiate the mountain track he mounted his guests on horses and they completed the journey by moonlight.

The visitors were accommodated in the little house, the host sharing a tent with his two valets. We do not know whether the visitors were comfortable in their homely surroundings. We do know that Napoleon did not sleep at all.

Marie Walewska had not travelled to Elba from motives of curiosity. Neither had she been tempted there by an affectionate longing to see him again. She had changed a great deal since the day when Marshal Duroc and Prince Poniatowski had laid siege to her bedroom, and earnest patriots had had so much difficulty in persuading her to violate her marriage vows. Both Duroc and Poniatowski were now dead but Marie Walewska had learned a great deal about life during the past seven years. She was, in fact, considerably wiser and sadder at twenty-five than she had been at eighteen and she had come to Elba to discuss money. Her object was to enquire whether or not her lover could persuade brother-in-law Murat to pay the Imperial mistress her pension arrears!

It is not surprising to learn that the pension was long overdue. Cavalryman Murat had other things to think about that summer. He and his vitriolic wife, Caroline, were now desperately engaged in trying to extract a modest profit from the French eclipse and insure themselves against a very uncertain future. The pension that the Emperor had arranged to be paid to Marie Walewska by the King of Naples could go hang. The former innkeeper's son and his cold-blooded wife needed every ducat they could lay hands upon.

Talks of money did not cloud the happy occasion however and the clearing among the chestnuts was the scene of a gay and enjoyable picnic the following morning.

Breakfast was eaten in the open, the child sitting beside Napoleon, despite his mother's protests that he would prove a great nuisance to his host.

Little Alexander-Florian did not justify his mother's fears and behaved himself very well. His father delighted in him and once the boy's initial shyness had disappeared he prattled away to this gentle, playful man, who seemed so interested in his mother's conversation. Napoleon spoke to him of his own childhood in Corsica, where he and his sister had once been given a sound thrashing for making fun of their grandmother.

'I don't make fun of my mamma!' replied the child and Napoleon laughed, pronouncing this 'a pretty answer'.

They spent the day walking the woods, where the child gathered armfuls of wildflowers. As night fell he escorted mother and son to the coast and Walewska sailed away, the richer by a gift of sixty-one thousand francs and one likes to hope, another pleasant memory.

They were to see one another again.

On 15 February yet another visitor disembarked at Porto Ferrajo, this time a Frenchman concerning whom Campbell, an English observer, noted in his journal, 'a man arrived under the guise of a sailor calling himself "Pietro St Ernest".'

The unlikely sailor's purpose in visiting Elba was not concerned with the payment of pension arrears. It had to do with rather more important matters, the seething discontent of the French nation, for instance, and the degree of support an ex-Emperor might count upon if he staked all on a desperate descent upon the mainland.

That same month the 'rotten old brig' constituting the principal item of the new Elba navy stole out to sea without its navigation lights showing. Its decks were packed with men, sunburned, moustached men, who had once tumbled down Kings and governments like rows of ninepins. The half-finished royal palaces of Elba were forgotten, for their would-be renovator now had his eyes on another palace, a building where Bourbon fleur-de-lys had recently been sewn over the bees that decorated the carpets.

On 1 March 1815, the tiny flotilla landed at Fréjus. Nineteen days later its commander entered Paris and the fat King who claimed to have reigned over France for nineteen years bolted for the coast.

Marie Louise received the news with horror. She sought an emergency consultation with her uncle, the Archduke John, but Uncle John had little comfort to offer. 'I hope for your sake and ours that he breaks his damned neck!' he growled.

This, and a stream of messengers who somehow found their way to her, gave the mistress of General Neipperg grave cause for concern. One letter, dated 28 March, a bare eight days after the eagle had perched upon Notre Dame, was couched in particularly strident terms. 'Meet me in Strasbourg', it screamed; 'I am master of the situation!'

CHAPTER XXIV

'My friends, you stifle me!'

Napoleon reached the Tuileries on the evening of 20 March and the palace was so crowded with adherents waiting to greet him that he was soon in grave danger of being suffocated by their enthusiasm.

He advanced inch by inch up the main staircase, a devoted follower retreating backwards in front of him in an effort to clear a passage through the press of courtiers. Even loyal mobs upset Napoleon. He cried aloud : 'My friends, you stifle me !'

How many among that hysterical throng were real friends and how many women who had basked in his favours or built fortunes on his bounty? Not many. Most of those who welcomed him back had nothing but scars to show for their loyalty.

Marie Walewska was there, having come posting up from Italy the moment she heard the news.

Madame Duchâtel, the object of his brief, passionate affair, of ten years before, was present and she was to remain faithful to the very end.

Georgina, the plump little actress, was loud in her protestations of loyalty and managed, somehow or other, to convey information of value to him.

For the rest his mistresses were either actively anti-Bonapartist, and loud in their denunciations of him, or disinclined to abandon a seat on the fence and jeopardize their fortunes and social positions by open espousal of his cause.

Madame de Vaudey, who had applied successfully to him time and again for money to settle her gambling debts, had recently made a petition of a different nature. She asked the

Bourbon authorities for a post-chaise in order to intercept Napoleon on his way to Paris and resolve Europe's dilemma once and for all by an act of assassination.

'La Bellilotte,' once Madame Fourès, who had paraded the streets of Cairo beside him and been hailed by the troops as the new Cleopatra, was still enjoying the social round, writing her novels, painting self-portraits and on the point of eloping with another man. So far had she strayed from the bower of infatuation with Napoleon that she was soon to publish a violent repudiation of the rumour that she had volunteered to accompany her former lover to St Helena !

Grassini, the opera singer, was still in Paris or thereabouts, but she sang him no arias of welcome. Perhaps she was saving her voice for the man who was to set the seal on Napoleon's doom at Waterloo in a few weeks' time. She was forty-two now but her great talent was still in demand, and so, it would appear, were her incidental charms.

Thérèse Bourgoin, the actress who had never forgiven Napoleon for the loss of her wealthy, middle-aged lover, was actively campaigning against him.

Poor Eléonore, who had just married her third husband and returned to Paris, was already enmeshed in a net of blackmail spread by her disreputable first husband. She had much on her mind at this time, too much to take part in a welcome-home party.

Marie Louise was safe in Vienna, where she had every intention of remaining until the Allied Armies had once again succeeded in cornering this terrible husband of hers.

Joséphine, Our Lady of Victories, was dead.

One other woman in Napoleon's past was resident in Paris at that time. She had no business at all to be there but had flatly refused to leave. The reason for this obstinacy on her part was not regard for Napoleon. It stemmed from the simple fact that Désirée Bernadotte, once Désirée Clary, found it impossible to exist outside the range of the Paris gownshops and out of earshot of the capital's salon-gossip.

Once upon a time this engaging little lady had flirted with the idea of marrying a penniless artilleryman. Instead she had married General Bernadotte and had become, in due course, Crown Princess of Sweden.

Désirée's continued presence in the French capital was evidence of Napoleon's essential tolerance and Désirée's appalling lack of tact.

Less than two years before her husband had led his Swedes into the camp of his country's enemies. Even less than a year ago he had been seen swaggering about Paris in the company of the invaders. These actions on his part did nothing to disconcert his wife. She continued to act as though her husband was still shedding his blood in French company. Some said that she was a spy for the allies but those who said this could have known very little about Désirée and nothing about Napoleon Bonaparte. Désirée did not possess sufficient intelligence to note down anything more important than the cut and colour of a rival's ball-dress, and Napoleon, strangely tolerant as he was with the vagaries of old friends, was not such a fool as to suffer a highly-placed agent to practise espionage under his nose. If the Crown Princess of Sweden had been in Paris for the purpose of reporting upon troop-movements there is not the slightest doubt but that she would have been under lock and key within an hour of her presence being made known to him.

She was not arrested and was not, so far as is known, placed under observation. She was still in Paris on 12 June, six days before Waterloo, pottering in and out of gown-shops and ordering a nankeen riding-habit from Leroy's, the principal fashion house.

It was not until the allies had again closed on the capital that we hear of her joining her husband in Stockholm and even then she went very unwillingly, bewailing a fate that separated her, by hundreds of miles, from shops and scenes that were her sole delight.

Désirée mourned Paris to the end. She never resigned herself to the Spartan pleasures of the north. Of the women in the life of Napoleon Désirée Clary was not the most alluring. She did, however, possess the strongest nerves and the thickest skin.

The moment it became obvious that the allied Sovereigns were resolved upon a renewal of war Napoleon displayed what was to prove his final burst of energy.

Women play no part in his feverish life during the Hundred Days. The tempo of life in Paris was too swift for dalliance.

Carnot had been sent for, Carnot, the Organizer of Victory in the far-off days of the guillotine and a threatened Republic. He asked the Emperor if he had returned to Europe with the blessing of any of the Powers and when told by Napoleon that this was not the case he shook his head.

'Then you have as much to do as you have already done!' he commented.

The Emperor did his best and in the circumstances it was a very good best indeed.

He first tried to persuade his opponents that he was sick and tired of war and had only returned to France on a tide of antipathy to the Bourbons. He would, he affirmed, be no trouble to anyone. He would frame a liberal constitution and rule quietly and justly, without recourse to war.

It was not to be. Britain and Prussia were already on the march and behind them, firmly united for once, were the legions of his Austrian father-in-law and ex-Marshal Bernadotte. Behind these again were the swarming battalions of the Czar.

It would have helped his prestige enormously if Marie Louise could have been persuaded to join him, or in event of being prevented from doing so by force, had made an attempt to escape from her father's custody.

The means to try were available. There were plenty of Bonapartists in Vienna and at least three of them, Governess Montesquiou, her adventurous son, and Napoleon's former secretary, Méneval, were still fanatically loyal to the Emperor.

The danger of their presence so near the King of Rome was not lost upon their gaolers.

The moment Napoleon's flight from Elba became known the French members of the household were either closely watched or dismissed. The Keeper of the Empress's Privy Purse came home in April and was closeted with Napoleon for two hours. He brought news of the Empress and of the King of Rome but he could not nerve himself to tell Napoleon of his wife's open association with Neipperg.

The anxious husband despatched two trusted agents to the Austrian capital, with instructions to get to the ear of Marie Louise by any means at their disposal. One of them succeeded in penetrating the allied lines but his enterprise was unavailing. Marie Louise was sitting tight in Vienna and did not even want to hear about Napoleon.

Then Méneval, a trusted member of the Empress's household, was dismissed and found his way back to Paris. Méneval was very devoted to his former master but he was a kind-hearted man and could only bring himself to hint at what had happened whilst Napoleon was exiled in Elba.

By this time it must have been clear to Napoleon that his wife had shamelessly betrayed him but it was not good policy to broadcast this news in Paris. It was far better that the public should continue to believe that the Empress and her son were being detained against their will, for this invested him with an air of martyrdom and the least scrap of sympathy was welcome to him in such a crisis.

Méneval did in fact bring him an unequivocal statement of the Empress's intentions. She had surrendered custody of her son two days before his father had returned to Paris and in so doing had written; 'I shall never consent to a divorce but I flatter myself that he will agree to an amicable separation. This has become inevitable but it will in no wise affect my feelings towards him of gratitude or esteem.'

The statement was almost certainly dictated by her

father's advisers or perhaps by Neipperg himself. Marie Louise's brain was not equipped to think such thoughts, much less commit them to paper.

Having failed in all his endeavours to persuade her to re-join him Napoleon turned over the possibilities of kidnapping his son. He offered a large reward to anyone who could succeed in whisking the four-year-old child from his Austrian captors.

The son of 'Mama 'Quiou' considered the ways and means of achieving this and there was a good deal of cloak-and-dagger talk and coach journeys in disguise. In the end, however, he made his escape from Vienna alone, only to be turned back at the frontier, arrested, and kept under guard until all was over and Napoleon was a fugitive.

To make doubly sure 'Mama 'Quiou' was also arrested and kept under guard.

Meanwhile the curtain was rising on the final scene and the Imperial army marched out to fight its last battles in the north-east.

Before it left the Parisians were regaled with a final display of Imperial splendour, the Emperor reviewing his troops in the Champ de Mai.

Escorted by heralds, squadrons of glittering cavalry and the veterans of the Guard, the Emperor came riding in his coronation coach. Instead of his familiar campaigning clothes he wore silk robes, the Imperial mantle and a hat crowned with ostrich plumes. He sat alone and those who saw him pass remembered that his first wife was dead, his second wife had gone over to the enemy and his son was a prisoner, surrounded by strangers. Many were sorry for him, too few had confidence in his ability to stem the tide of fortune and turn it in his favour.

They could have been wrong, at least for a limited period.

Within a fortnight of his last pageant he had smashed the Prussians at Ligny and turned on the British holding the ridge that guarded Brussels. After that things went awry and by sunset on 18 June this pale, plump adventurer was being jostled down the road to Paris again, surrounded by the wreck of a beaten army.

By 21 June he was in the capital, a city where jittery politicians were only anxious to be rid of him. He made another half-hearted attempt to abdicate in favour of his captive son but nobody took him seriously and in the end he drifted aimlessly out to Malmaison.

His escort consisted of a few men with a price on their heads and two women who had shared his years of triumph, women whom no reverse of fortune could tempt into the ranks of the neutrals. One was his mother. The other was his stepdaughter and sister-in-law, Hortense, the girl who had wept and wept when she heard that he was going to marry her widowed mother.

It was Hortense who had accompanied him on the occasion of his pilgrimage to Malmaison a few weeks before.

Together they had walked through rooms where every item of furniture, every curtain, carpet and wall-hanging was evidence of Joséphine's matchless taste. When he paused outside the room in which she had died he told Hortense that he preferred to go in alone, and when he emerged she saw that he was weeping.

Now Joséphine lay buried at Reuil, close by, but there was not even time to visit her tomb. The victorious allies were pouring into the suburbs of Paris and he had been declared an outlaw. The Prussians had orders to shoot him on sight.

Even so he could hardly drag himself away. Where could he go and what could he do? He half made up his mind to flee by frigate to America but by the time he reached the coast the British cruisers were blockading all the exits to the Atlantic.

Even his intimates had fallen away. His mother talked of accompanying him across the sea but he told her that she was far too old for such a jaunt. He was desperately short of ready money and Hortense gave him her jewelled necklace, sewing it inside a silk belt as if he had been a young adventurer setting out on a journey across a strange continent.

Hortense stayed at his side throughout every moment of these anxious days, only leaving him to go into her own exile when he made up his mind to surrender to the British Navy.

In the last week of maddening indecisions we hear nothing of Walewska or any of the beautiful women who had hovered so hopefully to catch his glance at the balls, levées and whist-parties. Only of Hortense, his stepdaughter and the impassive Madame Mère, who had never been persuaded that the Empire was more substantial than a handful of Corsican rock sand.

The others, men and women alike, were scattered, making their peace with Blücher and Wellington or spurring just ahead of the Bourbon firing-squad like Marshals Soult and Ney.

His friends had not pressed closely enough.

CHAPTER XXV

Tropical Siberia

Chance visitors to the room Napoleon occupied at Long-wood, his official St Helena residence, were at once struck by the repellent drabness of the room.

There was little about the folding camp-bed, the unre-markable furnishings or the mean little fireplace to suggest that this was the bedchamber of a man who had once ruled half the world. The sole reminders of the occupant's former position in life were the portraits.

On the wall, immediately over the grate, was Isabey's por-trait of Marie Louise. To the right, nearer the door, was Joséphine's portrait. Round the room, on each side of these pictures, were no fewer than six portraits of the King of Rome. There were no portraits of any of the multitude of women he had courted. He had, it would seem, outgrown promiscuity.

There was much else that he had outgrown by the time he stepped into the ship's barge of the *Northumberland* and was ferried across the anchorage to the rock that was to provide a sombre backcloth for the epilogue.

He had aged a great deal during the last eighteen months and his corpulence had increased to a degree that almost ex-cused the extravagances of the English cartoonists.

His capacity for work had dwindled from that of twenty men to that of a mere two or three and was to be reduced even further as the iron of exile corroded his faculties.

There was no real need for the British authorities to insti-tute such elaborate precautions against a second flight and a third bid for world dominion. The morbid fear of assassina-tion was a greater deterrent to his ambition, or such as remained of it, than the line of British sentries who marked bounds on the island.

Aside from stoutness his physical health was not what it had been. He, who had been able to spend days and nights in the saddle with only intervals of two and three hours for sleep, now lay abed for hours and sometimes did not even dress until well after midday! Such dreams as he had of re-entering the lists were not related to the immediate future but to the middle of the young century, when his son should have attained maturity and his father's name had become powerful legend.

He talked of his past campaigns as though they had been fought in the days of Alexander the Great. 'Sometimes,' said Madame de Montholon, a member of his suite, 'it was as though I was in another world, listening to the Dialogue of the Dead.'

Yet there was one aspect of his character that had not changed and this was his remarkable ability to respond to the freshness and the gaiety of children.

It is this facet of Napoleon that sheds a single ray of light on the steamy wretchedness of the exiled community. It shines like a lamp in the murk and dreariness of the petty household squabbles, infantile jealousies, preoccupations with what might have been and grinding opposition to the tyranny of the British Governor and his petty-minded masters in London.

It is this aspect of Napoleon alone that opens a window on the drabness of Longwood and admits a whiff of fresh air to a circle of sour, frustrated men, whose chief occupation was to sit around and discuss the relative charms of fat and thin bedfellows or argue who was to blame for some half-forgotten error of policy or battle tactics. Perhaps, in addition, this interest of Napoleon's in the young and eager did something to brighten the lives of the two women whose duty it was to act the parody of Imperial splendour in this tropical twilight, women who continued to address one another by high-sounding titles even while they wondered which of them would be invited to dine with the Emperor that night.

Napoleon arrived at the rock on 18 October 1815, but his official residence was not ready for occupation until 10 December.

In the intervening weeks he was accommodated in a merchant's pavilion, not far from the sole anchorage of the island, and this merchant's home possessed an Ariel in the person of a mischievous, hoydenish, laughing fourteen-year-old, Miss Betty Balcombe, the younger daughter of the family.

It is this English Miss Betsy whom Bonapartists should acknowledge as the person who did most to prevent the complete deterioration of a great mind.

William Balcombe, a purveyor in the employ of the East India company, settled on St Helena in 1807, when his second daughter, Betsy, was six years of age. His wife's facial resemblance to Joséphine struck Napoleon the moment he made her acquaintance and if one compares the two women's portraits today the resemblance is certainly very striking. Both have the same fine-spun hair, submissive mouth and well-shaped nose, the slightly prominent cheekbones and winning expression of gentleness.

There was nothing submissive or gentle about Mrs Balcombe's younger daughter. She had grown up in the freedom of one of the loneliest spots of the inhabited world. She was saucy, bold, tomboyish and utterly irresponsible. Napoleon, who loved to see such qualities in children, was captivated by her at their first interview.

They met the day after his arrival and Napoleon was delighted to discover that the girl spoke fluent French.

He at once set about testing her standard of education, firing a series of questions at her, all of which she answered without the least show of shyness.

One question, however, was to name the capital of Russia

and when she replied 'Moscow' he at once demanded to know who had set it on fire!

This frightened even Betsy but she was equal to the occasion. After saying that she did not know and being sharply informed 'that she knew very well' she told him the city had been fired by the Russians 'in order to get rid of the French!'

This ingenious reply made him laugh heartily and they became allies on the spot, skylarking in and around the pavilion up and down the rocky garden, much as the First Consul and young Georgina had romped in the library at St Cloud or the Emperor and Empress had played on Biscayan beach in the last days of their marriage.

They were always together and squeals of laughter outraged the ears of the little knot of courtiers who watched these extraordinary scenes. They found it difficult to accept this child's easy familiarity with a man who had won sixty battles and had made and deposed Kings before sitting down to luncheon.

Sometimes their fun and teasing outraged those who watched, as when Betsy whipped his ornate sword from its scabbard and whirled it above her head, making furious passes at him and backing him against the wall where she held him until he was rescued by her mother and sister! For this he rewarded her by pinching her sore, newly-pierced ear and pulling her nose.

Sometimes his teasing would goad her to tears, as when she bluntly accused him of cheating at whist and he punished her by scampering off with her ball-dress and locking himself in his room, laughing uproariously at her wild pleas to restore it in time for a dance.

How much happier his years on St Helena might have been had he continued to camp at The Briars with the kindly Balcombes, instead of moving out to the gloomy residence that was to become a hive of discord and intrigue.

His friendship with the Balcombes survived the move for Mr Balcombe had not only become his accredited purveyor but a sympathetic ally, so much of an ally indeed that Sir

Hudson Lowe, the Governor, finally had the family removed from the island.

They left in March 1818, under suspicion that Balcombe had been concerned in the transmission of clandestine correspondence to and from Europe.

Nothing reveals Sir Hudson Lowe's pettiness of soul more clearly than his subsequent handling of this affair.

Accused of persecuting the prisoner beyond the limits of his instructions Lowe subsequently appealed to Balcombe for a testimony to the contrary. Having received it he promptly dropped the charges of complicity against the merchant. Up to that time suspicion had materially affected Balcombe's career.

Once cleared of the charges the genial purveyor became Colonial Treasurer of New South Wales, an appointment that proves his alleged traffic in illicit mail could not have been viewed very seriously by the British Government.

Betsy left the island with her father and later joined him in Australia, subsequently marrying a Mr Abell and publishing her recollections in 1844. The book was extremely popular and ran into four editions.

Her association with the ex-Emperor paid her a strange dividend in middle age. She was favourably remembered by Napoleon III and given a tract of land in France's recently colonized Algeria.

St Helena was described by the French exiles as a tropical Siberia, with heat instead of extreme cold, and maddening restriction of movement instead of a vast and desolate emptiness. During the six years they were there the French never ceased to campaign against the rigours of their conditions.

Taking their cue from Napoleon (who regarded this counter-attack as a final campaign for the recognition of his dynasty) the exiles fought their captors with a courage and persistence worthy of a far better cause.

In fact their situation, irksome as it was under the inflexible régime of a narrow-minded Governor, was neither particularly uncomfortable nor unduly restrictive. The climate was disagreeable and Lowe's degree of surveillance was doubtless irritating but within certain bounds the little court was allowed to function unhindered and few of its complaints arose from actual hardship.

It is because of this atmosphere of ceaseless strife that it is almost impossible to discover for certain what happened on St Helena. No single account – and there are dozens of them – is an unbiased story and each is packed with rumour, accusation, counter-accusation and sometimes complete falsehood.

No one living in the island during the six years that Napoleon was there left it with an unsmirched reputation. Tittle-tattle and scandal gushed from this rock like jets of poisoned vapour. It was said that enmity far more deadly than any incurred on the battlefield bred like bacteria in the stifling atmosphere of the court, the Governor's residence and the barrack-rooms.

Napoleon's associations with the few women on the island, and more particularly his relationship with the two French-women who accompanied their husbands into voluntary exile, are difficult to assess. There were observers enough but unfortunately not one of them can be trusted.

Napoleon's last love-affairs, if indeed they can be called love-affairs, are hazy with contradiction.

The group of Imperialists who followed their master to St Helena were not prominent personalities, whose names had been household words in Paris under the Empire. There were five officers, three of whom were generals, and two women courtiers. There were also three valets and other servants, in addition to a resident physician.

The best known of the group was General Bertrand, who had served Napoleon all his adult life and become Grand Marshal of the Palace in place of Duroc.

Next to him, in order of precedence, came Count Montholon. Both these devotees brought their wives with them. Bertrand's wife, a tall, slender, affectionate woman, was the daughter of an Irish exile. She had an Irishwoman's charm and the lively temperament that usually accompanies it.

She had shared Napoleon's Elba exile and her husband's dual loyalty was the biggest problem of her marriage, so much of a problem indeed that when she heard they were all going to St Helena she tried (though not very seriously) to throw herself out of a porthole into Plymouth Sound! She was 'saved' by her husband's firm grip on her legs. Savary, who witnessed this incident, was not going to St Helena and could afford to regard it as a huge joke, but the misgivings that prompted the Countess to dive through the porthole remained with her during the long voyage out in the *Northumberland*. Maitland, the *Northumberland*'s captain, had a great deal of trouble with her.

On arrival she seems to have acclimatized herself far more easily than did the others and she remained with Napoleon to the end, setting an example of loyalty and devotion that was unrivalled among that desperate community.

There were, of course, the usual rumours about her reputation, and after her rival, Countess Montholon, had left St Helena, Napoleon is supposed to have conceived a violent passion for Madame Bertrand and quarrelled fiercely with his doctor, Antommarchi, because that surgeon could not be talked into persuading Madame Bertrand to replace Madame Montholon as his mistress.

Napoleon's passion for Madame Bertrand is almost certainly exaggerated. He was fond of her, and Count Bertrand's blind devotion to his chief would have removed any barrier to the open association, but by this time Napoleon's physical condition had greatly deteriorated and there was a consequent change in his attitude towards the women about him. A violent quarrel with the doctor concerning Madame Bertrand did take place but it probably had some other and deeper origin.

There is less doubt about his liaison with Albine Montholon for her reputation is one that invites speculation.

Albine was thirty-five when she landed at St Helena. She was a haughty, sensual woman, who had crammed a great deal of experience into her life, having been twice divorced for adultery. She had married her third husband, Count Montholon, under a cloud of social disapproval.

It is alleged that Albine Montholon became Napoleon's regular mistress and that her husband, the insanely devoted count, saw nothing shameful or embarrassing in this situation. It is also stated that the Countess gave birth to a daughter, whose father was undoubtedly Napoleon, and that she left the island in July 1819, as a result of this scandal.

Regarding this association, however, there is far more doubt than is customary as regards Napoleon's entanglements with ladies of his household. Some of the more reliable narrators of the exile make no mention of the liaison or the love-child and one cannot help thinking that the association would have been far better documented had it assumed the alleged proportions. If it existed at all then it was a casual, half-hearted affair, like his association with Eléonore or some of the less celebrated women of the theatre. It was certainly not a grand passion like that he had once entertained for Duchâtel or Walewska.

The strongest argument in favour of the affair and of the true identity of the father of the female child (listed in the island's *Who's Who* as 'a child of Montholon') is the fact that Napoleon left this lady's husband two million francs 'as proof of my satisfaction for the filial attentions paid me during six years ... and as an indemnity for the losses his residence at St Helena has occasioned him.'

One cannot help pondering on the exact nature of Montholon's 'losses'. They must have far exceeded the faithful Bertrand's. He only got five hundred thousand francs!

Napoleon's natural affability with chance acquaintances stood him in good stead during his exile. Up to the time that his bounds were reduced, and he began sulking at Longwood, he formed a number of firm friendships among the islanders.

To do this he had first to overcome their awe of him. For years they had been fed on horrific stories and grotesque caricatures, in both of which he had been represented as a bizarre monster. Their surprise, on finding him a plump, pleasant and often jocular inquisitor, was great and gratifying.

One young acquaintance of Betsy Balcombe stood in such terror of the famous prisoner that she had to be bullied into meeting him. Betsy exploited this wonderful opportunity by persuading Napoleon to justify her friend's fears. She urged him to greet her friend with a series of his famous grimaces.

This kind of prank was exactly suited to his curious sense of humour and he was glad to oblige, making the most horrible, facial contortions and almost scaring the poor child out of her wits. Betsy stood by, helpless with laughter. No other grown-up she had met was so accommodating to young people as 'Old Boney'.

There were two young women on the island whom he made no attempt to frighten. Instead he invented complimentary nicknames for them. Pretty Miss Robinson became 'The Nymph', and news of their friendship soon spread across the island, endangering her reputation. Napoleon was scornful when he heard about this. 'Mon Dieu!' he protested. 'I never once dismounted from my horse when talking to her!'

Another young woman who caught his fancy was christened 'La Bouton de Rose'. She was the daughter of a farmer and they often met and chatted during his walks across the farmland. She retained happy memories of the ex-Emperor when she married and left the island a year or so before he died.

The Nymph also married and brought her new husband up to Longwood to meet Napoleon when she too was about to leave in 1817.

There is no truth in the rumours that either of these young

women misbehaved themselves, not even to the extent that the lively Betsy did by throwing her dignity to the winds whenever encouraged to do so by the prisoner.

When the Balcombes left the island Napoleon sent Betsy a box of bonbons as a parting gift. Characteristically Sir Hudson Lowe confiscated them. He probably suspected that each bonbon contained a message in code for the despairing Bonapartists in Paris.

Time slipped away and Europe slowly settled down after twenty-two years of almost continuous warfare.

In the main Napoleon's family and friends did their utmost to swim with the ebb tide. If, from time to time, echoes of his last campaign from St Helena reached them they did little or nothing to further its progress on the Continent.

Sister Caroline, a merry widow since her husband, Murat, had got himself shot in a fatuous attempt to imitate Napoleon's descent from Elba, soon married again and chose, of all places, Vienna for the scene of the ceremony. Murat had been a fool, a fop and, in the final days of the Empire, a despicable traitor, but Napoleon almost choked with fury when he heard of his sister's cold-blooded behaviour.

Marie Louise continued to present her lover with illegitimate children and each of them was made a Prince or Princess by her approving father.

The other Marie, Marie Walewska, did not prosper. Her aged husband, the old Count who had been so flattered by his wife's sudden popularity in 1807, had died before Waterloo and soon after Napoleon had left for St Helena Marie married a distant cousin of Napoleon's, a dragoon who had served with distinction in the Imperial Guard. Man and wife were exiled for their loyalty to Napoleon during the Hundred Days.

In due course they obtained permission to return to Paris and it must have seemed then that the pattern of Marie's life would follow that of nearly all Napoleon's former mistresses – a 'suitable' marriage, a firm renunciation of the turbulent past and a respectable and prosperous old age.

It was not in Walewska's cards. All too soon her tragic destiny caught up with her and at the age of twenty-eight years she died. Her death occurred within six months of her confinement and took place, in December 1817, at the house that Napoleon had given her in the celebrated Rue de la Victoire.

Death had been very active among Napoleon's old friends in the last few years. His former aide-de-camp, Junot, the gay hussar who had been so impressed by dusky beauties of the Nile and had flirted with Joséphine's maid during the long coach ride down into Italy, had gone raving mad as a result of a wound in the head and had died on his estate in 1813.

Chief of Staff Berthier, he who had been called 'the Emperor's wife' and had knelt before the adored Madame Visconti's portrait in the desert, had thrown himself out of a window when he saw Russian troops marching against the man he had forsaken.

Wild, unpredictable Ney, whose gallant conduct during the terrible Russian retreat had rung through Europe, had faced a Bourbon firing squad like his hated rival, Murat.

Kindly Duroc, the palace Marshal who had knocked so persistently on Marie Walewska's bedroom door, had been killed in battle. Marshal Brune had been torn to pieces by a Bourbon mob, Marshal Bessières killed in action, and Prince Poniatowski, the Pole who had persuaded Walewska to sacrifice herself for her country, drowned during the retreat from Leipzig. Marshals Augereau and one-eyed Masséna, two other veterans of the great days in Italy, had both died within two years of Waterloo.

There were, however, a number of old friends who did not die but who skilfully adapted themselves to changed times and altered circumstances; Constant, the valet, was one of these. He had learned the art of making himself invisible during the performance of his duties at the Tuileries and he now put his experience to good use, slipping away during the first abdication and recommending a successor to go to Elba and St Helena. Constant had work to do. He was already writing his memoirs.

'La Bellilotte,' the blonde Cleopatra of the Egyptian campaign, was also counted among the survivors. About this time she was eloping with an adventurer but her mind was not wholly occupied by romance. She was busily investing money in South American trade.

A third survivor was Georgina, terribly fat by this time but still getting deeper and deeper into debt as she drifted to the bottom of the playhouse bills.

Eléonore, the unlucky beauty who had proved to Napoleon that he could become a father after all, was also involved in money troubles. Her son, Léon, was not yet old enough to engage in blackmail but Eléonore's first husband, the rascally Revel, was still doing his best to make the marriage of 1805 show a handsome profit.

One other piece of Imperial flotsam was not finding life very easy during his father's exile.

Napoleon II, once styled the King of Rome, was still a prisoner in Vienna. He was deprived of the last of his French attendants when his nursemaid was handed her passport, in 1816.

The attractive, sensitive, five-year-old child was the hope of every Bonapartist in the world and as such he was guarded as carefully as a desperate criminal.

His Austrian tutors worked very hard to make him forget his native tongue and speak only German but the boy had plenty of spirit and it was not easy to wipe the memory of his identity from his impressionable mind.

Grandfather Francis and his staff went on trying and ultimately the boy's resistance was worn down. He might never have existed for all the notice his mother took of him. She was enjoying life with Neipperg and never saw her first child again until, at the age of twenty-one, he lay on his deathbed.

There had been a slight change of plan about the child's

future after Waterloo. Instead of becoming the Prince of Parma and the heir to his mother's realm as was originally promised, he was made Duke of Reichstadt, an insignificant Germany Duchy. There was no reference at all to Napoleon in the diploma issued to his son.

Living in exile proud old Madame Mère, his Corsican grandmother, indulged in a short, scornful laugh when she heard about this piece of flummery. 'We have had our revenge upon Austria,' she commented, 'for when they gave Marie Louise to my son it was not in the character of a wife but that of a mistress! My grandson will never have a finer name than his father's!'

It was true but it was beginning not to matter.

A thousand leagues away, on an isolated Atlantic rock, the man who made that name so famous had reached a stage in his journey where he was able to get titles, etiquette and courtly fiddle-faddle into correct perspective.

He was dying, and dying in great pain, for his incompetent surgeon had diagnosed his complaint incorrectly and had given tartar emetic to a patient suffering from cancer of the stomach!

He had made his will long ago. Now he added a string of codicils. As his strength began to fail, and news went out to the islanders that all would be over in days or hours, no hush fell upon court and captors for there were now plenty of fresh excuses for wrangling. What surgical treatment should he be given? What diet? What name and rank should be inscribed upon the coffin?

He lay in great pain, pleading for a spoonful of coffee which had been forbidden him. Before he lost the power of articulate speech and his senses slipped away altogether the British and French bystanders had some inkling of the trend of his thoughts. Over and over again he muttered the words 'little King, little King ...' Then all thoughts of his son left him and the major preoccupation of his life regained exclusive possession of his mind. There were no more whispered requests for his son's name, no mention of Joséphine, of his mother, of his Austrian wife, or any of the women who had held him in their arms. At three o'clock on the morning of 5 May 1821, he spoke his final words. They were 'at the head of the army'.

So it was that the instrument that had lifted him to power remained with him to the very end.

At forty-nine minutes past five in the afternoon of the same day he died and the news was rushed across to Plantation House, to be relayed thence to every court, cottage and coffee-house in Europe.

They buried him in one of his favourite spots and accorded him full military honours. A guard was maintained over the tomb, a formality that the garrison continued to observe all the years that he lay there.

His heart had been extracted at the autopsy and Antommarchi, the surgeon, had strict instructions to send it to Marie Louise. He disobeyed the instruction, and it was as well that he did for when he travelled to Vienna, and tried to deliver Napoleon's last messages to the former Empress, she flatly refused to see him. She was on the point of marrying Neipperg and regularizing her life. Her husband's name had been deliberately omitted from the funeral mass she ordered, so what on earth could she have done with his pickled heart!

Two women might have mourned him sincerely but both Joséphine and Marie Walewska were dead. One only remained to hear from Antommarchi the details of his last days, last words and last wishes.

For two days the surgeon talked to the stern-faced peasant who had given birth to this restless genius. Dry-eyed she made Antommarchi recount every single detail of the final scene at St Helena. Then she folded her hands and went back to live among her memories, surviving him by fifteen years and steadfastly refusing Bourbon permission to return to Paris.

In the splendid days she had pooh-poohed his prattle of stars and destiny but as she grew blind and began to wither something of his starlight must have touched her at last. When they told her that they were raising Napoleon's statue once more in the Place Vendôme she smiled and murmured: 'So? The Emperor is in Paris again!'

Bibliographical Note

In his entertaining *Napoleon and His Marshals* the late A. G. Macdonnell says: 'I am profoundly suspicious of almost all bibliographies. Nothing is easier than to hire someone to visit the British museum and make an impressive list of authorities ... I propose therefore to confine myself to the simple statement that every single word of this book has been taken from one or other work of history, reference, reminiscence or biography.'

The same applies to the present volume. I have been dipping into Napoleonic memoir for the last thirty years and it would require a bolder man than I to tabulate and publish the hundreds of footnotes that would be necessary to indicate the sources of material.

I feel, however, under some kind of obligation to push these enjoyable dishes towards readers, in the hope that they may derive from them some of the pleasure that has fallen to me since I picked up a tattered *Life of Napoleon* on a threepenny bookstall. I therefore list the principal books that I read before beginning this chronicle and, in so doing, recommend each of them as a very agreeable fireside companion.

They are:

Memoirs of Napoleon, his Court and Family by the Duchess d'Abrantès (Madame Junot)
Memoirs of Napoleon Bonaparte by M. de Bourrienne, his private secretary
St Helena Who's Who by Arnold Chaplin, MD

The Love Affairs of Napoleon by Joseph Turquan, translated by J. Lewis May (John Lane Co, 1909)

Napoleon and his Court by C. S. Forester (Methuen & Co Ltd)

Napoleon the Last Phase by Lord Roseberry (Arthur L. Humphreys, 1900)

Napoleon and His Marshals by A. G. Macdonnell (Macmillan & Co, 1934)

Napoleon by Emil Ludwig, translated by Eden and Cedar Paul (George Allen & Unwin, Ltd)

Napoleon and the Fair Sex by Frederic Mason (William Heinemann, 1894)

Napoleon's Son by Clara Tschudi, translated by E. M. Cope (George Allen & Unwin, Ltd)

Joséphine, the Portrait of a Woman R. McNair Wilson (Eyre and Spottiswoode, Ltd)

Memoirs of Baron de Marbot translated by A. J. Butler (Cassell & Company)

Memoirs of Sergeant Bourgogne translated by the Hon J. W. Fortescue (Jonathan Cape)

Brumaire, the Rise of Bonaparte by J. B. Morton (Werner Laurie, Ltd)

Napoleon Bonaparte, His Rise and Fall by J. M. Thompson (Basil Blackwell, Oxford)

The Empress Joséphine by Joseph Turquan, translated by Violette M. Montagu (John Lane, The Bodley Head)

A Life of Napoleon Bonaparte by I. M. Tarbell (McClure, Phillips & Co, New York)

New Letters of Napoleon I (William Heinemann)

Romances of the French Revolution by G. Lenôtre (William Heinemann)

A Favourite of Napoleon, the Memoirs of Mlle Georges (Eveleigh Nash)

The Duke of Reichstadt by Edward de Wertheimer (John Lane, The Bodley Head)

Napoleon in His Time by Jean Savant, translated by Catherine John (Putnam)

Robert K. Massie

NICHOLAS AND ALEXANDRA (illus.)

60p

This is the world-famous bestseller – a moving and enthralling story of the last Tsar and his beloved Empress – on which the magnificent film is based.

'Contains every imaginable ingredient for a runaway literary success . . . grandeur and misery; romantic love; a glittering court; Byzantine intrigues; mysterious illnesses and evil influences; war and revolution; the violent, and horrible, death of almost everyone concerned.' – THE SPECTATOR

Elizabeth Longford

VICTORIA R. I.   £1

Illustrated

'A wonderfully vivid portrait built up with skill from massive research and presented with a beguiling artistry' – C. V. Wedgewood, LIFE

'Nearly two generations have elapsed since Queen Victoria died, and yet this is the first complete and authoritative biography . . . She has done a first-class piece of work, one that will stand comparison with that model of royal biography, namely Sir Harold Nicolson's *King George V* . . . She makes her Victorian statesmen come alive – no easy task. A most admirable biography' – Sir Charles Petrie, ILLUSTRATED LONDON NEWS

'Easily the best life of Victoria that has yet appeared' – Dr J. H. Plumb of Cambridge University writing in the NEW YORK TIMES

'It is hard to imagine how Elizabeth Longford's detailed and vivid volume could have been bettered . . . Her book is scholarly, yet racily readable, witty yet wise'
         – James Pope-Hennessy, SUNDAY TIMES